# Time and Ways of Knowing
# under Louis XIV

# The Bucknell Studies in Eighteenth-Century Literature and Culture

General Editor: Greg Clingham, *Bucknell University*

Advisory Board: Paul K. Alkon, *University of Southern California*
Chloe Chard, *Independent Scholar*
Clement Hawes, *The Pennsylvania State University*
Robert Markley, *West Virginia University*
Jessica Munns, *University of Denver*
Cedric D. Reverand II, *University of Wyoming*
Janet Todd, *University of Glasgow*

*The Bucknell Studies in Eighteenth-Century Literature and Culture* aims to publish challenging, new eighteenth-century scholarship. Of particular interest is critical, historical, and interdisciplinary work that is interestingly and intelligently theorized, and that broadens and refines the conception of the field. At the same time, the series remains open to all theoretical perspectives and different kinds of scholarship. While the focus of the series is the literature, history, arts, and culture (including art, architecture, music, travel, and history of science, medicine, and law) of the long eighteenth century in Britain and Europe, the series is also interested in scholarship that establishes relationships with other geographies, literatures, and cultures of the period 1660–1830.

## Titles in This Series

http://www.departments.bucknell.edu/univ_press

# Time and Ways of Knowing under Louis XIV

## Molière, Sévigné, Lafayette

### Roland Racevskis

Lewisburg
Bucknell University Press
London: Associated University Presses

Associated University Presses
2010 Eastpark Boulevard
Cranbury, NJ 08512

Associated University Presses
16 Barter Street
London WC1A 2AH, England

Associated University Presses
P.O. Box 338, Port Credit
Mississauga, Ontario
Canada L5G 4L8

The paper used in this publication meets the requirements of the American National Standard for Permanence of Paper for Printed Library Materials Z39.48-1984.

Cataloging-in-Publication Data is on file
with the Library of Congress.

*For the Rondeau family,*
*in loving memory of Dail*

# Contents

# Acknowledgments

I AM DEEPLY INDEBTED TO JOAN DEJEAN, WHO OVERSAW MY WORK IN the earliest stages of this project and who provided invaluable advice and inspiration along the way. For their tough-minded readings of the manuscript, I express my heartfelt gratitude to Michael Koppisch, Karlis Racevskis, and my reader at Bucknell University Press. A number of mentors and colleagues generously offered words of insight, encouragement, and challenge over the years: many thanks go to Janet Altman, Kevin Brownlee, Roger Chartier, Lance Donaldson-Evans, Herbert Garelick, Lynn Hunt, Lawrence Kritzman, Maurice Laugaa, Michèle Longino, Gerald Prince, Derek Schilling, Downing Thomas, Steve Ungar, and Charles Williams.

I thank my mother, Maija, my wife, Lynnette, and my entire family for their support. They have all lived with this project and have all contributed more than they may know to its fruition.

For technical consulting, my thanks go to *RANEC*.

The writing of this book would never have been possible without the generous support provided by the Mellon fellowships program at the University of Pennsylvania, the College of Liberal Arts summer fellowships program at The University of Iowa, and the University of Iowa Office of the Vice President for Research.

Finally, I gratefully acknowledge permission to reprint material, in modified form, from the following articles:

"Time, Postal Practices, and Daily Life in Mme de Sévigné's Letters." *EMF: Studies in Early Modern France /EMF Critiques* 7. Edited by David Lee Rubin and Julia V. Douthwaite. 29–47. Charlottesville: Rookwood Press, 2001.

"Mapping Spaces and Keeping Time: The Problem of Longitude Under Louis XIV." In *Classical Unities: Place, Time, Action*. Edited by Erec R. Koch. 125–34. Tübingen: Narr (*Biblio 17*–131), 2002.

"Dynamics of Time and Postal Communication in Madame de Sévigné's Letters." *Papers on French Seventeenth-Century Literature* 26, no. 50 (1999): 51–59.

9

# Introduction

*For what is time? Who could find any quick or easy answer to that? Who could even grasp it in his thought clearly enough to put the matter into words? Yet is there anything to which we refer in conversation with more familiarity, any matter of more common experience, than time? And we know perfectly well what we mean when we speak of it, and understand just as well when we hear someone else refer to it. What, then, is time? If no one asks me, I know; if I want to explain it to someone who asks me, I do not know.*
—Saint Augustine, *The Confessions*

TIME IS AT ONCE ONE OF THE MOST FAMILIAR AND INEFFABLE ELE-ments of human experience, an idea and an intuition with which we live closely but which somehow escapes our conceptual grasp. Well-worn though it may be, the path to Saint Augustine is still worth taking: we know what time is, but when we are asked to tell exactly what we think it is, we inevitably find ourselves at a loss.[1] This cognitive deficit, this ignorance, entails a desire to know more, to pursue the slippery question of time yet a step further. It is perhaps such a feeling of loss and of desire that lies at the origin of this book.

The task of telling time and telling about time has been undertaken for centuries and constitutes a significant component especially of literary endeavors. It is one of the central tenets of the present study that works of literature provide the most suggestive and nuanced representations of a given culture's and a given epoch's characteristic ways of thinking and living time.[2] Ways of knowing about time have changed throughout history, with every culture and with every thinker and writer who has attempted to give an account, however implicit, of the temporalities of human experience.

In the pages that follow, I take as objects of focus the multiple temporalities constitutive of the literature and culture of Europe, and particularly of France, in the second half of the seventeenth century. Early modern France was marked by significant changes in the use, measurement, and the ideation of time, changes whose results are still with us today. I shall examine some of the fundamental presuppositions of the

11

modern thinking of time by tracing certain of their initial manifestations in the early modern period. This study, I hope, will contribute to a historicized thinking of time in our twenty-first-century present. To seek the origins of modern temporal notions, I take as my starting point the revolutionary technological discoveries of the Dutch scientist Christiaan Huygens (1629–95), a pioneer of precision timekeeping, and then move on to discuss ways in which a newly exacting attention to time affected literature, government, and daily life in seventeenth-century France. Temporal experience at court, the use of the postal system, and the reading of an early periodical publication will serve, respectively, as contexts for my readings of the three authors—Molière (1622–73), Sévigné (1626–96), and Lafayette (1634–93)—whom I situate at the conceptual center of this project. Due to the ubiquity of temporality as a literary issue, my choice of authors is to some extent arbitrary. While Molière, Sévigné, and Lafayette were all extremely skilled at creating textual temporal constructs, many other authors—La Bruyère (1645–96), La Rochefoucauld (1613–80), Pascal (1623–62), Racine (1639–99), and Saint-Simon (1675–1755) to name only a few—developed literary temporalities that are equally worthy of further study.

What has brought together the authors I have chosen is a set of historical contexts, which I discuss below, and which are linked to the problem of precision time-measurement in administration, in thinking practices, and in lived experience. The historically contextualized particularities of Molière's premieres at tightly timed fêtes at Versailles, of Sévigné's letters traveling through the early modern mails, and of Lafayette's *La Princesse de Clèves* emerging as an unprecedented kind of proto-journalistic publicity stunt, all contribute to raising the question of the nature of early modern temporality. Each historically situated literary phenomenon allows points of entry into the cultural-historical question of temporality at the intersection between literature and history. The simultaneously philosophical, historical, and literary question of time that this book examines has called for an interdisciplinary approach that includes discussions of historical facts, close readings of literary texts, and interpretations of the temporal constructs in evidence within the cultural record of seventeenth-century Europe. While developments in cultural history and the history of science serve to focus the reading of the multifaceted literary question of temporality, textual analyses provide a conceptual framework for interpretation that the historical facts by themselves can only suggest. Nonetheless the initial step for such interpretations involves taking a close look at the technological

innovations that rendered possible significant changes in ways of thinking about and representing time.

Huygens ushered in a new era of precision in time-measurement
when he successfully applied Galileo Galilei's (1564–1642) invention of
the pendulum as a regulator to a clock mechanism in 1657. This advance permitted a new degree of accuracy for clocks and a new way
of audibly tracking the passage of time. Stuart Sherman describes the
significance of the entry into the English language of the pendulum's
constant *tick, tick, tick*: "The phrase performs compactly what was in
fact newest about Huygensian time: its capacity to track and report
newly small durations—minutes, seconds—in regular, perceptible, continuous succession. It proposes as language a temporality to match the
one the pendulum clock propounds as sound: time as steady series."[3]
With Huygens, time becomes a series of movements governed by an
escapement, the mechanism that regulates the motion of the clock's
motor according to the isochronic or regular oscillations of the pendulum. Instead of being conceived as a continuous movement, the measure
of time becomes an experience of steady discontinuity, the breaking-up
of the passing of time by the alternating gears of the clock mechanism
coming into contact with the teeth of the escapement. The resulting experience is one of time analyzed, or broken down, an experience henceforth to be reinforced aurally by the ticking of the pendulum.

Sherman's study of the importance of Huygens's inventions for
thinking and talking about time serves as an almost constant point of
reference for the chapters that follow. Owing a great deal to Sherman's
work, my inquiry into the cultural history of chronometry and the literary representation of time aims to complement Sherman's study of early
modern England by focusing on early modern France. In this regard,
my purpose is to bring out the significance of French contributions,
within a European context, to the development of seventeenth-century
chronometrical technologies. While Sherman convincingly examines
the impact of new technologies of time-measurement in seventeenth-
and eighteenth-century England, he does not take fully into account the
fact that Huygens did much of his most important work in France,
where he lived, with the exception of two journeys abroad, for some
16 years, from 1665 to 1681. Jean-Baptiste Colbert (1619–83) made
Huygens a founding member of the Académie Royale des Sciences in
1666. The period of Huygens's residence in Paris followed closely on
his invention of the pendulum clock—the accomplishment that had initially caught Colbert's attention—and saw also his invention of the spiral spring in 1675. This latter innovation was the most salient result of

Huygens's collaboration with French scientists and clockmakers during the 1660s and 1670s. It was a device that miniaturized the regular oscillations of the pendulum and thus rendered possible an unprecedented degree of accuracy for watches.

I follow on Sherman's idea that the use of watches in the early modern world corresponded to a progressive privatization of the activity of measuring time. The ability to keep track of time privately and individually, with accuracy to the minute (which the spiral spring made possible), provided a newly effective "tool for self-tracking" and a new way of accounting for "the idiosyncratic motion of the solitary self through space and time."[4] It is this idiosyncratic motion, at once an external modality of action and an internal dynamics of thought and feeling, that the following chapters explore.

My study begins with a brief history of chronometry in seventeenth-century France, especially under Louis XIV (1638–1715). It is an account of what clocks and watches were like during the time when Molière, Sévigné, and Lafayette wrote, and an inquiry into the ways their construction and use may have influenced the conceptualization of time. This cultural history is based on Sherman's insight that "[e]very clock proposed a temporality—a way of conceiving time, using it, inhabiting it—by its look and sound, its modes of motion and of definition, its placement and its purpose, within a culture composed of multiple temporalities operating separately and simultaneously."[5] I aim to take this idea one step further and to argue that a culture, defined within a historical period, can be described as a set of temporalities, some distinct and unrelated, others overlapping, still others in continuity one with the other. Complementing my historical analyses will be a study of how different theoretical approaches to time may be used in making sense of the historical data and in combining cultural/historical contexts with the literary readings of Molière, Sévigné, and Lafayette that follow. All of these authors, and the members of the nobility and wealthy bourgeoisie who could afford early modern timepieces, lived in a world of rapidly improving practices of chronometry.

The topic of human constructions of temporality is one so fraught with ambiguities and complexities that it is above all in esthetic objects composed of language—literary texts—that one may find answers to some of the most slippery questions of intellectual history. Paul Ricœur remarks that "speculation on time is an inconclusive rumination without the insights provided by narrative activity."[6] Harbored deeply within the recesses of subjective thinking and feeling, our most suggestive intuitions about time may only be accessible to the unpredictable angles of approach provided by the esthetic activity of figuration. While the methodical gathering of historical data can give us a fuller idea of how technologies of time changed during a given period, the subjective experience of time can best be approached through the mediation of the complexities of the esthetic object, in this study the literary text. Thus I draw on what Ricœur calls "the particular capacity of metaphorical expressions to describe a reality inaccessible to direct description."[7]

The present analysis combines historical approaches to and collections of verifiable facts about the science of time-measurement on the one hand, and literary interpretations on the other. The fundamental idea driving this project is that cultural history is in one sense a combination of multiple temporalities, of different kinds of "structures of feeling" about time, to borrow a term from Raymond Williams.[8] From the deep temporalities of the history of civilizations, to the private history of individual observations of daily life, to the narrative indices of psychological time, the cultural record presents to the literary historian an interweaving of temporalities of various dimensions. The tracing of these temporalities, in turn, gives an account at once historical, literary, and epistemological and can only be accomplished through an interdisciplinary approach. By alternating between historical context and textual analysis, my study aims to describe the nature of temporality in seventeenth-century France.

The works I have chosen to interpret all contain rich textual representations of time in historical context. Molière's *Le Tartuffe* is a theatrical performance of temporal exactitude that was produced within a tightly scheduled *fête* at Versailles. It was a dramatic creation that placed rigorous time constraints on Molière and all of the courtly participants in the event, the aristocrats whose daily lives followed exacting schedules under the Sun King. Mme de Sévigné's letters give mercurial narrative accounts of the private experience of time as it passed; while writing these texts, the marquise remained constantly preoccupied with the changing operations of the French postal system, an organization that followed increasingly precise schedules in the seventeenth century. Madame de Lafayette's *La Princesse de Clèves* elaborates a novelistic account of subjective and intersubjective time that accomplished numerous innovations in techniques of narration. The work itself was the object of considerable discussion and of a carefully timed publicity campaign in one of Europe's first "literary magazines," *Le Mercure galant.* From the dynamics of the royal *fête* to postal operations to early forms of journalism, the historical contexts that are implicated in the processes of literary production of some of France's best-known works all suggest time as an object of critical focus. It is in terms of this focus that I have developed the interpretive framework for close readings of textual time structures in the works of Molière, Sévigné, and Lafayette.

The choice of these authors has not been based on any outwardly temporal characteristics of their texts.[9] Although Sévigné's letters, for example, are dated in succession, it was not their diurnal form that motivated their inclusion as this book's third chapter; rather, as is also the case with Molière and Lafayette, it was by reason of the suggestiveness and literary quality of textual representations of time in Sévigné that her letters were identified as a principal object of focus. Their historical contextualization, structured by a study of seventeenth-century postal procedures under Postal Superintendent Louvois, provides a historical and conceptual backdrop against which I develop close readings, the interpretive results of which then open onto the domain of cultural history.

What is most interesting about early modern time is that one may observe there a dialectical tension between the emerging possibility of regular time-measurement and the individual subject's adherences, reactions, and resistances to this epistemological and technological trend. In other words, in the latter half of the seventeenth century in France, clocks and watches had come to exert an increasing amount of influence on both public and private life, but these instruments had not yet been distributed and used widely enough to dominate the individual's experience of time. In comparison with the relatively rudimentary technologies of time-measurement of the Renaissance and the eventual regimentation of life as a result of the changes effected by industrial society (such as the Taylorist restructuring of work), the seventeenth and eighteenth centuries can be viewed as a "middle period when precise clocks and watches, conspicuous but not yet ubiquitous, proffered to their owners a temporality closely calibrated, but not yet controlling: when the metaphorical societal 'metronome' was audible but not yet dominant."[10] It is in this kind of "middle period" that one can observe some of the most intriguing complexities of subjective reactions to larger epistemological trends, at a time when those trends were starting to impose themselves but had not yet become so ingrained as to be invisible or taken for granted.

This "middle period" in the development of the science and thinking of time entails a considerable amount of historical complexity, which E. P. Thompson described in his search for the roots of industrial capitalism: "[T]he historical record is not a simple one of neutral and inevitable technological change, but is also one of exploitation and of resistance to exploitation."[11] This cautionary note warning us against the reductionism of a linear representation of cultural history is very much *à propos* for the current project. The historical record of the perception of time is full of ambiguities and complexities that destabilize any monolithic view of trends in time-measurement and in the thinking of time. I attempt instead to point out elements of the cultural record that resonate with literary accounts of the human experience of time and open these representations to the complexities of interpretive activity. My historical and textual analyses are informed by a number of cultural historians' studies of the gradual transition from feudalism to administrative centralization that France was undergoing in the seventeenth century. The works of Roger Chartier and Michel Foucault have been especially useful for this approach to temporality in the seventeenth century, a historical moment when broad changes in the structure of society created a kind of substratum on which subjective self-conceptions and individual conceptions of time were constructed.

Subjective awareness of temporality constitutes one of the innovations of early modern culture and literature. Roger Chartier finds proof of this in the fact that "[p]rivate activities and intimate feelings were not a subject of writing before the second half of the seventeenth century."[12] Emerging practices of individual thought affected the formulation of subjective experience during the reign of Louis XIV in unprecedented ways. While this régime is generally known for its rigid codes of social organization (see my discussion of this in chapter 2), and while an increased intensity of behavioral control pervaded daily life under Louis XIV, paradoxically the period corresponding to his reign also gave rise to new possibilities for private, subjective experience, to be lived separately from the constraints of social life.

The break from feudal practices that Louis XIV's administration accomplished through the organization of what would eventually become centralized institutions created new possibilities for the king's subjects. Philippe Ariès assesses the effects of new administrative controls on private experience: "The king's court assumed responsibility for certain governmental functions that had previously been decentralized, such as maintaining law and order, courts of law, the army, and so on. Space and time thus became available for activities without public significance: private activities."[13] No longer bound by ties of loyalty to locally powerful representatives of the nobility of the sword, individuals grew dependent on the nobility of the robe and the functionaries executing the orders of a (still only relatively) centralized bureaucracy. No longer perpetually responsible to a feudal lord, the individual gained "space

and time for private activities," in the interstices of increasingly regularized institutional contact.[14] In the chapters that follow, I would like to
identify and describe some of the time structures of both institutionally
mediated and private experience in the second half of the seventeenth
century in France.

My temporal analysis follows on the work of historians of private life
who have argued that new domains of subjective experience constitute
a central component of early modernity in Western culture. Chartier
identifies the seventeenth century as a key moment for the historical
observation of the distinction between public and private spheres of existence: "The opposition between intimacy and representation was perhaps most intense, in certain countries at any rate, when the state
attempted to regulate all aspects of social life—not only the social life of
its subjects but even more that of its administrators and rulers. France
in the mid-seventeenth century is of course the prime example."[15]
Seventeenth-century subjects were obliged to trace the boundaries between public and private activity and personal identity. One indication
of the separation between public and private domains of existence can
be found in experiences of social and individual time. By reorganizing
their time, subjects produced a separation between exposure and self-
contemplation:

> In order for private life to flourish, various obstacles had to be overcome.
> In particular, a clear boundary had to be drawn between the function of
> public representation and the private sphere of intimate retreat. Many peo-
> ple in the ancien régime held office and wielded authority; all of them, from
> the sovereign on down, had to divide time and space, roles and practices,
> between the public and private spheres.[16]

Seventeenth-century subjects were obliged to reconceptualize the
spaces and schedules of daily experience in their interaction with new
forms of government and representations of authority. New divisions of
time and space were products of the effort to separate conceptually the
domains of the public and the private. This cognitive tendency to divide
time led to an intensified attention to small time quantities in temporality, in ways of thinking and experiencing time.[17]

Tracking time ever more closely in daily life, individuals in early
modern France initiated a reflection on the temporal dynamics of inner
experience that continues in the philosophy and literature of our own
times. Detailed time-consciousness was facilitated by Huygens's innovations. Those privileged enough to own newly accurate timepieces had

the ability, for the first time in history, to chart the minutes of their own daily lives with a portable device. The development of private thought thus included new possibilities in mapping the microitineraries of private experience.

In his study of time and narrative in early modern England, Stuart Sherman considers that Huygens's timepieces initiated a "new chronometry" and acted as an agent of privatization, or of "chronometric autonomy."[18] The privacy of the watch pocket and the cover of the watch itself established the activity of time-measurement as an individual affair. The use of the minute to chart daily life, unprecedented until the seventeenth century, contributed to new forms of focus on subjectivity.

Paying attention to a "temporal unit exotically small" as the minute allowed the owners of early modern watches to take account of their daily schedules with an exclusive precision and thus shored up the sphere of purely private existence as an integral part of human experience. Sherman refers to one particular way in which "Huygensian precision conduces to privacy. It has to do with the status in the late seventeenth century of the minute as a unit of measurement, and with its consequent eligibility as a means of self-definition, a tool for self-tracking."[19] With the new watches available in Europe and England during the second half of the seventeenth century, individuals were first capable of temporally measuring "the idiosyncratic motion of the solitary self through space and time." This kind of temporal self-awareness required a specific focus on small time increments. Restricted temporal units framed within microdiachronies of daily experience constituted a new domain of consciousness.

Fragmented into constitutive components, time was conceived in a new complexity by early modern subjects. With early precision timepieces, the regular sound of isochronous oscillations

> made available to sense and thought a new experience of time as it passed; [the clock's new sound-series] proffered a new and concrete means for coming to grips with an old elusive mystery. Where church bells and clock towers had for centuries tolled time intermittently and at a distance, Huygens's clocks, ticking steadily, translated time into a sound both constant and contiguous.[20]

An entire dimension of temporal experience, the moments of recent past and near future that made up the lived experience of the present, opened up for subjective examination with Huygens's inventions. A closer attention to small spans of time imbued "hitherto emptier and more shapeless tracts of time (minutes, quarters, hours) with steady, sharp definition."[21] Detailed consciousness of time increments contributed significantly to shaping daily life during the emergence of new forms of privacy in the seventeenth century.

In order to take account of relatively small time structures of subjective contemplation, communication, and social interaction, this study draws on a number of philosophical and theoretical approaches to micro-time. The time frame that serves as an object of analysis in the following chapters can be called the relative present, a limited diachrony of cognitive references to moments of recent-past and near-future time that closely surround the subject's experience of the present. The immediate temporal horizon of the relative present frames the newly precise and minute early modern time-consciousness that it is my aim to describe.

In the subjective sphere, new uses of time created possibilities for temporal self-measurement, while at the same time producing a potential for intersubjective dynamics of power, mediated through a control of time. Increased precision in cognitive approaches to time made possible more calculated applications of microschedules in social interaction and in administration.

Michel Foucault has shown how, from the early modern era of the seventeenth century through high modernism, institutions have used meticulous scheduling procedures to control specific activities. New organizational principles in education reflected the development of disciplinary time: "From the seventeenth century to the introduction, at the beginning of the nineteenth, of the Lancaster method, the complex clockwork of the mutual improvement school was built up cog by cog."[22] Foucault traces the origins of the Gobelins tapestry school to an edict of 1667. This institution would put into practice "a new technique for taking charge of the time of individual existences; for regulating the relations of time, bodies and forces."[23] The articulation of time structures with specific bodily attitudes and required tasks imposes patterns of power, of institutional intentionality, directly on bodies, through the "meticulous, often minute, techniques [that] . . . defined a certain mode of detailed political investment of the body, a 'new micro-physics' of power; . . . since the seventeenth century, [these techniques] had constantly reached out to ever broader domains, as if they intended to cover the entire social body."[24] Foucault's terms—"meticulous," "minute," "detailed," "micro-physics"—refer to a practice of intense focus on small time quantities in this "political investment of the body." A study of the microtemporal dynamics of subjective experience contributes to describing the rhythms of this "micro-physics of power" in early modern France.

For Foucault, the disciplinary applications of time to activity that were in evidence in the seventeenth century culminated, in the domain of education, in the pedagogical theories of La Salle which aimed at "the supervision of the smallest fragment of life."[25] In the area of military training, the historical record contains such documents as the punctilious blueprint for bodily movements contained in the Ordinance of 1 January 1766, for the regulation of the exercise of the infantry. Foucault discusses the precision with which gestures are described in this ordinance, which counts motions in seconds and even parts of seconds.

The epistemological tendency toward a focus on small units of time in the construction of disciplinary procedures grew from utilitarian concerns:

> [I]t is a question of extracting, from time, ever more available moments and, from each moment, ever more useful forces. This means that one must seek to intensify the use of the slightest moment, as if time, in its very fragmentation, were inexhaustible or as if, at least by an ever more detailed internal arrangement, one could tend towards an ideal point at which one maintained maximum speed and maximum efficiency.[26]

The conception of time as a resource which could be broken down quantitatively and arranged in pursuit of procedural efficiency pervaded reforms under Louis XIV. In court life and in processes of communication, cognitive practices of temporal fragmentation were deployed in order to attain an increasing rapidity of actions and functions. Micro-time played a central role for knowledge during the classical age.

As Foucault points out, however, it would be erroneous to locate the origins of minutely analytical utilitarianism in the seventeenth or eighteenth century: "The classical age did not initiate it; rather it accelerated it, changed its scale, gave it precise instruments."[27] This book aims to chart some of the accelerations of thinking and action that French court society underwent during the first two decades of Louis XIV's reign. My discussion of clocks and watches takes account of some of the "precise instruments" that were technically improved and began to serve more people in their daily lives.

But the study of instruments and their uses does not suffice for a topic as complex as time and its conceptualization. Herein lies the significance of artistic (for the purposes of this study, literary) production contemporary to technological advances in time-measurement. Sherman comments on the need to study temporal figurations in approaching the abstract topic of time: "By its impalpability time requires close attention to its artificial forms."[28] Ricœur emphasizes literature's privileged relation to time. The ambiguities and subjective dimensions constitutive of literary texts contribute to "fiction's power to re-figure this temporal experience susceptible to the aporias of philosophical speculation."[29] While the explicit and methodical nature of philosophical discourse can lead, in an inquiry on time, only to intractable contradictions, fictional and figurative narratives provide approaches to time in its most elusive manifestations.

Following on Ricœur's insight, then, the readings of Molière, Sévigné, and Lafayette that follow undertake a reflection on time mediated by literary interpretations. More specifically, these critical readings of seventeenth-century French texts will focus on verb tenses, rhythms of utterance, punctuation, figures of rhetoric, semantic fields descriptive of temporal awareness, gaps or ellipses that call readerly attention to the passage of time in dialogue, and other aspects of literary textuality and temporality. Placed in the historical context of evolving methods of time-management under Louis XIV, these literary texts provide a commentary, from the subject's point of view, on the temporal dynamics of early modern life.

My aim is to provide an account of the ways in which one particular era in our civilization established a conceptual framework for understanding time. It is an understanding, I would like to argue, that is of particular relevance to our present time-consciousness. An appreciation of the mutability and diversity of time concepts appears particularly crucial at the start of the third millennium of human history, a moment when an unquestioning adherence to a growth-oriented economics of time may eventually threaten to destroy the earth we inhabit. The historical study of variations in time concepts in our past can act as a corrective to our tendency to take time as an absolute and to forget that culture, art, and life's experience are composed of an interweaving of numerous temporalities. One of today's more important critical tasks, I believe, is to decipher and to distinguish the different ways in which our daily lives and experiences are structured by the individual and collective notions that serve to found our social world. Time, clearly, is one of the most fundamental of these ideas.

# Time and Ways of Knowing under Louis XIV

# 1

# Watches, Culture, and Society in Seventeenth-Century France

*Pour la mécanique et pour l'horlogerie, le XVIIe siècle fut aussi le grand siècle.*
— Laurent Defossez, *Les Savants du XVIIe siècle et la mesure du temps*

## FROM DECORATION TO FUNCTION: A BRIEF HISTORY OF EARLY MODERN WATCHES

THE EVOLUTION OF THE EARLY MODERN WATCH CAN BE SEEN AS A progression from an overarching concern for decoration to an increasing focus on accuracy. The watch as a material object of historical study manifests a defining trend of the early modern period in Europe, a tendency toward greater valorization of technical precision. In this chapter, I trace some of the most significant developments in the science and craft of horology in seventeenth-century France, where some of the major technological breakthroughs occurred.

These advances marked the early years of Louis XIV's reign, a period beginning in 1661 and ending prior to the revocation of the Edict of Nantes in 1685, when horological preeminence shifted to England and Switzerland. While France and England contributed to the evolution of the watch, and while Switzerland would eventually become the world leader in watchmaking, the precise national origins of the watch remain a subject of dispute among historians. There is evidence to suggest that history's first watch was invented by the German technician Peter Henlein, in Nuremberg in 1510.[1] Other indications point to Julien de Coudray, working in Blois, France in 1518, though the oldest known French watch was signed by Jacques de la Garde in 1551. Still others claim that there were watches in Italy as early as 1500.[2] But regardless of which European nation can claim the fame of having served as the birthplace of the watch, there is no doubt that portable timekeeping devices underwent significant changes and improvements during the following century, and that a number of the most important developments took place in France.

The early watches of Renaissance Europe were above all decorative objects to be worn by wealthy lords and ladies.[3] The etymology of the French word for watch, *montre,* points to the importance of displaying this object: *montre* is the substantivized form of the verb *montrer,* meaning to show. Originally, the term *montre* designated the face of a watch, the part that showed the time. Later, the word referring to the single part of the device became a synecdochal indicator of the entire device, the part for the whole.[4] While the face of the watch showed the time, and this only approximately in the sixteenth century, the watch as a whole served as an indicator of financial and social status: being only inconsistently functional, watches were worn mostly for show.

Watchmakers working in France would bring the decorative qualities of portable timepieces to new heights in the first half of the seventeenth century. The master enamel painters of Blois benefited from an artisanal innovation that permitted elaborate decorations to be drawn on the cases of watches: "[I]n about 1630, Jean Toutin invented a way of painting pictures in colour without having to run the enamel into separate chambers, which not only considerably simplified the task of the casemaker, but gave the enameller much greater freedom of design."[5] The covers of enamel-painted watches became known throughout Europe for the exquisite detail and lively colors of their portraits, landscapes, and allegorical scenes. While Blois established itself as the leading center for the fabrication of these colorful timepieces, Lyon, Rouen, and La Rochelle also grew in importance for decorative painting and horology. The climate of tolerance for Protestantism that grew out of the Edict of Nantes, signed by Henri IV in 1598, created safe havens in France for the largely Protestant artists and technicians who came from throughout Europe to practice their craft.

Meanwhile, in a separate and perhaps more significant sphere of activity for the evolution of watches, innovations in the mechanics of chronometry developed simultaneously with the decorative achievements of enamel painters. While the latter strove for elegance and beauty, mathematicians and astronomers, seeking new standards for measuring terrestrial and celestial phenomena, worked for accuracy. In a letter of 1 September 1639, Galileo told fellow scientist Giovanni Battista Baliani of the progress he was making in the precision of time-measurement:

That the use of the pendulum for the measurement of time is a most exquisite thing I have stated many times; as a matter of fact I have brought together diverse astronomical operations, in which by means of this measurer
I have achieved a precision infinitely more exact than that which was possible with any other astronomical instruments, as well as even with quadrants,
sextants, armillaries, and whatever else, having diameters . . . divided evenly
not only into degrees and minutes, but into parts of minutes as well.[6]

Having first conceived of the pendulum as a chronometrical instrument
when observing the swinging of a lamp in the arch of a cathedral in
Pisa, Galileo sought to put this device to more specific uses in tracking
astronomical phenomena.[7] The one invention that eluded Galileo, however, was the application of the pendulum to a clock mechanism.

The next generation of scientists after Galileo would draw on his
achievements and further the science of precision timekeeping. During
Louis XIV's reign, Paris would host a number of these scientists and
technicians and become a center for the emerging scientific domains of
the Newtonian era. Indeed, the interest in clocks and watches had already been in evidence at the French royal court before Louis XIV's
advent to the throne. In the "lettres patentes du roi" of November 1652,
horology is praised as a kind of art synthesizing several domains of scientific endeavor:

[Cet art] fait découvrir les degrés du soleil, le cours de la lune, les effets des
astres, la disposition des moments, des secondes, des minutes, des heures,
des jours, des semaines, des mois et des années, les productions des métaux,
les qualités des minéraux . . . toutes les sciences contribuent au succès favorable de ces objets.[8]

[This art permits the discovery of the successive positions of the sun, the
movement of the moon, the influence of stars, the disposition of moments,
seconds, minutes, hours, days, weeks, months, and years, the uses of metals,
the properties of minerals . . . all sciences contribute to the remarkable success of these objects.]

As in Galileo's description, units of measurement are emphasized. Here,
time quantities from "moments" to "années" are arranged in order of
increasing dimensions. The notion of increments is at the heart of this
celebration of horology, not only in terms of time but also in terms of
the spatial discovery of "les degrés du soleil." The statement also points
out the practical advantages of accurate means of time-measurement:
"[L]e coup d'une horloge adroitement disposé préserve la personne

d'un malade des attaques funestes de ses douleurs, quand le remède lui est proportionnellement donné à l'heure prescrite par le médecin." [The sound of a carefully utilized clock protects a patient from the pernicious attacks of his pains, when he is provided with the remedy in carefully timed doses by his physician.] The discussion then moves from medical to military questions—"une bataille se trouve ordinairement au point de sa gloire par le secours d'un juste réveille-matin" [a battle often achieves the height of its glory with the aid of an accurate alarm clock]—and ends with a global assessment of the value of watches for human life: "[L]'invention de la montre doit effectivement passer pour le principal mobile du repos, de la douceur et de la tranquillité des hommes." [The invention of the watch must be recognized as the main reason for to the calm, peace, and tranquility of all men.] In a number of areas of scientific and technical inquiry, watches represented an epistemological tendency toward accuracy in the conceptual apprehension of the world. This new approach to conceptualizing reality was described as a boon for humanity and given a high priority for further exploration.

In Charles Perrault's (1628–1703) polemical treatise, the *Parallèle des Anciens et des Modernes* (1688–97), the science of clocks and watches functions as a metaphor for the inventiveness of Moderns over against the precedents set by Ancients in the construction of knowledge. Perrault's Chevalier, speculating on the origins of watches, marvels at the advancement of technology during his own century: "Ce serait un plaisir de voir la première montre qui a été faite, je ne crois pas qu'on la pût voir sans rire, car je suis assuré qu'elle ressemblait plus à un tourne-broche qu'à une montre."[9] [It would be a pleasure to see the first watch ever made, I do not believe that one could see it without laughing, for I am sure that it more closely resembled a roasting spit than a watch.] Later in the dialogue, the abbé goes on to examine the question of original inventions versus relatively modern, recent innovations:

> Je veux bien . . . que l'inventeur de la première montre dont nous avons parlé, ait eu plus de génie et qu'il mérite plus de louanges, que tous les horlogers qui sont venus depuis; mais je prétends que d'y avoir ajouté la pendule, et d'avoir ensuite rendu cette pendule portative, inventions admirables, que nous devons à Monsieur Huygens, sont quelque chose de plus spirituel et de plus ingénieux que l'invention toute nue de la première montre. . . . ces premières montres n'approchaient nullement de la justesse et de la propreté de celles qui se font par les moindres de nos horlogers.[10]

> [I freely admit that . . . the inventor of the first watch of which we spoke had more genius and deserves more praise than all the clockmakers to come

after him; but I would contend that adding the pendulum to this device, and then making this pendulum portable—the admirable inventions of Mr. Huygens—is something much more ingenious than the mere invention of the first watch. . . . these early watches could hardly approach the accuracy and the neatness of those that the least skilled of our clockmakers produce today.]

In the *Parallèle*, the watch and the stages of its technical improvement become a representation of modernity as a whole, of the development of the sciences and of knowledge in general. The use of the watch as a frame of reference indicates not only its symbolic value as a metaphor for modern technologies of the time, but also its general recognition, near century's end, as an object of use and exchange in seventeenth-century culture, one representative of the possibilities for technological improvement that modern science offered.

Perhaps the most significant promise of technological advancement that still remained only a possibility at the end of the century was the determination of longitude. Under Louis XIV, interest in the improvement of clocks and watches was largely motivated by the problem of the calculation of longitude at sea, a central preoccupation for early modern navies aiming to expand the frontiers of their activity. France's economic and political fortunes clearly stood to improve with innovations in the science of tracking longitude, a technique for which watches would prove to be of central importance. Thus the watch took on a special significance, owing to the generalized kind of association with modernity that it acquired in Perrault's writings.

## Mapping Spaces and Keeping Time: Chronometry and the Problem of Longitude

The development of the science and industry of chronometry in early modern France was closely tied to navigation. Precision timekeeping was a key to tracking the position of a ship at sea by means of calculations of longitude, and these techniques were indispensable to the growth of France's navy under the direction of Louis XIV's highest minister, Jean-Baptiste Colbert. Colbert's active interest in maritime commerce was to be the motivating impulse behind a long-term search for a solution to the problem of longitude.

To know longitude by means of chronometry was to be able to sail safely and efficiently. Not to have this information at hand made sea travel at best a risky and inefficient business: ships could languish for weeks in open seas, missing landfalls (or achieving them prematurely), and exposing their crews to hunger, thirst, and disease.[11] Avoiding such dangers with precision navigation would serve France's interests abroad and, it was hoped, pose a serious challenge to the English and the Dutch, for whom France's naval enterprise at the beginning of Louis XIV's reign had become something of a laughing stock. Whereas Richelieu (1585–1642) had taken a keen interest in improving and expanding the French marine, Mazarin (1602–61) had thoroughly neglected it. While naval budgets at times approached 5,000,000 livres a year in the 1640s, between 1656 and 1660 budgets averaged only 312,000 livres.[12] At the time when Colbert began reviving Richelieu's efforts in 1661, more than 6,000 French sailors were employed abroad, by the Dutch and the Italians, and France could only claim to have some 18 warships; by the end of Colbert's administration of the navy, France could boast about 276 *bâtiments de guerre*.[13] So rapid was the pace of expansion in the early years of Louis XIV's reign that contests were held in some of France's major ports to see who could build a ship in the least amount of time: Rochefort produced a frigate in 30 hours, Brest in 22, and Marseille in only 7.[14] Though one might have hesitated to climb aboard especially the latter vessel, this competition simply highlights the well-known fact that Colbert was at the center of a concerted effort toward naval expansion.

The prospect of posing a strong challenge to the Dutch and of finding new resources in what would be France's first colonies was an exciting one for Colbert, but striking out on the high seas without accurate maps was always a gamble for those in his employ.[15] Latitude, of course, was not the problem: with a sextant, a compass, and a view of the sun at noon, an explorer could measure the angle between the sun, the vessel, and the horizon and thus determine the number of degrees north or south of the equator that gave his latitude.[16] Longitude, however, was an entirely different matter. To determine his position on the globe's vertical meridians, the sailor would need to measure not only space but also time. Since the earth spins through 360° in 24 hours, each hour of time difference between the local time at sea and the time of day at the port of origin would be equivalent to 15° of longitude. Whereas today one could take any cheap jogging watch to the middle of the Atlantic and know the time of day in Paris, in the seventeenth century there was no way of holding on to or keeping Parisian time once one had ventured far enough into the seas. There was no *garde-temps* [timekeeper] accurate, consistent, or durable enough to keep time from escaping the mariner's grasp. Pendulum clocks were thrown off by the bobbing and pitching of the vessel, and the inner mechanisms of watches were prone to expansion, contraction, and oxidation resulting from changes in temperature and barometric pressure as well as exposure to salt water and sea air. What was needed was a new kind of timepiece, impervious to movement and to the elements, consistent, accurate, and portable, and what this new kind of device urgently needed was an inventor.

As we know, Huygens first successfully applied Galileo's idea of the pendulum to a clock mechanism in 1657. While Salomon Coster, the clockmaker who executed Huygens's directions, and Galileo's son Vincenzio Galilei both contested Huygens's claim to the invention, Huygens provisionally silenced these disputes with the publication of his *Horologium oscillatorium* [*The Pendulum Clock*] in 1658.[17] His work attracted the attention of Louis XIV and Colbert, there being no question that Huygens was the closest to solving the problem of longitude through chronometry. Colbert founded the Académie Royale des Sciences (today the Institut de France) in 1666 and made Huygens a founding member of the society, bringing him to Paris in April of that year and awarding him an annual pension of 6,000 livres.[18] Huygens lived first in the Bibliothèque Royale and later in the Observatoire de Paris, which was founded in 1667 to support new work in astronomy that was to contribute to the quest for longitude. Huygens would stay in Paris until 1681, by which time an increasingly generalized intolerance toward Huguenots obliged the Protestant scientist to return to his native Holland, four years before the revocation of the Edict of Nantes in 1685.

Huygens's years in a Paris not yet dominated by religious persecution were highly productive. In 1675, his invention of the spiral spring, a device that miniaturized the regular oscillations of the pendulum within the restricted confines of watches, made possible a new degree of accuracy for portable timepieces. In his announcement of the invention in the *Journal des savants*, Huygens stressed its significance for the determination of longitude:

> Ayant trouvé une invention longtemps souhaitée, par laquelle les horloges sont rendues très justes ensemble et portatives, je crois que ce sera faire chose agréable au public de lui en faire part. . . . Les horloges de cette façon étant construites en petit seront des montres de poche très justes et en plus grande forme, pourront servir utilement par tout ailleurs, et particulièrement à trouver les longitudes, tant sur mer que sur terre, puisque leur mouvement est réglé par un principe d'égalité.[19]

[Having come upon an invention that has been pursued for quite some time, an invention as a result of which clocks are made both accurate and portable, I believe it would please the public if I were to communicate this. . . . These kinds of clocks constructed in miniature will be very accurate pocket watches. In a larger form, these devices will be widely useful, particularly for the determination of longitude, on land and at sea, since their movements will be regulated by a principle of equality.]

Huygens's chronometers had been tested at sea as early as 1664, on a voyage to the Cape Verde Islands off the western coast of Africa, and they were determined to be useful, albeit only relatively accurate tools for charting the ship's course. With the new spiral spring, Huygens had made a significant step forward, but the obstacle of the elements remained. A timepiece both accurate and durable enough to measure longitude consistently would only come into existence in the mid-eighteenth century (1730–70), a time during which English clockmaker John Harrison (1693–1776) perfected his series of revolutionary marine chronometers.[20] In the meantime, although progress was made, the quest continued.

While the pursuit of accuracy in timekeeping remained central to the search for longitude, Colbert and Louis XIV were always open to other possible solutions. In 1667, an anonymous German inventor claimed to have discovered a fail-safe method for determining longitude at sea. His invention was a kind of odometer, a spinning water wheel attached to the keel of a ship, registering the distance traveled. Louis XIV granted the inventor a patent immediately and paid him 60,000 livres on the basis of the proposal alone. In addition, Louis XIV promised to pay four sous on every ton of merchandise carried by every vessel to use the device. He also promised the inventor a sum of 8,000 livres a year for the rest of his life. All of this was on the condition that the inventor successfully demonstrate the marine odometer to a team of experts including Colbert, Abraham Duquesne (1610–88), who had just been named *lieutenant général des armées de mer* [Lieutenant General of the Navies], and, from the Académie Royale des Sciences, Huygens and the Abbé Jean Picard (1620–82).[21] While the evaluating committee praised the invention, they did not neglect to point out that the device's accuracy would be fatally compromised by the strong currents that any ship would encounter at sea, forces that would either immobilize the wheel, as in the case of a counter-current, or inordinately accelerate its revolutions. Although the invention did not receive official approval, the promise of this possible step toward a solution to the problem of longitude greatly benefited the inventor, who, when all was said and done, left Louis XIV's court wealthier by the sum of 160,000 livres.

Parallel to the possibility of a solution provided by mechanical devices, early modern administrators, sailors, and cartographers looked with their contemporary astronomers to the skies for points of reference in the determination of longitude. In 1610, Galileo, the first scientist to use telescopes for research,[22] opened up a new range of possibilities when he discovered that the moons revolving around the planet Jupiter could be observed, timed, and charted.[23] The movements and eclipses of these satellites were both predictable and relatively rapid, much more so than the eclipses of the moon, which proved to be a cumbersome tool for astronomical observations serving measurements on earth. The Jovian satellites, on the other hand, disappeared and reappeared in patterns so frequent and consistent that they constituted a kind of celestial clockwork, a steady frame of temporal reference that could be consulted from various points on the surface of the earth. Galileo drew up tables for predicting and tracking the eclipses of the Jovian satellites, and his method would eventually become generally accepted as a way of calculating longitude, but only on land.

Astronomical observations, requiring clear skies and optimal conditions for the use of sophisticated instruments, had their limitations when it came to sea travel. Whereas most ships' captains could handle a sextant, the kind of meticulous observation required for Galileo's method was beyond the grasp of an average crew at sea. Not only would a team of astronomers have to be on board to make the necessary calculations; their delicate instruments would need greater stability than a moving ship would allow, and one could not always guarantee that the weather would cooperate. The Jovian satellites proved nonetheless to be a privileged object of investigation for scientists in the second half of the seventeenth century.

Most notably, Giovanni Domenico Cassini (1625–1712), superintendent of the waterworks of Bologna, published a set of *Ephemerides*, tables of observations on the eclipses of Jupiter's moons, in 1668, and thereby caught the attention of Colbert.[24] Cassini's success as an astronomer earned him an invitation to the Académie Royale des Sciences and a *pension* of 9,000 livres a year. Cassini came to France in 1669 and became a naturalized citizen in 1673, taking on the gallicized name of Jean Dominique.[25] He was appointed director of the recently founded Observatoire de Paris, where he worked with Huygens, the Abbé Picard, and other noted astronomers to map the skies (Cassini also worked on a map of the moon from 1672 to 1679) and the earth. Isaac

Thuret (d. 1706), who would eventually be named Horloger du Roi in 1684, was put in charge of clock maintenance at the Observatoire in 1672. The observatory had some of the best clocks in the world, including a pendulum clock that could consistently mark half-seconds, quite a feat for the time. While there was a movement to trace the world's prime meridian through Paris, the Royal Observatory in Greenwich, England, built in 1675 and host to a distinguished rival group of scientists in Charles II's Royal Society of London, gradually became the de facto standard for measurements of longitude and time in maritime commerce during the following centuries and was established as the world's prime meridian in 1884, at the International Meridian Conference in Washington, D.C.[26]

In the seventeenth century, with the problem of longitude still unsolved, the race for technological superiority with England (which included as well the competition for maritime commerce with Holland) involved not only precision timekeeping but also measurements of space, as scientists continued struggling to find a way to determine longitude consistently and precisely at sea and observed the Jovian satellites on land. The Abbé Picard was assigned the task of determining the amount of arc between two selected points, measuring a meridional line between Malvoisine, near Paris, and Sourdon, near Amiens. He determined the number of degrees of arc between these two terminal points by means of the observation at each location of the angle between two stars. The discrepancies of the observations at both points were calculated as a specific amount of arc, which was then translated into a linear value for a degree of longitude. A figure for the circumference of the earth was then deduced from these findings. Without a way of determining longitude at sea, this was the best that scientists could do on land.[27]

When in 1679 Louis XIV ordered the Académie Royale des Sciences to draw up a new map of France based on all the latest precision technologies for measuring terrestrial space, Picard's findings were combined with a newly revised version of Cassini's *Ephemerides*. Looking over the updated map of his domain, Louis XIV complained that he was losing more territory to his astronomers than to his enemies. Nevertheless, a new kind of accuracy was being gained, a newly precise conceptual hold on time and space that resulted from Colbert and Louis XIV's efforts to bring some of the world's best scientific minds to Paris. As the world seemed to be shrinking into the restrained forms of mathematically determined spatial parameters, the prospect of exercising a greater degree of control over the spaces of France's domestic realm and its potential interests abroad became increasingly real. A sufficiently clear indication of France's expansionist zeal during the early years of Louis XIV's reign can be seen in the founding of the Compagnie des Indes occidentales [West India Company] and the Compagnie des Indes orientales [East India Company] in 1664, the Compagnie du Levant [Company of the Rising Sun], based in Marseille in 1670, and the Compagnie du Nord [Company of the North] in 1669. Through the latter, Colbert aimed to compete with the Dutch on their own thoroughly established marine turf in the Baltic Sea. This competition would become sufficiently acrimonious to lead to the war with Holland of 1672–78.

Both military and economic objectives motivated the project of mapping spaces and keeping time with increasing precision under Louis XIV. The major milestones in the temporal arena, Huygens's pendulum clock of 1657 and his spiral spring regulator device of 1675, had their analogues in the new maps being drawn up by Cassini and his cohort. Perhaps the culmination of these newly precise achievements in cartography was Cassini's *Planisphère terrestre* of 1696, a large-scale circular world map, eight meters in diameter when laid out on the floor of the Observatoire.[28] This map incorporated the findings of astronomical observations taken from more than forty locales, including Québec, Santiago, the Cape of Good Hope (with the assistance of Edmond Halley [1656–1742]), Goa, and Peking.[29] New geographical knowledge represented in this map included the revised extent of the Pacific Ocean and topographical details such as the marking of the Mississippi River, based on data available by the mid-1690s.

While this comprehensive map did not have the benefit of reliable measurements of longitude at sea, it nonetheless represented a major improvement on earlier world maps and a departure from early practices of mapmaking. From late-Medieval and Renaissance cartography to the end of the seventeenth century, significant changes in the conceptualization and representation of space occurred. In the late fifteenth and early sixteenth centuries, mapmakers like Martin Behaim (1459–1507) and Diogo Ribeiro (d. 1533) played the combined role of geographer, explorer, merchant, and scholar, using strong symbolism in their drawings and evocations of the unknown to appeal to the imagination of the mapreader. Thus the mapmaker was a kind of visionary, a holder of a mysterious authority in the spatial understanding of the world. Paul Zumthor sees the work of the Cassini family as the turning point in the history of cartography, since it represented a transition from a practice based on the evocativeness of symbols to the pretended neutrality of calculations: "It was only during the century that ran its course between

1670 and 1770, with the Cassini family, father, son, and grandson, that the elements of modern cartography—based on triangulation, the regularity of proportions, and a strictly codified sign system—would liberate themselves from the burden of traditions."[30] In fact, the transition toward modern mapmaking was already being prepared by such Renaissance mapmakers as Gerard Mercator (1512–94), whose world map of 1569 was the first attempt to project a representation of the earth on a flat surface, as a practical tool for navigation; and Abraham Ortelius (1527–98), author of the *Theatrum Orbis Terrarum* (1570), one of the first attempts at a comprehensive world atlas.[31] In skillfully manipulating the conditions of publication and reception of their work in a marketplace determined by a new print culture, these cartographers departed from the quasi-mystical claims to knowledge of early mapmakers and constructed the identity of the cartographer as a professional, objective observer and author, whose work would serve the practical purposes of merchants and explorers. With Cassini, drawing on the work of Galileo, Huygens, and the Abbé Picard, a new degree of accuracy became possible, and the ultimate criterion for conceptualizing space became the strict adherence to mathematical observation.[32] Even if Louis XIV lost territory in the process, he gained in accuracy, and that gain would give him a potential advantage in the race against the English and the Dutch.

Accuracy and the ability to display it in maps meant power. J. B. Harley, applying Michel Foucault's analyses of historiography to the history of cartography, makes the point that maps are always discursive constructs and manifestations of the will to power of those who commission them.[33] For Harley, the transition from richly illustrated, evocative maps to ones which foreground the geometrical calculations guaranteeing their accuracy is a move, not away from symbolic representation, but toward a different kind of symbolism, a system of signs that articulates claims to objectivity and rational control of the physical world: "Far from being incompatible with symbolic power, more precise measurement intensified it. Accuracy became a new talisman of authority."[34] Seen in this light, the scientific pursuit of longitude contributed to the representation of royal authority as the seat of the conceptual power of spatial and temporal quantification.[35] Louis XIV was among many political figures whose portraits were included on early modern maps as a way of associating the rational representation of space with political authority. In 1665–66, a reissue of the Dutch cartographer Joan Blaeu's world map of 1648 placed a portrait of Louis XIV in the middle of the map, in a position subtending the union between the earth's two hemispheres. A Dutch wall map of 1660 by Pieter van den Keere and his anonymous collaborators situated a portrait of Charles II (1630–85) in precisely the same position. This cartographical iconography bears witness to the competition between France and England for political, economic, and scientific control of the world by means of the ability to map it accurately—in other words, through the determination of longitude, the techniques for which they were racing to perfect.

Perhaps an even more powerful manifestation of Louis XIV's role in early modern mapmaking is the absence of his or any other portraits in Cassini's *Planisphère terrestre* of 1696. To use Harley's term, the new "symbolic realism" resulting from the findings of the Académie Royale des Sciences offered to the viewer a world adorned only by topographical features and meridians, traced in the highest degree of specificity available at the time. But the ultimate goal still had not been reached. Even Cassini's masterful world map at century's end did not mark the oceans and what lay beyond them (from the European perspective) with the accuracy that John Harrison's marine chronometers would render possible only in the mid-eighteenth century. In analogous temporal terms, even Huygens's pendulum and spiral spring could not keep time without fail. It was as if space and time continued just barely to elude the grasp of Louis XIV, Colbert, and all those who labored under them to gain a firm conceptual hold on the earth's dimensions. This situation of just falling short fueled further activity and continued a veritable explosion of scientific research during the second half of the seventeenth century.

## ONIONS, PATENTS, AND EDICTS:
## THE CHALLENGES OF INNOVATION

The scientific and administrative quest for longitude led to major advances in such domains as cartography and precision chronometry. Gone were the days when a watch mechanism would be prone to hours of inaccuracy even in the mundane meteorological conditions of landlocked life. For pre-Huygensian timekeeping, as Catherine Cardinal explains, "the functioning of watches was very imprecise. They were observed to run approximately 30 minutes fast during the hours that followed winding and they ran equally slow when the winding mechanism was almost completely unwound. The necessity of frequent rewinding explains the presence of a small sundial inside the covers of numerous watch cases."[36] The backup sundial, a mark of material culture on the threshold between the ancient and the modern, the natural (solar) and the artificial (mechanical), would progressively disappear as watches increased in accuracy during the seventeenth and eighteenth centuries. Still in the seventeenth century, the sundial attached to watches served to compensate for losses in accuracy concomitant with the unwinding of what was often a length of pigskin that would be wound up and then released to turn the inner mechanisms of the watch. As watches increased in precision, this sundial, the mark of the ancient, disappeared, giving way to modern timepieces, independent of sun and sky, which then began steadily to improve and serve more utilitarian purposes.

Like the outmoded technology that disappeared during the reign of Louis XIV, the ornate enamel decorations characteristic of watches at mid-century appeared less often for a time, giving way to the more somber, utilitarian style for watches that can be observed in the *oignons*, the timepieces associated with Louis XIV's reign.[37] With improvements in accuracy continuing, the enamel painting of elaborate miniatures, independently of and on watches, would see a kind of renaissance in the eighteenth century, as part of the style typical of Louis XV's reign. The *oignons*, situated at a point of transition in the science of horology and in the public and private uses of timepieces, were named for their rather clunky appearance: "The typical *oignon* is a hefty watch with a diameter of 58 to 60 mm, the thickness of which, taking into account its curved glass, is from 37 to 40 mm. These dimensions are at the origin of the name given to these watches."[38] Larger than the enamel-painted gems made famous in Blois or than the *montres de fantaisie* [specially shaped watches], in shapes like those of a flower, a bee, or even a skull (a manifestation of the reflection on time and death characteristic of the still life in painting, taken to the domain of watchmaking), the *oignons* of Louis XIV's reign represented the possibility of greater accuracy. The emphasis in the design of the watch was on the device's inner mechanisms, and a more monochrome exterior of silver- or gold-studded Moroccan leather became prevalent in the decoration of the watches' covers.

Perhaps the most significant of the inner mechanisms causing a swelling of watches in their appearance and resulting from increased concern for accuracy was Huygens's spiral hair spring.[39] The spiral spring provided regularly alternating motion for the escapement, the device that breaks up the continuous movement of the motor into even portions. The escapement temporarily stops the gear that is driven by the watch's motor, one tooth at a time, allowing the movement to escape at regular intervals. The key for the effective functioning of the escapement is a consistent means of driving the oscillations, something the spiral spring provided in 1675.

Also during the period 1670–75, a fourth gear was added to the innards of watches. This allowed the watch to run for up to 30 hours with each winding, a considerable improvement over the 12 hours that watches could run continuously before. During this time, then, the watch was first made capable of operating for a period greater than a day. A day in the life had thus become a measurable entity.[40] The changes in functioning of watches marked Louis XIV's reign with the monochrome *oignons*, bulky, laden with their innovations in both the tracking of short durations and the ability to run over longer durations.

The 1670s were a time of major technological improvements and a significant period for the career of Huygens, living on the banks of the Seine under the auspices of the recently established Académie Royale des Sciences. As was the case for the pendulum clock, however, Huygens encountered considerable difficulties in trying to obtain a patent, or "privilège," for his spiral spring. Huygens had commissioned a prototype based on his calculations and instructions from Isaac Thuret in January of 1675. The very same month, Thuret produced a second prototype and announced it to Colbert as his own invention. Huygens eventually prevailed and was granted the "privilège" when Thuret himself admitted to having tried to steal the rights to the device. But Huygens's troubles were far from being over. A certain Abbé de Hautefeuille accused Huygens himself of having stolen the invention. In England, Robert Hooke (1635–1703) claimed to have first come up with the spiral spring.[41] Hooke worked intensively with watchmaker Thomas Tompion (1639–1713), presenting devices to the king in the hopes of being granted a patent, to no avail.

Although Huygens was officially recognized for his major innovation of 1675, he was weary of the legal battles for rights to the invention and decided to relinquish the "privilège," thus allowing rival clock and watchmakers to work freely with the technology. Huygens sought temporary refuge from the travails of his professional life in France by traveling to Holland the following year:

> Leaving Paris the first of July, 1676 for Holland, after an illness of five months, I left all clockmakers free to work on this invention, seeing that the patent had cost me a number of appeals in order to have it registered with the Parliament and that, even afterwards, I would always have new lawsuits and difficulties.[42]

As an inventor, Huygens dealt with a steady stream of legal challenges for the rights to his work; as a Huguenot, he faced perhaps even greater obstacles.

Along with enduring the pressures of the race for technical breakthroughs in horology, technicians like Huygens, many of whom were Protestants, increasingly met with religious persecution as Louis XIV's politics began to undermine the provisions for tolerance established under Henri IV by the Edict of Nantes (1598).[43] Catherine Cardinal describes the difficulties that Huguenot technicians and craftsmen had to confront in the latter half of the seventeenth century:

> The repressive measures taken against Protestants began with the personal reign of Louis XIV. In 1661, the king formed a commission for verifying the conduct of the Reformed Church. Several acts of repression came in succession: in 1667, a ban on conducting burials during the daytime; in 1669, the elimination of bipartisan houses of justice, a decree stipulating that at least half the members of a union had to be Catholics; then, a ban on practicing various occupations; after 1676, the creation of the treasury of conversions dubbed the Pelisson treasury, followed by *dragonnades* [sending of troops to Protestant regions]. These measures provoked a first wave of emigration in 1680–1683. The revocation of the Edict of Nantes on 18 October 1685 resulted in more departures for other countries. Emigration picked up again after 1698, the year when Louis XIV authoritatively reaffirmed his decrees.[44]

While Louis XIV took a keen interest in technological improvements early in his reign and invited Huygens to Paris because he was impressed by the Protestant scientist's achievements, the Sun King was also moving toward a total renunciation of tolerance for Protestantism. As a result, while during the initial years of Louis XIV's reign applied sciences like horology flourished, later in his reign the emigration of a number of key Protestant technicians and artisans contributed to France's fall from preeminence as a center for horology. Because there were so few experts in the newly developing technologies of time-measurement, and because many of these experts were Protestants, the Revocation of the Edict of Nantes had a devastating effect on technical endeavor in France. Carlo M. Cipolla estimates that "[t]o destroy or to build up the industry it was enough to dismiss or to attract a dozen craftsmen."[45] While the Sun King had aimed early on, under the influence of Colbert's politics of maritime expansion, to attract these experts, later in his reign his politics tended to exclude them, and England and Switzerland began to outshine France in the science of keeping time.

Judging from the intense interest and indeed the pride that France took in the science of horology, the loss of some of the science's most prominent practitioners must have come as a blow to Louis XIV's court. Even in 1652, Parisian preeminence in clock and watchmaking had been a matter of both economics and nationalistic pride:

> [L]es maîtres jusqu'à présent reçus en notre dite ville se sont rendus si habiles que leur industrie surpasse de beaucoup celle des étrangers tant à la beauté de leurs ouvrages qu'en la bonté qu'ils se sont particulièrement étudiés d'y garder . . . dont nous tirons un avantage de si grande conséquence, que les plus considérables de notre cour, les marchands et tous nos peuples ont perdu le désir d'en chercher ailleurs.[46]

> [The master clockmakers we have welcomed into our city until now have become so skilled that their industry surpasses by far that of foreigners, both in regard to the beauty of their works and to the quality that they have labored to maintain in their products . . . from which we gain such a considerable advantage, that the most prominent members of our court, the merchants, and all of our people no longer wish to seek these items anywhere else.]

Huygens's presence in France was both a continuation and a culmination of this trend toward social and political valuation of the science of horology, and his departure can be considered the beginning of the end for early modern French clock and watchmaking. The innovations that he achieved were highly valued by Louis XIV and his ministers at a time when religious intolerance still was not strong enough a force to override the desire for technological advances. France took pride in the science of horology, and individuals privileged enough to take part in new activities of precision timekeeping valued watches as objects both precious and practical, as indices of social rank and tools for the development of new ways of thinking time and experiencing daily life.

## USES AND DISTRIBUTION OF WATCHES

What emerges from the historical study of the cultural valences of clocks and watches in the 1660s and 1670s is a sense that precision timekeeping was of central concern not only for scientists and artisans, but also for members of Louis XIV's court and political and cultural figures of the time. Truly accurate early modern timepieces were rare in the initial stages of their development, and their distribution early in the

Sun King's reign was thus limited to the most privileged sectors of society. As a result, my analysis of how the valorization of accuracy and quantification of small units of time affected ways of knowing and thinking about time mainly limits itself to economically privileged social strata. Time conceptions built around what I call microdiachronies, or sets of small time units arranged in the perception and understanding of experience, were only beginning to take shape among the scientific and literary intelligentsia of the seventeenth century. These ways of thinking would become more widespread as precision time technologies were more widely distributed in the eighteenth century and beyond. Already in the seventeenth century, evidence can be found for a progression toward wider distribution.

To go back to the early seventeenth century, the postmortem inventory of Cardinal Mazarin's possessions gives some indications of the value that watches held during the time leading up to Louis XIV's reign. This listing includes a number of *montres sonnantes*, watches with an alarm, several with cases made of gold and with enamel-painted faces.[47] The cost of these watches ranged from 150 livres, for a watch with a silver cover, to 1,000 livres, for the watches encased in gold and featuring sound along with their timekeeping functions. One other indication is given in the Mazarin inventory, of a clock decorated with diamonds: "Une horloge sonnante garnie d'or d'émaux dapli[e] couleur violet, garni[e] de 44 petits diamants et de son étui de velours rouge, prisée ensemble la somme de trois cents livres" [A clock with alarm, decorated in gold with violet enamel, furnished with 44 small diamonds and its case made in red velours, priced at the sum of 300 livres].[48] Such a collection of timepieces could only have been in the possession of one of France's highest ministers.

The work of Annik Pardailhé-Galabrun has shown, however, that watches and clocks were slowly increasing in their distribution and availability, even in the seventeenth century.[49] Pardailhé-Galabrun points out that the number of Parisian clock and watchmakers increased dramatically from the sixteenth to the eighteenth century. In the first half of the sixteenth century, there were only "6 clockmakers, 5 of whom were master clockmakers. According to the statutes of their community, dating from 1544, they were able to make clocks or alarm clocks, large or small watches, and other works of their art. . . . The number of master clockmakers reached 180 in the 18th century."[50] During this period, watches were placed in the same category as these "other works," that is jewels, since they were decorative, luxury items. Their rarity and high cost made them available mostly to such wealthy nobles as Charles Damas, comte de Charolais, the inventory of whose possessions was taken during the year of his death in 1640, and included "a watch made of copper with a gold case, a watch with a silver case and alarm, a copper watch."[51] Following her analysis of the inventory, Pardailhé-Galabrun reminds us that "watches were still fairly rare objects during this period."

For the period of Parisian history covering the years 1690–1726, the results are different. A survey of 59 members of the clergy, for example, shows that "approximately 40% of these priests owned an instrument for time-measurement: watches, pendulum clocks, or clocks."[52] The timepiece becomes at this point an indicator of the relative wealth of members of the clergy. A number of merchants also began owning timepieces by the turn of the century, as is indicated by inventories of their possessions, including "a clock from England with a repetition mechanism, in its case, priced at 250 livres, at the home of a clothier, a Parisian bourgeois, in 1719, a clock with ebony case and console stand in gilded wood, signed Curlot, estimated to be worth 140 livres, at the home of another clothier."[53] Marie-Anne des Essarts, the wife of a wealthy bookseller and publisher named Frédéric Léonard, left behind, after her death in 1706, "a watch with chain in gold, enamel and diamond, evaluated at 350 livres."[54] The wealth of the bourgeoisie expanded, making these luxury items more readily available as these objects were being distributed more widely. In 1710, "Jeanne Dameron, nanny of the Duke and head housekeeper of the Duchess of Bourbon, owned . . . 'a watch, made by André Moris in Paris, in its leather case furnished with small gold studs and a string of 60 small pearls, the whole item priced at 70 livres.'"[55] Pardailhé-Galabrun finds similar data for "L. Michel Gersaut, butler for the marquis de Vince," who in 1710 owned "a watch in its silver case."[56] In discussing these inventories, Pardailhé-Galabrun points out that "these two types of domestic employees were at the top of the social ladder in this category of servants." Thus by the turn of the century, not only did the clergy and the bourgeoisie begin owning clocks and even watches, but also some of the most privileged of the servants of noble households in Paris were able to acquire a relatively inexpensive watch, like Jeanne Dameron's 70-livre model. As it became less of an ornamental object and began serving more utilitarian purposes, the watch also gradually became more widely available in different sectors of society by century's end.

The seventeenth century is therefore a crucial in-between period for horology, a time when clocks and watches were undergoing revolutionary improvements, like the pendulum and the spiral spring, but were

overall still limited in distribution to the wealthiest inhabitants of
France, albeit with change on the horizon. The emergence of new technologies and the growing use of clocks and watches constituted a series
of events in the cultural history of France that had an initial impact in
society's most privileged sectors, an impact that would become generalized in the eighteenth century, when 40% of Parisian households, for
example, had a clock.[57] In the time period before such generalized distribution of clocks and watches, the way in which these objects constructed the human experience of time elicited various reactions,
interpretations, and commentaries. To recall the remarks of Stuart
Sherman, every timekeeping device proposes a temporality, or a way of
understanding the idea of time that the device represents. These temporalities were new and vital to intellectual life and subjective experience
in the seventeenth century, a time when new domains of private life
were beginning to take shape.

## THE LOVER'S WATCH

During the 1660s and 1670s, several works of popular literature focused on the personal experience of love and/in time. This literary fashion took the form of lovers' clocks and watches. In 1666, a Marseillais
writer named Balthazar de Bonnecorse (1631–1706) published a work
of epistolary fiction, combining poetry and prose, entitled *La Montre*
[The Watch].[58] The book enjoyed considerable popularity and was published in four editions in Paris. It also appeared in Bordeaux, Grenoble,
and in Holland.[59] Bonnecorse, a wealthy nobleman, was a friend of
Georges (1601–67) and Madeleine de Scudéry (1607–1701), who
helped his publishing career, and of La Fontaine (1621–95) and Pellis-
son (1624–93). Although his writings could not be considered great literature, they had a public impact sufficient to inspire imitations of the
Lover's Watch in 1678, in the pages of the *Mercure galant*. Aphra Behn
(1640–89), the first English woman to make her living as a writer, composed an adaptation of Bonnecorse's work, called *La Montre: or the Lover's Watch*, which was first published in 1686.[60]

Despite his successes and influence, however, Bonnecorse is mostly
forgotten today, remembered only as one of Boileau's many victims.
Boileau (1636–1711) veritably skewered Bonnecorse in his ninth *Epître*,
where it is a question of "tous ces vains amas de frivoles sornettes, /
*Montre*, miroir d'amour, amitiés, amourettes, / Dont le titre souvent est
l'unique soutien / Et qui, parlant beaucoup, ne disent jamais rien" [All

of these vain collections of frivolous nonsense, *The Watch*, the mirror of love, friendships, and trysts, whose titles are often their only redeeming quality, and which, speaking a lot, never say much of anything].[61] Although Boileau himself admitted to not having read *La Montre*, but only to having scanned the title and first page, his harsh sarcasm has branded Bonnecorse ever since as a talentless charlatan.

Although Bonnecorse was certainly no La Fontaine (far from it), his invention of the Lover's Watch is not without its moments of literary verve. For the purposes of this study, what is most significant about *La Montre* is its representation of time and personal identity, of the rhythms of emotional life during the very period when horology was undergoing a kind of technological revolution in France. The charming volume and its second part, published by Claude Barbin in 1671, are valuable documents for the study of the representation of time, timepieces, and private life in the seventeenth century.[62]

This love story describes the hours of a day in the life of a lover named Damon, whose demanding lady, Iris, writes to him from a faraway place, while he pines away for her. He has asked her for some sign of affection, and by way of response she sends him a kind of epistolary timepiece:

> Je veux enfin sortir d'affaire, je suis fille de parole; et pour vous payer (une discrétion que Damon lui avait demandé), je vous envoie une Montre de ma façon. Il pourrait être que vous n'en avez point vu comme celle-ci: ce n'est pas une des ces montres, où il y a toujours quelque chose à racommoder: elle est bonne, elle est juste, et elle le sera tant que vous m'aimerez, et tant que je serai absente: dès que vous cesserez de m'aimer, la corde se rompra; elle n'ira plus; et dès que je serai de retour, l'usage en sera presque inutile. (7–8)

> [But, to let you see I am a maid of honor, and value my word, I will acquit myself of this obligation I have to you, and send you a watch of my fashion; perhaps you never saw any so good. It is not one of those, that have always something to be mended in it; but one that is without fault, very just and good, and will remain so, as long as you continue to love me. But Damon, know, that the very minute you cease to do so, the string will break, and it will go no more. 'Tis only useful in my absence, and when I return, 'twill change its motion.][63]

In her writing, this lady marks every hour of her admirer's day and recommends the tasks and activities—reading her letters, writing responses, getting dressed, socializing with friends, eating, sleeping, dreaming—that he should pursue during his day. The whole text is a time construction, representing a subjective, affective experience of time.

Damon's lady specifies the way in which he should make use of this figurative watch that she has sent him: "ma montre servira moins à vous montrer les heures, qu'à vous enseigner comment vous devez les employer" [my watch will not serve so much to indicate the hours, as to teach you how to make use of them] (9). Iris places emphasis on the subjective experience of time and on the use of time as the proper execution of a lover's duties. According to the literary device of the lover's watch, love and proper devotion to love take the form of a particular kind of attention to time in daily life. The quasi-monastic regimen of dutiful love takes shape around the hours indicated on Iris's creation:

> Mais je dois vous expliquer ma montre. Elle marque les vingt-quatre heures qui composent le jour et la nuit. Au-dessus de chaque heure vous trouverez écrit ce que vous devez faire durant cette heure-là. Toutes les demi-heures sont marquées par des soupirs: parce que le propre d'un Amant est de soupirer jour et nuit: outre que les soupirs sont des enfants qui naissent à toute heure. Toutefois afin que ma montre soit juste, il faut que l'Amour la conduise, et que le mouvement soit enfermé dans votre cœur. (12)

> [But I ought to explain to you my watch. [It] points you out . . . the four and twenty hours, that compose the day and the night: over every hour, you will find written, what you ought to do, during its course; and every half-hour is marked with a sigh, since the quality of a lover is, to sigh day and night: sighs are the children of lovers, that are born every hour. And that my watch may always be just, Love himself ought to conduct it; and your heart should keep time with the movement.] (Behn 286–87)[64]

Iris places her imaginary watch within the most intimate emotional and physical space of her lover—she wants the watch to become coequal to his heart, so that even his most visceral experience of rhythm and time in life will be dependent on his love for her, a love taking the form of a timepiece and a daily schedule. Damon's duties are marked on each hour of the clock, as follows:

> VIII. Agréable rêverie [Pleasant rêverie].
> IX. Dessein de ne plaire à personne [Intention not to be pleasing to anyone].
> X. Lecture de Billets [Reading of love letters].
> XI. Heure à écrire [The hour for writing].
> XII. Devoir indispensable [Indispensable duty].
> I. Entretiens forcés [Obligatory conversations].

II. Heure du repas [Mealtime].
III. Visites d'amis [Visits from friends].
IV. Conversations générales [General conversations].
V. Visites un peu dangereuses [Slightly dangerous visits].
VI. Promenade sans dessein [Aimless stroll].
VII. Retraite volontaire [Voluntary retreat].
VIII. Demandes empressées [Hurried requests].
IX. Fâcheux souvenir [Unpleasant memory].
X. Réflexions [Reflections].
XI. Repas du soir [Evening meal].
XII. Complaisance [Indulgence].
I. Impossibilité de dormir [Insomnia].
II. Conversation en songe [Conversation in a dream].
III. Caprices à souffrir en songe [Caprices to be tolerated in the dream].
IV. Jalousie en songe [Jealousy in the dream].
V. Rupture en songe [Separation in the dream].
VI. Racommodement en songe [Reconciliation in the dream].
VII. Songes divers [Various dreams].

When the watch has gone through twenty-four hours of time, it is time once again for Damon to awake and to resume his regimen of devotion to Iris. This demanding lady places clear and precise time constraints on Damon's activities, even throughout the duration of his nightly slumber. She does, however, allow him a certain freedom during meal-times, telling him that this is a kind of private time or free time that not even she will regulate. But meals are also social occasions, and, as is the case especially following the evening meal, they involve a certain amount of obligatory conversation, patience, and indulgence of others, duly included on the face of the watch.

Socializing is a significant category of the lover's daily chronology. While social life is associated with mealtimes, it also includes the obliga-tory conversations following religious duties, the "devoir indispensable" at church. While, as Iris seems to indicate, socializing can at times be tedious and take the form of an obligation or, more precisely, a time constraint, life in society also presents its perils, as in the case of the dangerous visits at five in the evening. For these, Iris takes into account the possibility that Damon's internal watch may be at risk of running a bit fast or slow: "Il n'est pas aisé de se gouverner juste en ces rencon-tres; le moyen le plus sûr est que vous vous imaginiez que je lis toutes vos pensées; que j'observe tous vos regards; et que j'écoute toutes vos paroles" [It is not easy to control oneself with precision in these encoun-ters; the surest way is to imagine that I can read all of your thoughts;

that I observe your gaze; and that I hear all of your words] (60–61). At one of the more fluid points in the lover's daily chronology, Iris imposes her desire for omniscience, omnipresence, and control from afar. This is the clearest instance of the use of the watch as an instrument of inter-subjective control.

Perhaps the most significant area of personal experience marked on the watch, however, consists of the activities of reading and writing, to which Iris demands that Damon devote two hours a day, from ten until noon, immediately before the rites of piety. Time takes shape in this tale through writing, and writing must without fail take up at least some part of the lover's time. This figurative watch is, after all, a kind of motor not only for the synchronization and continuation of amorous interior experience, but also of epistolary communication. Iris wishes above all that Damon remain in contact with her from afar.

Damon carries out his duties diligently, and, in the second part of *La Montre*, he practices his own brand of horology in evaluating and supplementing the device that Iris has sent him:

> J'avoue que votre montre est juste, son mouvement règle celui de mon cœur; et j'observe si exactement ce qu'elle marque, que vous me louerez de mon assiduité lorsque vous apprendrez que je compte jusques aux minutes. Vous me dites que je la conserve chèrement, et cependant vous me l'avez envoyée sans boîte. Je veux lui en donner une; mais il faut auparavant que je vous en envoie le dessein, et que je vous consulte sur une matière si délicate. (4)

> [I admit that your watch is accurate, that its movement regulates that of my heart; and I observe all that it marks so exactly that you will praise me for my assiduity when you learn that I even count each minute. You entreat me to keep it and cherish it, yet you have sent it to me without a case. I want to make one for it; but first I must send you its design, so that I may consult you on so delicate a matter.]

The design that Damon favors is, predictably, in the shape of a heart. Further, he creates a cover for the watch through which one can see the face of the watch. In a sense, then, the lover wishes to see time only through love:

> Enfin, cette boîte sera à peu près comme ces ouvrages de filigranne, dont le travail n'empêche pas qu'on n'y voie ce qu'ils renferment. Vous pourrez donc voir au travers de ce cœur toute votre montre, et vous avouerez sans doute que le désir que j'ai qu'elle règle tous les moments de ma vie, n'est pas

moindre que celui de conserver un ouvrage qui m'est infiniment précieux. (44)

[This case will be like these filigree works which allow one to see what they contain just beneath the surface. Thus you will be able to see your entire watch through this heart, and you will no doubt recognize that my desire that this device regulate each moment of my life is no less important than my wish to preserve an object that is infinitely precious to me.]

Presenting himself as the perfect lover, Damon goes his lady one better, adding to the watch in such a way as to protect it, as a material object, and to enhance its functioning on a figurative level. He places love in the foreground to improve his understanding of time, a deeply subjective way of knowing his day's hours, minutes, and moments. Starting with the stipulations created next to each hour of time by Iris, Damon subdivides this time and imposes even more exacting constraints on himself, insisting to his lady that he is counting all of the minutes tracked by the watch and that he wants this device to control every single moment of his daily life. On the face of the Lover's Watch, then, we can see a combination of a concern for precision in the tracking of time and for a fuller understanding of the subjective experience of private time.

Within the following decade, the Lover's Watch, while being published in ulterior editions, also had an influence on one of history's first "literary magazines," Jean Donneau de Visé's *Le Mercure galant* (see chapter 4). In the March 1678 issue of the *Mercure galant,* a picture of a clock appeared, the face and its hours all surrounded by pictures of cherubs and hearts, with Cupid and his arrows in the center of the clockface, pointing to the different hours, each bearing a different caption.[65] This picture reappeared in the April issue, accompanied by a story explaining the composition and the meaning of this "Horloge d'amour" (306–45). It is a story of a certain Cavalier and a Belle who agree to be together at a masked ball. The lovers decide to let each other know all they do while disguised, so as not to betray one another. They also agree to accompany one another when going to such events. A hidden Rival overhears them making their pact and hatches a plan to create a misunderstanding between the two lovers. Later, the Rival leads the Cavalier to believe that the Belle will be at a certain ball, where the lovers had not planned to be together. Distraught, the Cavalier goes to the ball but cannot find his Belle, who, for her part, finds out that he has been there without telling her. Her extreme jealousy makes her spend "comme lui une très-méchante nuit" [as he did, a very unpleasant night] (313).

Determined to break with his Belle, the Cavalier goes to see her: "Le lendemain dès neuf heures du matin, l'Amant va trouver sa Belle" [The next day at nine in the morning, the Lover goes to see his Belle] (314). She has her own side to the story: "La Dame soutient qu'il faut être aussi bonne qu'elle est pour le souffrir un moment après qu'il est capable de l'oublier au point qu'il a fait. Il jure que depuis le soir précédent elle a occupé tout son temps sans qu'il ait songé qu'à elle seule" [The Lady argues that she must be quite generous to tolerate him for even a moment, when he has been capable of forgetting her to the extent that he has. He swears that since the preceding evening she has taken all of his time and he has thought of nothing but her] (315).

The Cavalier tries his best to prove what he is saying, that he has occupied all of his time in thinking about her, and thus not in being unfaithful. The best proof, the best alibi, comes in the form of a schedule, which he constructs on the spot: "il demande une écritoire et du papier, afin que justifiant l'emploi de tout son temps par articles, la Belle puisse examiner à loisir de quelle manière il a toujours pensé à elle, sans qu'aucun autre soin ait pu l'occuper" [he asks for a writing desk and paper, so that by justifying his schedule point by point, the Belle may examine at leisure the way in which he has constantly been thinking about her, without being occupied by any other care] (315–16). He draws for her a clock face, "une espèce de cadran" (316) accompanied by text that explains all that he has thought and done since last seeing his Belle: "il sort en l'assurant qu'il ne s'était jamais rendu un compte si juste ni si véritable que celui qu'il lui laissait" [he leaves, assuring her that he has never given such a truthful and accurate account of himself as the one with which he leaves her] (317). The reflexive verb places emphasis on the activity of temporal self-tracking. With the adjectives "juste" and "véritable," the Cavalier makes claims to truth and accuracy, or to truth through accuracy, in the composition and communication of his explanatory self-referential timepiece.

The Belle, who expected merely a standard lover's *billet*, is surprised to see this elaborate design and finds it to be quite gallant. The clock or watch is entitled "Compte d'un Amant rendu à une Maîtresse de l'emploi de son temps pendant douze heures" [An Account, given by a Lover to his Mistress, of the use of his time during twelve hours] (318). Some of her friends come by to look at it, and she is quite pleased, until she notices that this lover's clock serves a purpose quite contrary to her love. The diagram, which instructs the reader to begin at nine in the

evening and continue around the clock, includes the following statements for their respective spans of time:

9:00–10:00 — Je suis venu chez vous à neuf heures du soir, et n'en suis sorti
qu'à dix [I came to see you at nine o'clock in the evening, and I only left
at ten].

10:00–11:00 — Depuis dix jusques à onze je me suis paré pour aller au bal
[From ten to eleven, I got dressed and ready to go to the ball].

11:00–1:00 — Depuis onze jusqu'à une j'ai tâché à me faire distinguer par ma
danse et je n'ai cherché qu'à plaire [From eleven to one I tried to distinguish myself in dance and I aimed only to please].

1:00–2:00 — Depuis une jusqu'à deux je suis revenu chez moi et me suis cou-
ché à une résolution de vous haïr toute ma vie [From one to two I came
home and went to bed, resolving to hate you for the rest of my life].

2:00–3:00 — Depuis deux jusqu'à trois, j'ai continué dans le même dessein
[From two to three, I continued with the same resolution].

3:00–7:00 — J'ai dormi depuis trois jusques à sept [I slept from three to
seven].

7:00–8:00 — Depuis sept jusques à huit je me suis habillé et me suis affermi
dans la résolution de vous haïr éternellement [From seven to eight, I got
dressed and reaffirmed my resolution to hate you eternally].

8:00–9:00 — Depuis huit jusques à neuf j'ai cherché des chevaux de poste et
je suis venu vous dire adieu pour jamais [From eight to nine I found
postal horses and came to tell you good-bye forever].

The solicitation of horses from the postal service, the fastest means of
transportation available, highlights this time-conscious, frustrated lover's desire for speed and efficiency in the difficult task of communicating his lover's spite to the Belle. When she realizes what message the
Cavalier has wished to give her on the face of his lover's watch, she
becomes embarrassed and quickly gets rid of her friends. She runs to
see her best friend and confidante; on the way to the latter's home she
runs into the Cavalier's best friend, who, as it happens, is madly in love
with the Belle's confidante. The Cavalier's friend, who goes in the story
by the name of "l'Ami," has never told the Belle's confidante of his love
for her and is trying to find a way to do so. At the Confidante's home,
a precious discussion ensues, about love, arguing, making up, and expressing one's love for one's lady. The Confidante wants above all to
love "un homme d'esprit," an intelligent and witty man. The anxious
Ami, constructing a microtemporal regimen of fervent love, claims that
love requires "qu'on dise mille fois en un quart-d'heure qu'on aime avec
la plus violente passion" [that one say a thousand times in a quarter of

an hour that one loves with the most violent passion] (326). The Belle's confidante seems to think this is fine, but fears that it may become a bit repetitive, for an "homme d'esprit," after all.

At this point, the Cavalier and the treacherous Rival both arrive on the scene. The Cavalier explains point by point, around the clock he has composed, why he wrote what he did, explicating each statement in terms of his love for the Belle, a strong emotion that has taken contradictory forms and made him say such cruel things. The Confidante praises the Cavalier's "esprit," his way of turning things around to justify himself and win back the love of the Belle. In so doing, the Confidante makes the connection between the measurement of time, the activity of narrative representation, and skill in argument. The Cavalier is a worthy lover because of his capacity to use language to give an account of time, in the relatively present time frame of the past twenty-four, heart-wrenching hours. The effect of the Cavalier's creativity and understanding of time, language, and love is not lost on the Belle, with whom, to the Rival's chagrin, the Cavalier is soon reconciled.

In a burst of inspiration, the Ami has left, borrowing the lover's watch of the Cavalier and saying he will return, which he eventually does: "L'Ami qui était sorti depuis trois heures, rentra dans le temps qu'ils se faisaient de nouvelles protestations de s'aimer toujours" [The Friend, who had been gone for three hours, came back during the time when they were making new promises to love one another forever] (337). The time of the Ami's absence is specified, as is the timing of his return. During these three key hours, the disorder of the past twenty-four hours has been put back into amorous order. The Cavalier and the Belle have regained control of their lovers' time, and meanwhile the Ami has used this time to undertake a project of his own, combining time-consciousness, drawings, and the use of language to describe time and love.

When the Confidante asks to see the lover's watch again, the Ami gives her instead a new picture of a clock, with the title "Tout Aime" [Love is Universal] written across the top (338). This is the "Horloge d'amour," with the following statements marked by their respective hours:

I: J'en tiens assez pour les autres [I have enough for everyone].
II: Mes coups ne lui feront point de mal [My blows will not do him any harm].
III: Je devrais l'avoir blessé plutôt [I should have wounded him earlier].
IV: Je finirai comme j'ai commencé [I will finish just as I started].

V: Il ne me méprisera plus [He will no longer disdain me].
VI: Il a beau s'en vouloir défendre [A lot of good it will do him to try and defend himself].
VII: Je ferai sa fortune [I will make his fortune].
VIII: Il me craint sans raison [He fears me without reason].
IX: Il attend mes coups tranquillement [He calmly awaits my blows].
X: Il en sentira plus d'un [He will feel more than one].
XI: J'en ai bien blessé d'autres [I have certainly wounded others].
XII: Il ne peut plus m'échapper [He can no longer escape me].

The words on the clock playfully evoke an amorous hunt, drawing the reader's attention to the time of love. The ingeniousness of his invention wins for the Ami the love of the Confidante, and the story ends happily, with the new and renewed lovers all embracing and shoring up ties.

During a time when clocks and watches were undergoing revolutionary improvements in accuracy and were being more widely used, at least among the relatively privileged echelons of French society, new imaginary uses of timekeeping devices were being constructed in the cultural domain of popular literature. With time becoming available as a measurable entity, new forms of subjective apprehension of time thus came into being, in the form of lovers' time. This kind of charting of hours and minutes contributed to the development of some rather precious love stories, while at the same time revealing an increasing concern for quantifying and keeping track of units of time in daily life. The Lover's Watch is a manifestation of a larger epistemological trend, toward the construction of new forms of early modern subjectivity inflected by a focus on time quantities in the relative present. This approach to time was both highly subjective and intently calculating.

As the study of early modern cartography and chronometry makes clear, the understanding of both space and time in France under Louis XIV was at a moment of transition, between the symbolic and the schematic, where the latter had not yet entirely superceded the former. Time was presented to the seventeenth-century mind in both symbolic and utilitarian ways—symbolically, in the figures of the hours incarnated by Molière's troupe during the *Plaisirs de l'île enchantée* [Pleasures of the Enchanted Isle] (1664) at Versailles; with a practical purpose, in the form of timepieces like the bulky *oignons* [onions], watches newly accurate with their expanded Huygensian innards, objects that could be used to track the daily motions of the self and of the collectivity.[66] Space took the form both of Madeleine de Scudéry's *Carte du Tendre* [Map of Tenderness] (1654), a mapping of regions to be explored in the intimate domain of sentiment, and of the new maps being created by the astronomers of the Académie Royale des Sciences. Fueled by the political and economic objectives of colonial expansion, research into new ways of mapping spaces and keeping time produced new modes of conceptualizing the world and of representing royal authority. The impact of sociopolitical reconceptualizations of time within the domain of individual existence was paradoxical: new conceptual tools for understanding space and time both imposed new structures on daily life and opened new avenues for subjective explorations of the everyday. This latter phenomenon, less objectively identifiable than the public and administrative forms of new practices of temporal and spatial measurement, can nevertheless be observed in literary texts and in personal accounts of daily life in early modern France, a key time and place for the transition to modern temporalities of thought and communication.

The second half of the seventeenth century in France was marked by accelerations of administrative activity, new processes of information acquisition, and new conceptions of time through which individuals traced the separation between their public and private lives. The political and economic need for a new chronometry motivated technological advances that, with greater distribution of early modern timepieces, had an impact on social life, as an increasing number of individuals gained access to the subjective experience of precision time-measurement.

While it has been the present chapter's purpose to examine some of the cultural and historical underpinnings of a technological and epistemological trend toward the valuation of precision and quantification in the human experience of time, the following chapters will link elements of the cultural record to literary representations of time. These textual constructions of temporality provide glimpses of the experience of the early modern subject, at a point of intersection between the interpretation of the work of art and the study of the cultural/historical record. The first of these literary/historical hybrids is to be found in the history of court life under Louis XIV and the textual/performative experience of time in Molière's theater.

# 2

## Time Structures in "Les Plaisirs de l'île enchantée" and *Le Tartuffe*

*Dans les grandes affaires on doit moins s'appliquer à faire naître des occasions qu'à profiter de celles qui se présentent.*

*Le calme ou l'agitation de notre humeur ne dépend pas tant de ce qui nous arrive de plus considérable dans la vie, que d'un arrangement commode ou désagréable de petites choses qui arrivent tous les jours.*

—La Rochefoucauld, *Maximes*

### TEMPORAL DYNAMICS OF ROYAL SPECTACLE

THE PREMIERE OF MOLIÈRE'S *LE TARTUFFE* AT VERSAILLES WAS A CAREfully timed literary event that took place in the midst of a variety of spectacles and performances.[1] The "Plaisirs de l'île enchantée" [Pleasures of the Enchanted Isle], a suite of ceremonial processions and tournaments, ballets, plays, feasts, games, and fireworks at Versailles, lasted from 7 to 13 May 1664. Officially dedicated to the Queen Mother Anne of Austria (1601–66) and to the Queen Marie-Thérèse (1638–83), the "Plaisirs" were unofficially known to be an offering to Louis XIV's mistress Mlle de la Vallière (1644–1710). Through a tightly scheduled series of perceptual pleasures, the king paid personal tributes while at the same time producing a representation for the entire court society of his absolute authority as a monarch. One way in which Louis XIV displayed his power was through his control of time. Just as the geometrical arrangement of Versailles offered to courtiers the image of Louis XIV's esthetic and rationalizing mastery over space, the schedules of both courtly festivals and court life represented a corresponding mastery over time. As every moment of the "Plaisirs" offered delights for spectators, events and their arrangement also repeatedly transmitted the king's message, that he was a sovereign in complete control of his realm.

This chapter argues for the importance of detailed time structures in conceptualizations of temporality during the initial stages of Louis XIV's rule, a time when the Sun King sought ways of symbolically establishing an unquestioned legitimacy. The rhetoric of time that anticipated, announced, and depicted the "Plaisirs de l'île enchantée" characterized Louis XIV as a mind in control of time's most minute increments and, by extension, of every moment of the courtier's being. As I discussed in chapter 1, Louis XIV was a strong patron for clock and watchmakers during the first two decades of his reign. The present chapter traces the links between the science of horology and the creation of meticulously scheduled rites of sociability at Versailles. This analysis of a pervasive awareness of small time units in seventeenth-century technology and social life contributes to explaining the significance of scheduling and of representations of time at Versailles, specifically in the "Plaisirs de l'île enchantée" and in the dramatic action of *Le Tartuffe*.

Situating *Le Tartuffe* within the context of a carefully scheduled and politically significant fête calls attention to time structures of action and utterance and to strategic uses of timing within the play itself. Tartuffe and Molière's other characters in this work reveal an acute, opportunistic consciousness of the small time increments shaping the rhythms of their words and deeds. A close attention to these temporal dynamics helps place Molière within the historical frameworks of court life at Versailles and, more precisely, of the fête during which the first performance of *Le Tartuffe* took place.

What today is perhaps Molière's best-known play emerged during a period when thinking practices were marked increasingly by detailed attention to and measurement of time. In consonance with this epistemological trend, *Le Tartuffe* contains nuanced representations of time and dramatized strategic uses of time in the words and actions of the play's characters. In the opening scene, Madame Pernelle produces exacting conversational structures, through careful timing, that both send her message of disapproval and situate members of Orgon's household within an evaluative hierarchy. Dorine, Valère, Cléante, and others keep careful track of the temporal dynamics of communication processes through which they remain informed of Tartuffe's machinations. Following the lead of the savvy Dorine, Orgon's family attempts to time their actions strategically in countering the treacherous tactics of the impostor. Tartuffe, a formidably time-conscious schemer, calculates his every move within strategic microdiachronies of power acquisition.

These characters' attention to and use of small time units attest, within the domain of literary production, to the importance of detailed time-consciousness in ways of knowing during the second half of the seventeenth century. My reading of *Le Tartuffe* will explore the subjective dimension of the temporal awareness that took both symbolic and political forms during the fête of 1664. The political meanings of such ways of thinking time were elaborated in the representation of Louis XIV as a monarch who held considerable power by means of his control of even the slightest increments of time. I argue that this kind of representation of authority was partly necessary because the power thus represented was actually only in a virtual state. At the beginning of his reign, Louis XIV anticipated and wanted others to anticipate the realization of an absolute power over both space and time.

As an initial step in the analysis of detailed time structures of projected authority and of experience both social and subjective at Versailles, this chapter's first section examines the rhetorical use of temporal contraction, in the anticipation of a near future of integral kingship and architectural achievement in the Sun King's new home. These near-future cognitive projections brought attention to microdiachronies of experience in the anxious atmosphere that immediately preceded the opening of the "Plaisirs de l'île enchantée."

*Projections and Pressures: Anticipating "Les Plaisirs de l'île enchantée"*

In May 1664, "Les Plaisirs de l'île enchantée" inaugurated Versailles as the symbolic center of royal authority for France. From this moment forward, Versailles would architecturally represent absolute power, even if, as was the case, this edifice remained unfinished. Royal spectacles enacted Louis XIV's political legitimacy, complementing the young monarch's principal legal action of 1664, the arrest and trial of Nicolas Fouquet (1615–80). The former minister of finances had been known to host guests at the château of Vaux-le-Vicomte, where the scenery and the events had been remarkable enough, to Fouquet's eventual chagrin, to threaten the Sun King's sense of symbolic superiority. Thus in the spring of 1664 Louis XIV aimed immediately to assume preeminent status in the domains of architecture and spectacle. The relative disorganization of Versailles at that time obliged the king's chroniclers to use a particular rhetoric of time that brought present attention to a near-future projection of perfection for the royal grounds. The goal was to produce a conceptual contraction of the temporal distance between an incomplete present and a desired future. This is the first instance showing the cognitive importance of small time units for symbolic expressions of royal splendor.

In an effort to ensure the significance of Versailles as a spatial representation of the king's authority, the written guide (or *livret*) to the "Plaisirs de l'île enchantée," penned by the architect and art historian André Félibien (1619–95), compensated for the palace's evident architectural paucity with a rhetoric that projected completion: "[Q]uoiqu'il n'ait pas cette grande étendue qui se remarque en quelques autres palais de Sa Majesté, toutes choses y sont si polies, si bien entendues et si achevées, que rien ne le peut égaler" [Although it does not have the luxuriant space that can be seen in His Majesty's other palaces, everything here is so polished, so well-planned and completed, that nothing can equal it] (Molière 1:751). The past participles "polies," "entendues," and "achevées" project Versailles into a future time frame of static perfection. This anticipatory language places itself against the insecurity about the royal dwelling contained in the qualifying clause introduced by "quoique." Uncertainty about the château produces an irony: the term "achevé," suggestive of completeness, describes a grand opening which, for all its splendors, is merely a kind of trial run for the facility. A past participle accounts for an act of architectural inchoation.

In the spring of 1664, Versailles was far from finished. An envelope of extensions onto Louis XIII's château would only begin taking shape under the direction of the royal architect Louis Le Vau (1612–70) in 1668.[2] Versailles was thus anything but "achevée," or, as the last words of the guide to the "Plaisirs" would have it, a "maison accomplie" [a completed home] (Molière 1:751). The most telling term in the projection of architectural perfection, then, would appear to be "entendue." This word's cognitive connotations point to a process of conceptualization. The composition of representational elements in the "Plaisirs de l'île enchantée" takes place in an anticipatory time frame, in which the thinking of the fête's participants is directed toward the future time of architectural integrity. One of the purposes of this festival of 1664 was thus the accomplishment of a temporal subterfuge, executed through a rhetoric of anticipation and projection. Time became a privileged object of manipulation in the structure and spectacle of kingly magnificence.

The extent to which Louis XIV and the festival's organizers actually succeeded in making courtiers believe that Versailles was the very symbol of completion remains questionable: "[D]espite four months of preparation and the veritable army of artists and craftsmen rushed in from Paris, virtually nothing [was] ready."[3] The suspension of disbelief required to accept the words of the guide must have posed a considerable challenge to members of the court, many of whom had to sleep in carriages and stables in between sessions of "pleasures."[4] In spite of the inconveniences encountered by participants and organizers alike, the show went on. The rhetorical mastery of time undertaken in the guide, which goes on to enumerate a series of carefully planned processions and performances, appears to be motivated by a desire to compensate for the logistical imperfections resulting from an exceedingly tight schedule of practical preparations.

Molière himself worked under severe time constraints in order to compose the fête's two theatrical premieres—*La Princesse d'Elide* and *Le Tartuffe*—the second of which would establish the literary-historical significance of this festival, as the initial context for what would eventually become a masterpiece. *La Princesse d'Elide* was the largely improvised result of rushed work: "He worked in haste, or perhaps completed hastefully a work already outlined; in any case, the first act and the first scene of the second act were in verse, and Molière, hurried by the king's orders, continued in prose."[5] This formally heterogeneous work, conceived and executed just under the wire, appears as a strange beginning to a staging of royal legitimacy and immutable perfection.

A recognition of uses and representations of time in the "Plaisirs de l'île enchantée" can contribute, however, to explaining the appropriateness of Molière's unfinished work to the proceedings of the fête. The refrain in the musical prologue to *La Princesse d'Elide* evokes a frantic atmosphere structured by a rapid organizational rhythm: "Allons, debout, vite debout: / Pour la chasse ordonnée il faut préparer tout. / Debout, vite debout, dépêchons, debout" [Get up quickly, get up quickly now: we must prepare everything for the organized hunt. Get up, up, hurry up, get up].[6] Alliteration and repetition reinforce the semantic content of the verses and provide an implicit commentary on the frenetic pace of preparations for the fête staging the play. The slothful Lyciscas, not quite ready for the quickening of activity that his compatriots demand, asks first for "un petit quart d'heure" [just a quarter of an hour] and then for "[u]n moment," but his requests are met only with the rhythmic repetition of "debout." The "chasse ordonnée" serves as a metaphor for the kind of organized activity that constitutes the "Plaisirs." The set of exhortations to quick action and preparation resonates with Molière's own writing process. He, like Lyciscas, might have appreciated some extra hours and minutes to versify the play but obeyed his sovereign in hastefully erecting the required theatrical edifice. Like Lyciscas, the *Princesse d'Elide* had to be on its feet quickly. Not even a moment of unproductive time could be permitted when the "chasse ordonnée" of royal spectacle was to be prepared. The good courtier hurried to the task of participating in the composition and reception of the sovereign's ceremonial representations, and each observable increment of time played a role in this work.

Quickening the planning process and neglecting time for rest, the organizers of the "Plaisirs de l'île enchantée" conceptually contracted time in order to make the anticipatory present of royal insecurity most nearly approach the near future of kingly solidity. The eventual completion of Versailles could be attained on the level of representation within the tightly controlled time frame of the fête. The show had to go on, in order to inaugurate Versailles successfully, and it had to be played out in measured increments in order to capture the full attention of potentially distracted or disgruntled courtiers.

*Practices of Ceremonial Scheduling*

The Paris *Gazette* specified that the king and queen arrived for the beginning of the festival "sur les six heures du soir" [about six in the evening].[7] Although a strong wind was blowing, the setting for the fête's visual adaptation of an episode from Ariosto's *Orlando Furioso* was preserved by a set of structures designed to protect the sorceress Alcine's palace from the elements. In the guide, Félibien insisted on the rapidity with which these scaffolds took shape, under the efficient direction of the architect Vigarani: "De hautes toiles, des bâtiments de bois, faits presque en un instant, et un nombre prodigieux de flambeaux de cire blanche . . . résistèrent à ce vent" [tall tents, wooden structures, produced almost in an instant, and a prodigious number of torches of white wax resisted the force of this wind] (Molière 1:752). With comparable swiftness, the festival's actors stopped before the queens and then cleared the way for the tournament's grounds to be prepared: "[T]ous ayant repris leur tour à gauche, au même ordre qu'ils étaient venus, ils sortirent du camp pour faire place aux pasteurs, qui en un instant posèrent la barrière, et favorisèrent, ainsi, l'ardeur que nos chevaliers avaient de signaler leur adresse" [Everyone having resumed their march to the left, in the same order in which they had come, they left the camp in order to make room for the shepherds, who in a single instant set up the barrier and thus encouraged the ardor with which our knights wished to show their skills] (*Gazette* 487). Again, Félibien places emphasis on the single "instant" of logistical accomplishment and indicates the necessity of this accurate use of time for the success of the proceedings.

The protective structures for Alcine's mythic palace and the arena for the tournament represented Versailles as an architectural whole. The performativity exemplified by the immediate construction of these ephemeral edifices aimed to suggest that the king's new home would also be, and in some sense already was, "vite debout," and would attain the dimensions required to reflect absolute royal authority. The use of minute time increments to form impressions of instantaneity and simultaneity factored into the organization of the "Plaisirs de l'île enchantée," and the perception of these moments of time was crucial for the success of the festival's visual effects.[8]

In his account of the first evening's events, Félibien points out that the coincidence of nightfall with the end of the tournament resulted from the scheduling of the fête: "La nuit vint cependant à la fin des courses, par la justesse qu'on avait eu à les commencer" [Meanwhile, night fell at the end of the races, because they had begun just in time] (Molière 1:762). The notion of temporal "justesse," of accomplishing acts at the last moment, pervaded the hasteful processes by which Versailles was symbolically inaugurated in May 1664. This emphasis on a critical moment receives further force in Félibien's narration from the simultaneity of nightfall with the fireworks that concluded the tournament. This spectacular display was itself juxtaposed in the fête's schedule to a striking entrance: "En même temps, on vit entrer par le portique de la droite une compagnie de trente-six concertants" [At the same time, a company of 36 musicians was seen entering through the portico to the right] (Gazette 488). The attention with which Félibien pinpoints events in time and the chronometrical accuracy with which he establishes their relation to each other in his narration point to the conceptual importance of small time increments for the "Plaisirs de l'île enchantée" and for its narrative representation. Meticulous marks of instantaneity and simultaneity account for concerted uses of micro-time in the scheduling of the fête's first day, and these marks had their analogues in Félibien's perceptions of the proceedings as he recorded their unfolding.

The second day of the festival began slightly later in the evening in the gardens of Versailles, "[l]e Roi et la Reine s'y étant rendus sur les huit heures du soir" [the king and queen having arrived at eight in the evening] (Gazette 492). The unveiling of Alcine's palace struck spectators in a single instant of time: "[E]lle ordonna que le palais où elle tenait Roger enchanté s'ouvrît. A l'instant, par un admirable artifice, le rocher se séparant aux deux bords de l'île laissa voir ce palais qui surprit également les spectateurs par sa magnifique structure" [She ordered that the palace where she held Roger under her spell be opened. Right away, by an admirable artifice, the rock separating on both sides from the island revealed the palace, whose magnificent structure surprised and delighted the spectators] (494). The element of surprise for the audience was attained through precise scheduling of visual effects. Part of what constituted this "admirable artifice" was its accomplishment "à l'instant." Similar immediacy was required to protect the stage set for *La Princesse d'Elide* from the strong winds that were still buffeting the grounds of Versailles. The necessity of a protective structure provided a pretext once again for foregrounding the promptness of the king's engineers: "Le Roi fit donc couvrir de toiles, en si peu de temps qu'on avait lieu de s'en étonner, tout ce rond, d'une espèce de dôme" [The king had the whole area covered in tarps, in a kind of a dome, in an astonishingly short time] (Molière 1:766). Félibien's emphasis falls squarely on the scant time required for the operation in question, and on the fact that it was the Sun King who was at the origin of the solution to the problem. The festival organizers' logistical efficiency impressed the audience, as evidenced by the term "s'étonner." The fête consistently pursued the goal of using exact scheduling and small time units to surprise and delight the courtiers and thus to establish the legitimacy of Louis XIV who received credit for every minute manifestation of the control of time.

Appropriately, the second day of the "Plaisirs de l'île enchantée" concluded with a spectacle that called attention, as the *Gazette*'s account of the event shows, to temporal dynamics of rapidity and virtual instantaneity. With her spell over the knight Roger having been broken, Alcine suddenly destroyed her palace, to the surprise and delight of Louis XIV's court:

> [E]lle mit le feu à son palais, avec un flambeau, de manière qu'il disparut incontinent, avec toutes les lumières. Aussitôt, on découvrit en sa place, un feu d'artifice, duquel il n'est pas moins difficile de faire une fidèle description que du reste, puisqu'à peine les spectateurs eurent le temps d'en remarquer les diverses beautés, dans la grande foule des feux qui remplirent durant [une] demi-heure, l'eau, l'air, et la terre de leur lumière, et de leur tintamarre. (496)

> [She set fire to her palace, with a torch, in such a way that it disappeared immediately, with all of its lights. Right away, in its place, fireworks were

seen, a spectacle that is just as difficult to describe faithfully as the rest, because the spectators barely had a chance to notice the various beauties of
this sight, in the great tangle of fires that filled the water, the air, and the
earth with their light and cacophony for half an hour.]

The temporal markers "incontinent" and "aussitôt" designate the immediacy of this dramatized destruction. The description then evokes the
rhythms of subjective experience of the spectators, who barely had time
to admire one aspect of the display before being struck by others. The
account of this evening of festivities that began at eight o'clock thus
concludes by evoking a carefully timed perceptual experience, 30 minutes of fireworks, that capped off a sequence of visual effects carefully
measured in time.

The *Gazette* then makes the connection between the rhythms of the
fête and the reasons behind royal authority. The "Plaisirs de l'île enchantée" set forth an uncompromising political agenda, in no small part
through a rhetoric of time. These festivities "doivent faire avouer que la
France n'est pas moins grande et magnifique dans la paix que conquér-
ante et glorieuse dans la guerre, depuis que son sceptre est dans les
mains d'un monarque, dont les jours sont tous remplis de merveilles qui
n'ont point d'exemple dans le passé, et qui n'auront rien de semblable
dans l'avenir" [make it necessary to admit that France is no less great
and magnificent in peace than she is conquering and glorious in war,
since the moment when her sceptre was placed in the hands of a monarch whose days are all filled with wonders that have no precedent in
the past, and that will never be repeated in the future] (496). The full-
ness of his daily schedule characterizes Louis XIV as a great monarch.
This fête of May 1664 has functioned to prove that his "jours sont tous
remplis de merveilles" by calling attention to various privileged moments of wonderment and their arrangement in the king's experience.
By evoking all of the king's days, the account of the fête applies the
extraordinary nature of the festival's marvels to the king's everyday life,
thus suggesting that for this monarch every moment of what most people would experience as mundane existence held the affective potential
of enchantment. This focus on the minutes and hours of splendors fill-
ing Louis XIV's days valorizes the present, in creating a radical disjunc-
ture between time frames of historical past and eventual future. The
rhetoric of time reveals the importance, for the representational establishment of singularity and spectacularity in Louis XIV's incipient
reign, of small time increments, located in a relative present of daily
experience.

*Le Roi-Horloge: Representations of Time at Versailles*

The timing of events in the "Plaisirs de l'île enchantée" contributed to the figuration of royal authority by placing Louis XIV at the helm of a systematic, hyper-efficient, and spectacular kind of time-management. While at the level of organization of events time created strong impressions on spectators, this effect was reinforced by a number of references to time itself. These were invitations to reflect on time extended to members of the court as part of the royal spectacle. The visual representations that made up the fête's processions included a strong thematization and allegorization of time. The description of Apollo's chariot, which assumed a prominent position in the first day of the Sun King's festival, contained numerous incarnations of time's various dimensions:

> Le Dieu y était accompagné des quatre Ages assis à ses pieds, sur de vastes degrés qui lui formaient un trône, ainsi que du Temps, qui gouvernait le Char, représenté par un vieillard ailé, avec un sable sur la tête, et une faux couchée à ses pieds: les douze signes du Zodiaque, et les douze heures du jour étant autour de lui, avec les hiéroglyphes qui les désignent. (*Gazette* 487)

> [The God was accompanied there by the four Ages seated at his feet, on huge steps that formed a throne for him, and also by Time, driving the Chariot, represented by a winged old man with an hourglass atop his head and a scythe lying at his feet: the twelve signs of the Zodiac, and the twelve hours of the day were around him, with the hieroglyphs that designate them.]

The ages of gold, silver, copper, and iron evoked a distant, legendary past, encompassed in the generalizing figure of time itself, with an hourglass atop his head. Actors from Molière's troupe stood for the twelve hours of the day, giving an imagistic form to the concern for the parameters of daily existence to which the "Plaisirs" ascribed new meanings. From the epochal to the everyday, all dimensions of time were set forth as domains within the Sun King's realm.

Juxtaposed to symbols of larger temporal dimensions, a picture of a clock on the duc de St. Aignan's shield evoked the hours and minutes of daily experience. The duke took part in a procession, adapted from Ariosto, which staged some of the court's most prominent nobles in heroic roles. In this display the "duc de St. Aignan [avait] pour corps de sa devise un timbre d'horloge frappé par le marteau" [duc de St. Aignan had on his coat of arms a clock bell being struck by its hammer] (*Gazette* 484). The measured rhythm of processional movement was thus visu-

Watch with enamel painting representing the Tower of Babel. Enamel attributed to J. Toutin. Mechanism signed M. Wentzel, Strasbourg, 1636. Photos Musée international d'horlogerie, La Chaux-de-Fonds, Suisse.

Enamel Watch, "Cléopâtre et l'aspic," watch cover. Signed Jean Bonbruict, Blois, 1650. Photos Musée international d'horlogerie, La Chaux-de-Fonds, Suisse.

Enamel Watch, "Cléopâtre et l'aspic," watch face. Signed Jean Bonbruict, Blois, 1650. Photos Musée international d'horlogerie, La Chaux-de-Fonds, Suisse.

Watches in form of *oignons* by Gribelin; Gloria; Yver; J.Ph. Dupressoir; Francois Joseph de Camus. Late 17th-early 18th ca. from Paris, Rouen, Angoulême. Gold, gilded brass, enamel, leather, silver. Photo Chuzeville. Copyright Réunion des Musées Nationaux/Art Resource, NY. Louvre, Paris, France.

Watch, "oignon," watch face. Case in gold-studded leather. Signed "Balthazar Martinot à Paris." End of 17th century. Photos Musée international d'horlogerie, La Chaux-de-Fonds, Suisse.

Watch, "oignon," back of watch. Case in gold-studded leather. Signed "Balthazar Martinot à Paris." End of 17th century. Photos Musée international d'horlogerie, La Chaux-de-Fonds, Suisse.

Testelin, Henri (1616–95). After Charles Le Brun. *The Establishment of the Academy of Sciences and the Foundation of the Observatory by Louis XIV.* Oil on Canvas, 3.48 × 5.9 m. Copyright Giraudon/Art Resource, NY. Châteaux de Versailles et de Trianon, Versailles, France.

ally doubled by the decorative ornament of a clock with a timed bell. The ringing of the bell announced the structuring of activity that would inflect everyday life during the reign of a rational monarch, one capable of controlling time, in his own doings and in the lives of his subjects.

In the part of the ceremony that announced the evening's tournament, the actor portraying Apollo marked the hour in verses composed for the fête by the poet Isaac de Benserade (1613–91):

> Il est temps de céder à la loi souveraine
> Que t'imposent les vœux de cette auguste reine;
> Il est temps de céder aux travaux glorieux
> D'un roi favorisé de la terre et des cieux.
> Mais ici trop longtemps ce différend m'arrête;
> A de plus doux combats cette lice s'apprête. (Molière 1:761)

[It is time to give in to the sovereign law that this august queen's wishes impose on you; it is time to give in to the glorious works of a king favored by the earth and the skies. But this delay keeps me here for too long; this tournament is prepared for a sweeter kind of combat.]

The anaphoric use of "il est temps" mimicked a clock in sounding the hour for the tournament to begin. The invocation of delay in the verse containing "trop longtemps ce différend m'arrête" referred to a temporal concept directly opposite to the kind of time that the "Plaisirs" exemplified. Battling against temporalities of inaction and deferral, the Sun God urged participants and spectators to continue the festival's proceedings. The terms "loi souveraine" and "travaux glorieux," situated at the end of verses beginning with "il est temps," established a strong link between the emphasis on time and the verbal expression of absolute power.

In the procession of characters from Ariosto, time and the dynamics of power were represented on the coat of arms of "[l]e prince de Marsillac, représentant Brandimart, ayant pour devise une montre en relief, dont on voit tous les ressorts, avec ces mots: *Chieto fuor, commoto dentro.* (tranquille au-dehors; agité au-dedans)" [the prince de Marsillac, representing Brandimart, having on his coat of arms a watch shown in relief, whose mechanisms are visible. The coat of arms is accompanied by these words: calm on the outside, agitated inside] (Molière 1:758). The image of a watch with its internal mechanisms revealed emphasized the simultaneously vigorous and utterly unperturbed consciousness of Brandimart. Behind a calm external appearance, myriad thoughts occupy the mind of this hero and play themselves out in the regular time increments figured by the watch's mechanical parts. Just as for Perrault the watch would represent knowledge in the modern sense, on Marsillac's shield the watch stood for an active thought process and a new kind of subjective self-presentation within the social context of court life at Versailles. This image of the courtier foregrounded a silent and efficient mind and a disciplined body, *chieto fuor*, held in check by an exacting conception of attitude and gesture.[9] Both the constraints of seventeenth-century social existence and the new temporal possibilities of interior, private life appeared in the modern image of the watch mechanism on Marsillac's shield. Clearly, the watch, which served as a decoration on the shield, was principally represented here as a useful object, the inner gears of which ensured consistent functioning. In a Hobbesian and Cartesian sense, and in anticipation of La Mettrie, man was being presented as machine in the allegorical figure of Marsillac, a result of a complex system of inner workings, "ressorts," the exactitude of which guaranteed heroic stature in modern life.[10]

In his *Dictionnaire universel* of 1690, Antoine Furetière gives numerous definitions for "ressort," one of which refers specifically to portable timepieces: "Dans les montres, c'est une pièce d'acier enfermée dans un barillet, laquelle en s'étendant fait mouvoir les roues" [In watches, it is a piece of metal enclosed in a cylinder, which by stretching drives the gears]. In a more general sense, a "ressort" designates "tout ce qu'on croit être cause du mouvement dans les machines" [everything one believes to be the cause of movement in machines]. The inclusion of the notion of belief ("tout ce qu'on croit") in this definition suggests that the term can designate unexplained aspects of natural or mechanical function. This connotation of mystery finds corroboration in the usage Furetière gives with regard to nature: "La nature a des ressorts inconcevables, pour produire tous les effets surprenants que nous voyons" [Nature has perfectly inconceivable inner workings, in order for it to produce all the surprising effects we observe]. To comprehend the inner workings of nature would seem to require powers of divination, or alternatively of Cartesian scientific inquiry, as is suggested by the definition that touches on the vocation of engineering: "Un ingénieur fait agir tous les ressorts de son esprit, en bande tous les ressorts pour inventer quelque nouvelle machine ou problème" [An engineer operates all the mechanisms of his mind, winds up all the springs in order to discover some new machine or problem]. Here the task of conscious application to new tasks ties the notion of a "ressort" to the development of early modern technologies, machines and devices, like timepieces, whose purpose was to place rational grids onto the natural world and harness more of its mysteries.[11]

Access to the "ressorts" lying behind and determining aspects of perceptual reality thus constituted a kind of privileged knowledge. The signifying processes put into operation during the "Plaisirs de l'île enchantée" effectively ascribed these ways of knowing to the king: "The fêtes also were impeccable mechanisms. They organized the disorder of space and time according to an order that only the king seemed to understand. Nothing could have been more concerted than this arrangement of distilled surprises."[12] Louis XIV's authority was buttressed, in the presentation of the "Plaisirs," by an exclusive attribution of knowledge. Only the king knew the secret principles governing the rigorous control of space and time at Versailles.

In his 1664 account of the "Plaisirs de l'île enchantée," the writer Jacques Carpentier de Marigny (d. 1670) claimed that the king not only had knowledge of "ressorts" but actually acted as one: "Grâce à Dieu, nous nous apercevons chaque jour de mieux en mieux qu'il est le plus grand et maître ressort qui fait mouvoir la machine" [By the grace of God, we realize better every day that he is the greatest and main spring that puts the machine in motion].[13] In Benserade's verses, the character of the Golden Age thus described the Sun King's advent: "Comment, depuis ce jour, d'infatigables mains / Travaillent sans relâche au bonheur des humains, / Par quels secrets ressorts un héros se prépare / A chasser les horreurs d'un siècle si barbare" [What? Since that day, tireless hands work constantly for the well-being of all people. By what secret mechanisms does a hero prepare himself to rid a barbaric century of its horrors?] (Molière 1:761). The adjective "secrets" emphasizes the privileged nature of the king's knowledge, which will impose order on the realm, in the near-future time designated by "se prépare."

In his description of Louis XIV's entry into Paris in 1660, Jean-Marie Apostolidès has shown that, even before his advent to the throne, Louis XIV played the symbolic role of the unifying element that would restore order to France. During the course of this ceremony, the disparate parts of the king's court become integrated into a single unit of continuous sovereign functioning.[14] In the "Plaisirs de l'île enchantée," one of this mechanism's most compelling images, Marsillac's coat of arms, showed this device's inner workings to be as inexorable as the march of time itself. As we have seen in the preceding chapter, the structured representations of time and mechanistic order in association with Louis XIV served to indicate that this king cultivated a concerted interest in the science of watch and clockmaking.

During the first two decades of Louis XIV's rule, Paris and Versailles stood as significant sites for the study and use of clocks and watches. Henri Testelin's painting entitled "The Establishment of the Academy of Sciences and the Observatory" serves as a visual representation of this era. In this work Louis XIV sits surrounded by Colbert and other ministers and scientists from the newly founded academy. The king and his subjects are depicted in the midst of a profusion of scientific tools — books, compasses, maps, globes, and a clock, situated left of center and just above the king's head. The clock's gold ornamentation makes it stand out from the painting's somber background and aligns this device, in the color scheme, with the serious faces of the king and his distinguished academicians. In the years of Louis XIV's initial establishment as absolute sovereign, the measurement of time, along with an attendant acuteness of time-consciousness, contributed to a rhetorical construction of a heroic sovereign figure and to the structuring of court life, the enactment of which provided a social mirror image for the Sun King's mastery of space and time.

*Temporal Dynamics of Court Life*

Daily activities at Versailles played themselves out according to meticulous schedules. While subjecting all courtiers to exacting time constraints, the king imposed the same rigors on himself. Saint-Simon observed that "[w]ith an almanac and a watch one could tell, three hundred leagues away, what he was doing."[15] In thus regulating himself, Louis XIV paid close attention to his own personal timepiece: "Louis XIV had made a kind of institution out of the king's watch. A distinguished clockmaker, who carried the title of *valet de chambre* to the king, would daily wind up this august mechanism."[16] The ceremony of winding the royal watch took place as part of a carefully orchestrated daily rite, the king's "lever," during which the monarch's most minute gestures conferred relative degrees of privilege on his aristocratic subjects, who waited in turn to observe as the king arose and readied himself for another day.

At seven-thirty in the morning, the first valet would awake and get dressed, before bringing lamplighters into the royal bedchambers a quarter of an hour later. At half-past, the first valet approached the king's bed, and, without touching the curtains, made the announcement: "Sire, voilà l'heure" [Sire, it is time]. The "premier gentilhomme" of the king's chambers would open the bed's curtains at a quarter past eight.[17] After fifteen minutes of prayer, Louis XIV arose from his bed and put on his slippers and robe and, while being combed by the head barber, began to be clothed. Norbert Elias gives a detailed account of this ritual: "The *maître de la garderobe* pulled his nighshirt by the right sleeve, the first servant of the wardrobe by the left; his dayshirt was brought by the Lord Chamberlain or one of the king's sons who happened to be present. The first valet held the right sleeve, the first servant of the wardrobe the left. Thus the king put on his shirt."[18] Every gesture involved in the process of dressing Louis XIV was measured and repeated in the same way from day to day. A specific rhythm of daily experience structured mornings at Versailles, as anxious court members observed the proceedings and remained constantly aware of the moments at which they might speak to the king. Those courtiers privileged enough to have access to the ceremony through which the king arose and was dressed, the "petit lever," could consult with him without having to request formal audience: "May they profit by it: this time does not last long. The *petit lever* is now over."[19] Slightly lower in the court hierarchy, those who observed the ensuing "grand lever" jockeyed for position in this highly symbolic schedule of royal daily life.

Similarly detailed time structures determined the experience of later hours in the day at Versailles. The "coucher" followed routines that were as strict as the "lever." Saint-Simon recalled having performed the honorific and carefully timed duty of illuminating the king's bed: "One took off one's glove, stepped forward, held the chandelier for a few moments while the king was lying down, and then returned it to the first valet."[20] The king's supper followed meticulously organized codes of action, as courtiers stood and watched the sovereign eat and drink. It required three servants and seven to eight minutes, for example, to bring the king a glass of wine diluted with water.[21]

Days were dotted with privileged moments, when court members aimed to obtain a few words of conversation with Louis XIV. One of these sets of seconds would habitually occur at one o'clock in the afternoon, as the king left a meeting with ministers to reenter his bedroom: "Numerous anecdotes reveal the importance of this instant in the eyes of all the gentlemen who had awaited this moment since the morning."[22] Another of these highly valued points in time came when the king descended the stairs, during the afternoon, in order to go walking or hunting.[23] These were opportune times to request royal favors or to file observations or complaints.

One wonders if the king did not tire of the constant acts of solicitation that punctuated his daily life. Perhaps he might have, had the scheduling practices encouraging the courtiers' perpetual scrambling not served his interests so directly. As nobles competed to situate themselves advantageously in the midst of the royal daily timeline, their activities assumed a fragmentary form. With their attentions focused on small units of time, court members pursued their individual micro-objectives with a fervor that could only reassure the king. Fragmented modes of activity and the mutually inhibiting spirit of competition rendered impossible the formation of the blocs of rebellious nobles that had threatened the monarchy during the Fronde (1648–53).

The scheduling of court life thus constituted one of Louis XIV's major innovations in the establishment of absolute royal authority. An inventor of meanings for minute actions, the Sun King took pains to introduce "new subtleties into the daily routine of court life, so that his every gesture might be seen as a sign of his favour, his displeasure or his indifference," such that "every moment [was] organized by strict etiquette."[24] Louis XIV's creativity in producing meticulous structures for routines of everyday life render the court over which he reigned a privileged object of study for the cultural historian: "In such a society the chance of preceding another, or sitting while he had to stand, or the depth of a bow with which one was greeted, . . . were not mere externals. . . . They were literal documentations of social existence."[25] The codified and carefully timed behaviors that characterized court life under Louis XIV attest historically to the increasing importance of detailed time-consciousness in early modern France. Minute details of movement and attitude were invested at court with political meanings constituted within a precisely constructed power hierarchy surrounding the king. In order to assess their position and potential within this social structure, nobles had to remain aware of the extremely small quantities of time in which power functioned. Louis XIV's purposeful patronage of innovations in the science of clocks and watches frames the social dimension of courtly convention within the epistemological changes exemplified by the development of early modern technologies. Representations and uses of time in the "Plaisirs de l'île enchantée" take on their full significance when viewed in the contexts of both technological and social practices of temporal precision under the Sun King.

Still, it would be simplistic to claim that conceptions of time in Louis XIV's court pointed the way unequivocally to thinking practices constitutive of high modern rationalism, bourgeois capitalism, and Taylorism in the structure of work. In fact, the investment of nuanced behaviors in the self-justifying perpetuation of figurations for royal authority harks back to feudalism. The measured actions of the nobility served no tangible, practical purpose. Time used in measuring bows and entrances pursued the ages-old goal of tightening ties of loyalty to the king.

Nevertheless, even in combination with historically regressive elements of Louis XIV's absolute rule, detailed consciousness of time reflected an increasing demand, in the Sun King's administration, for efficiency and rational organization: "To make the dealings of people with each other calculable . . . an analogous means was used to that by which a work-process is made calculable in economic society."[26] In Louis XIV's court, one can thus observe an early and stylized form of the kinds of time conceptions that would lead to the increasingly rigid scheduling of work in industrial societies. Time as constructed in bourgeois capitalism is by no means identical to time as it was experienced at Versailles, but evidence of modern time-consciousness exists in the historical record, in a complex interweaving of practices both atavistic and innovative.

The temporal complexity of the "Plaisirs de l'île enchantée" provides a richly suggestive representation of the ambiguities of time under Louis XIV. The use of machines and the rhetoric of a radical monarchical modernity served to point France in a forward-looking direction, while at the same time the setting for these announcements of a new era evoked a mythic past, an *illo tempore* to which spectators were invited to direct their rêverie. The Golden Age, as dramatized in the fête, spoke both from a deep past of folklore and from a present of early modern hopes and political objectives.

The coexistence, in representations of temporal consciousness at Versailles, of progressive and retrograde views on time throws early modern temporal conceptions into a stylized relief that provides different angles of approach to the cultural history of court life, subjective existence, and thinking practices in the seventeenth century. By focusing on time structures and the meanings they generate in the specific context of political representation and socially mediated reception at Versailles, I have sought to develop a historical context for framing a reading of a significant literary element of the "Plaisirs de l'île enchantée," the premiere of *Le Tartuffe*. This is only one part of the story, however. The fragmentary nature of historical data and the ineffable character of time-consciousness as an object of analysis require interpretive activity as a complement to the exegesis of historical material. Moving from context to textual content facilitates the task of interpretation which is central to analyzing temporalities and their potential valences in terms of social and subjective experience. The section that follows extends the task of interpretation through a literary-critical reading of time structures in Molière's *Le Tartuffe* in the context of the play's premiere at Versailles.

## TIME STRUCTURES OF *LE TARTUFFE*

### *Interlude: Placing Molière in Context*

The spectacles given at Versailles in May 1664 attested above all to the court's taste for change.[27] Spectators wanted to see rapid movement and lively variety in the displays and dramatic works contributing to their pleasures, such that, according to Jacques Schérer, the dramatist's goal was "to defamiliarize [Schérer's term is *dépayser*] the spectator, to take him from one surprise to another."[28] The esthetic objective of providing often disjunctive sequences of images, actions, and words required an attention to small spans of time in the orchestration of the theatrical event. As the second half of this chapter argues, Molière developed a meticulous approach to time in the composition of *Le Tartuffe*. Recognizing this way of thinking time in Molière's play allows us to place this work within the cognitive atmosphere of detailed time-consciousness that pervaded Louis XIV's court at the time of the "Plaisirs de l'île enchantée," and to make temporal sense of play and fête as an esthetic/epistemological whole.

The tight timing of Louis XIV's inaugural fête, along with the numerous visual and sonorous representations of time traversing the event, suggest a temporal reading of *Le Tartuffe*. Seen in this perspective, this complex theatrical work offers ample commentary on time-consciousness under the Sun King. More specifically, *Le Tartuffe* stands as literary testimony to the epistemological shift that inflected thinking practices in Louis XIV's France, taking these toward an increasing appreciation of small time quantities and of their potential disposition for strategic purposes.

By its very nature, the work of theater must confront the temporality of the ephemeral. The singularity of performance places theater in a constricted time frame governed by dynamics of instantaneity. The temporal specificity of *Le Tartuffe*'s first performance brings our attention to the play's insertion into the rhythms of events at Versailles in May 1664: "Thus Molière's plays seem 'trapped' in their own being by this necessity of being perceived in the instant, forever lost, in which they appeared, in this movement that traced the convergence of several art forms."[29] Reinserted within a set of historical circumstances, viewed through the kaleidoscope of baroque entertainments that surrounded its emergence, *Le Tartuffe* appears as an aggregate of richly suggestive microdiachronies. Contextualizing this play within the temporality of performance functions to reinsert moments of theater into the spaces of textuality. If, as Artaud claims, theater must be understood in contexts larger and more dynamic than mere textual constructs, then the total spectacle (*Gesamtkunstwerke*) that was the "Plaisirs de l'île enchantée" frames Molière's theater in exemplary fashion.[30]

Apart from its inevitable insertion in the instantaneity of event, the theatrical work must rely on mere instants of time to achieve comedic effect. For Poulet, "[t]he comic is . . . the perception of an ephemeral and local fracture in the middle of a durable, eternal world."[31] Within an atmosphere of detailed time-consciousness, Molière's *Le Tartuffe* solicited perceptions of numerous privileged instants of comic time.

## *Madame Pernelle: Scheduling Bedlam*

*Le Tartuffe* begins with an imperative of a verb of motion: "Allons, Flipote, allons, que d'eux je me délivre" [Come, Flipote, come along. Let me be getting away from them].[32] The repetition of the injunction to action recalls the "Vite debout" sounding the beginning of the prologue to *La Princesse d'Elide*. Carried into the subjunctive clause concluding *Le Tartuffe*'s famous first line, the performativity of the imperative completes a sentence that announces an impending exit, an action serving to send a strong message of disapproval. Elmire's reaction opens dialogue with an evaluation of rapidity: "Vous marchez d'un tel pas qu'on a peine à vous suivre" [You walk so fast one can hardly keep up with you] (1.1.2). The speed with which Madame Pernelle moves communicates a message as well, a statement on the current state of affairs in her son's household. The daughter-in-law feels compelled to request an explanation for Madame Pernelle's rate of exit: "Mais, ma mère, d'où vient que vous sortez si vite?" [Why must you be in such a hurry to go, mother?] (1.1.6). The time that Madame Pernelle uses to depart seems scant to Elmire, whose query leads her mother-in-law to impose a conversational time structure onto this Bedlam, this "cour du roi Pétaut."[33]

Dorine's attempt to interject stops after a single syllable, accomplished in a brief breath of utterance, "Si . . ." [If . . . ] (1.1.13). Damis, as a member of the family, whose temper and potential to torment his father displease Madame Pernelle to no end, is allotted a slightly more generous syllable containing a labial sound, "Mais . . ." [But . . . ] (1.1.16). Mariane, "l'eau qui dort" [standing water] (1.1.23), whose only bad quality consists in her potential to have bad qualities, occupies the relatively privileged linguistic space of two syllables in this dialogue, and accomplishes the grammatical goal of verbal utterance with her hesitant "[j]e crois . . ." [I think . . . ] (1.1.21). On the next rung of the conversational hierarchy produced by Orgon's mother, the unfailingly respectful but suspiciously well-dressed wife utters three syllables: "Mais, ma mère . . ." [But mother . . . ] (1.1.25). Finally, Cléante, whom Madame Pernelle admits to respecting, places the few moments of his permitted speech into an entire hemistich: "Mais, Madame, après tout . . ." [Oh come, after all madam . . . ] (1.1.33). From Dorine to Cléante, every resident of Orgon's house has taken a place in Madame Pernelle's ritual of conversation and interruption, a carefully staged set of actions and words that serves to represent her authority as judge of the household.

In the opening scene of *Le Tartuffe*, meaning is conveyed through the recognition and careful disposition of speech and action in small units of time. Opening in the verbal mood of rapidity, the play's first scene transmits a conversation which calls attention to the microdiachrony of a set of minimal utterances, the aggregation of which gives a lively rhythm to this theatrical work's comical *incipit*. Georges Poulet's observation that disjunctive instants are required for the production of comic effect accurately describes the microdynamics of time through which Madame Pernelle places her kin in a meticulously subdivided order of differently articulated negative opinions.

The rudeness of Madame Pernelle's interruptions, combined with the harshness with which she treats Flipote, whom she resoundingly slaps at the conclusion of this scene, announces the familial strain of violence that will throw both Damis and his father into rages later in the play. There is, however, a significant difference between mother and son. Orgon's anger causes him to lose control of situations, thus creating the power voids into which Tartuffe insinuates himself. The clearest case in point is the expulsion of Damis from the household (3.6). Both Damis and Orgon lose their temper in this scene, while Tartuffe remains calm and develops a hyperbolically self-deprecating rhetoric that serves to protect and preserve all of his privileges. Madame Pernelle, on the other hand, manages to channel her anger into a temporal/punitive strategy for limiting others' communication. The hapless Flipote's corporal punishment points to the disciplinary nature of Madame Pernelle's other uncivil behaviors. Her interruptions in the play's first scene, accomplished in small increments of time, can be seen as a disciplinary imposition structuring the conversation she wishes, rather vociferously, to conclude. Power resides in the ability to make oneself heard while controlling the communication of others. The disadvantages of these tactics will only surface near the end of the play, when Madame Pernelle's persistent blindness to the truth about Tartuffe makes her appear ridiculous even in comparison to her son, who has by then been disabused. In the opening scene, however, the strategic limitation of others' speech works quite well, and the matron clearly has her say.

Ironically, in the process of monopolizing conversation and creating constraints for others, Madame Pernelle identifies Dorine as the party responsible for such restrictions: "Ma bru, l'on est chez vous contrainte de se taire, / Car Madame à jaser tient le dé tout le jour" [I have to hold my tongue when I'm at your house for Mistress Chatterbox here holds forth all day long] (1.1.142–43). Madame Pernelle uses her consciousness of the constrictive capacity inherent in time structures to impose a linguistic order on the "cour du roi Pétaut" she wishes to exit, and she manages as well to lay the blame on Dorine, and more generally on the communicational disorder in Orgon's home, a bedlam that Dorine's utterances are made to represent. Madame Pernelle thus defines her own interventions as a justifiable, inevitable response to an unsatisfactory state of affairs. Against the king of vagrancy and disorder, she places the authority of her moral judgments.

The rest of the household certainly has a good laugh at Madame Pernelle's expense. Courtiers at Versailles undoubtedly shared in this mirth as they watched Louis Béjart in drag, chastising anyone and everyone onstage. But behind the comical mask of the irate mother there lies nonetheless the serious implication that power operates along lines of carefully timed communication. Madame Pernelle's upper hand in the play's opening scene foreshadows Tartuffe's tactics while developing an implicit commentary on speech, time, and power relationships in seventeenth-century society. By structuring her utterances and those of others in an exacting time frame, she accomplishes her rhetorical goal within a rapid dynamics of communication that announces the fast-moving and at times dangerous nature of dialogue in *Le Tartuffe*. News travels quickly, both outside and within Orgon's household. In order to maintain one's position within the social order depicted by the play, one must think, speak, and act quickly and strategically. Not to do so, in a world of Tartuffes and gossiping neighbors, can lead to the most dire consequences. This is what Madame Pernelle's opening remarks point out, behind the risible façade of her bad temper: she knows how word travels, and she intends to put words in an order protective of morality and reputation.

*Time Structures of Communication and Gossip*

Madame Pernelle's opinions of her interlocutors in the first act have been formed by the gossip she has heard in her social circles. While the free-wheeling conversational practices through which she has been informed remain unquestioned as rites of sociability and expressions of the collectivity's values and judgments, speech within Orgon's household falls under a severe critical lens:

> Ces visites, ces bals, ces conversations,
> Sont du malin esprit toutes inventions.
> Là, jamais on n'entend de pieuses paroles;
> Ce sont propos oisifs, chansons et fariboles:
> Bien souvent le prochain en a sa bonne part,
> Et l'on y sait médire et du tiers et du quart.
> Enfin les gens sensés ont leurs têtes troublées
> De la confusion de telles assemblées;
> Mille caquets divers s'y font en moins de rien,
> Et comme l'autre jour un docteur dit fort bien,
> C'est véritablement la tour de Babylone,
> Car chacun y babille, et tout du long de l'aune;
>
> (1.1.151–62)

[This giddy round of balls, assemblies, and routs is all a device of the Evil One. In such places one never hears a word of godliness, nothing but idle chatter, singing, and nonsensical rigmaroles: often enough the neighbours come in for their share and slander and gossip go the rounds. Even sensible heads are turned in the turmoil of that sort of gathering, a thousands idle tongues get busy about nothing and, as a learned doctor said the other day, it becomes a veritable tower of Babylon where everybody babbles never-endingly]

Here Madame Pernelle cites the definition of gossip as idle talk, speech that follows its own timeline, out of sync with the rituals of religious duty. The gossip in Orgon's house is thus deemed not only to be disorderly but also ungodly and even satanic. In opposition to this pernicious kind of communication, Madame Pernelle appeals to the information she has gathered from the neighborhood prudes in order to set things right. As Ross Chambers has pointed out, gossip that creates scandal serves to reinforce the *doxa* of a particular social group.[34] We find out later in the play that Tartuffe has been manipulating the collectivity surrounding Orgon's home, and thus shaping Madame Pernelle's opinions from the very beginning. In the process of trying to seduce Elmire, Tartuffe excuses himself for having participated in these rumors: "les bruits que j'ai faits / Des visites qu'ici reçoivent vos attraits / Ne sont pas envers vous l'effet d'aucune haine, / Mais plutôt d'un transport de zèle que m'entraîne" [anything I have said against those who were paying homage to your charms was not spoken in malice against you but rather [as a result of] the intensity of my pious zeal] (3.3.907–10). Madame Pernelle's uses of communication, then, are a direct result of Tartuffe's machinations. The hypocrite is thus virtually present onstage, between the lines of dialogue, from the very opening scene of the play, fueling Madame Pernelle's criticism of ungodly discourse in Orgon's home.

In a more descriptive and less explicitly moralizing way, Madame Pernelle characterizes ways of talking in Orgon's household in terms of an excessively rapid rate of communication: "Mille caquets divers s'y font en moins de rien" [a thousand idle tongues get busy about nothing] (1.1.159). She is not only bothered by the perceived vacuity and heresy of these "caquets," but also shocked that such an agglomeration of acts of speech could take shape in such a brief span of time, "en moins de rien." Her consciousness of the myriad microtemporal links in this perpetually unbroken communicative chain spurs her to try and impose a new order on the household.

By way of response, Dorine, who as we have seen is held responsible for much of the chattering in question, describes the activities of the gossips from whom Madame Pernelle has received her (mis)information:

> Ils ne manquent jamais de saisir promptement
> L'apparente lueur du moindre attachement,
> D'en semer la nouvelle avec beaucoup de joie,
> Et d'y donner le tour qu'ils veulent qu'on y croie:
>
> (1.1.107–10)

[They never miss a chance of seizing on the least glimmering suspicion of an affair, of gleefully spreading the news and twisting things the way they want folk to believe]

Dorine's emphasis falls on the rapidity with which the spreaders of gossip act. The terms "saisir," "promptement," "semer," and "nouvelle" describe hasteful communicative and cognitive activities. The dubious thinking practices involved in grasping new information, vaguely discerning its possible implications, and rhetorically altering one's own account of the news all fall under Dorine's critical eye. The rapidity of communication leads to fragmentation of evidence, neglectfulness in verification of facts, and to the proliferation of conjecture.

The savvy maid knows of the potential both for abuse and use in the communication network operating within and surrounding Orgon's house. She negotiates this system often strategically, in her efforts to act in Mariane's best interests. While Orgon presses his daughter to accept his proposal that she marry Tartuffe, Dorine appears on the scene to disrupt this attempt to coerce Mariane into consenting. Orgon shows his awareness of Dorine's timing: "La curiosité qui vous presse est bien forte" [You must be mighty curious] (2.2.457). Implied in the verb "presser" is the notion of haste that ascribes an excessive rapidity to the effect created by the maid's curiosity. Having just announced the plan to marry Mariane to Tartuffe, Orgon is surprised that Dorine knows of it already: "Mais de ce mariage on m'a dit la nouvelle" [when I heard about this marriage] (2.2.461). Dorine's entry in the second scene of the play's second act serves a disjunctive purpose: by disrupting the present conversation, she protects Mariane from her father's attempt to extract a statement of consent. The rapid dynamics of the communication network through which the maid has been informed come into association with conversational disjunctions, as was the case for Madame Pernelle's strategies of utterance in the opening scene of *Le Tartuffe*.

Attempting to dissuade Tartuffe from marrying Mariane, Cléante prefaces his own remarks with an observation on the timing of his advice amid the circulation of gossip:

> Oui, tout le monde en parle, et vous m'en pouvez croire,
> L'éclat que fait ce bruit n'est point à votre gloire;
> Et je vous ai trouvé, Monsieur, fort à propos,
> Pour vous en dire net ma pensée en deux mots.
>
> (4.1.1185–88)

[Yes, everyone is talking about it and, believe me, the sensation the news has made has done your reputation no good. This is an opportune time to tell you briefly and bluntly what I think about it.]

Cléante takes stock of what is being said in the recent past and the relative present designated by "parle" and "fait." The collectivity which

Cléante calls "tout le monde" is thus in the process of discussing these matters in an unfavorable light, even as Cléante speaks to Tartuffe. Cléante wishes to insist that his own words have considerable importance for being part of a generalized expression of opinion regarding the pressing matter of plans for Mariane's betrothal. The advice he is about to give gains value in being "fort à propos," timed with precision and encapsulated in the brief time frame of Cléante's "deux mots."

Cléante situates the potential repercussions of Tartuffe's actions in the imminent time frame structured by the communication of opinions about his conflict with Damis. Cléante's terms evoke a constricted diachrony of prior event and preceding and current gossip, in the midst of which quick and efficient speech and action take on the utmost importance. Similarly to Dorine, Cléante realizes that time is of the essence when negotiating the communicational networks of the community to which Orgon's household belongs. With a critical eye and a rational manner of interpreting news and events, all characteristic of his *honnêteté*, Cléante aims to elicit a prompt, effective response from Tartuffe. Cléante's use and construction of time in his plea for explanation and reconciliation produce an attempt to place a time constraint on Tartuffe, in the name of good sense and reputation. Tartuffe responds, not in the timely way Cléante seems to demand, but rather with his own style of reference to and reflection on time, a cynical method for manipulating speech, opinion, and actions.

## Tartuffe's Uses of Time

Tartuffe uses the pretense of strict adherence to a ritualized schedule to break off communication with Cléante: "Il est, Monsieur, trois heures et demie: / Certain devoir pieux me demande là-haut, / Et vous m'excuserez de vous quitter si tôt" [It is now half past three, sir. Certain pious obligations require my presence upstairs without delay. Excuse my leaving you so soon] (4.1.1266–68). Cléante can respond only with the interjection "Ah!" as Tartuffe attends to the observation of religious duty. The single syllable of utterance allotted Cléante after Tartuffe's tactical announcement recalls the power that Madame Pernelle exercised over her interlocutors in the play's opening scene. Just like Madame Pernelle, Tartuffe knows that truncating the utterances of others, while giving free rein to one's own ideas, is the quickest way to gain the upper hand. As we will see, Tartuffe's understanding and use of carefully timed conversation goes well beyond the range of Mme Pernelle's rhetoric of admonition and develops a keenly subjective method of temporally nuanced manipulation, seduction, and power acquisition. Tartuffe's awareness of time and the rhythms of pious display allows him to deflect Cléante's potentially compromising observations. This same tactical knowledge permitted him initially to win Orgon's admiration and to begin his infiltration of the household. Initially, the impostor used a regular schedule of activity to pass himself off as a zealot: "Chaque jour à l'église il venait, d'un air doux, / Tout vis-à-vis de moi se mettre à deux genoux" [Every day he used to come to church and modestly fall on his knees just beside me] (1.5.283–84). Tartuffe's routine appearances in church were matched within the time frame of the day's rituals by consistent efforts at the strictest appearance of devotion:

> Il attirait les yeux de l'assemblée entière
> Par l'ardeur dont au Ciel il poussait sa prière;
> Il faisait des soupirs, de grands élancements,
> Et baisait humblement la terre à tous moments;
> Et lorsque je sortais, il me devançait vite,
> Pour m'aller à la porte offrir de l'eau bénite.
>
> (1.5.285–90)

[He would draw the eyes of the whole congregation by the fervour with which he poured forth his prayers, sighing, groaning, kissing the ground in transports of humility. When I went out he would step in front of me to offer me the Holy water at the door.]

Every moment of Tartuffe's activities carried particular significance in the context of his attempts to ingratiate himself to Orgon. Through calculated use of timing in symbolic actions, Tartuffe has formed the bond with his host that will permit him to attain subsequently a position of considerable influence in Orgon's household.[35]

While Orgon remains oblivious to the motivations underlying Tartuffe's pious displays, Cléante describes the hypocritical behavior of those who merely wear the mask of the zealot, "[c]es gens qui, par une âme à l'intérêt soumise, / Font de dévotion métier et marchandise" [men who put self-interest first, who trade and traffic in devotion] (1.5.365–66). By transforming pious duty into a business opportunity, Tartuffe applies to prayer and ceremony a "temps des marchands" [merchants' time], to use Jacques Le Goff's term.[36] A symbolic system of gestures, sighs, bursts of reverent emotion, kissing the ground, and the offering of holy water, functions according to a precise schedule of actions, in order to accomplish the practical goal of creating an alliance with a wealthy bourgeois. While enacting a temporal formalism for godliness

inherited from ages-old practices, Tartuffe displays a practical, mercan-
tile understanding of time in order to achieve his earthly objectives.

When Orgon criticizes Valère for his infrequent churchgoing—"Je
ne remarque point qu'il hante les églises" [I don't see him at church
much] (2.2.525)—Dorine's response reveals her awareness of Tartuffe's temporal strategies: "Voulez-vous qu'il y coure à vos heures
précises, / Comme ceux qui n'y vont que pour être aperçus?" [I suppose
you'd have him run there at the very moment you get there yourself
like some folk who only go there to be noticed] (2.2.526–27). Dorine
understands fully the importance of timing in Tartuffe's gestures, just as
she has from near the beginning of the play remarked on the temporally
patterned effect exercised by Tartuffe over his host: "Son cagotisme en
tire à toute heure des sommes" [he . . . gets money out of him constantly
by means of canting humbug] (1.2.201). The servant's awareness of
Tartuffe's time-consciousness casts an irony onto Tartuffe's supposed
"trop peu de soin des choses temporelles" [his indifference to temporal
matters] (2.2.489). Not only is the impostor indeed interested in earthly
delights, such as food and sex; he also keeps close track of temporal
matters like the timing of acts of devotion in church and the strategic
use of time in avoiding threatening conversations.

Tartuffe even admits to his awareness of and interest in the immediate time frame of earthly life when he speaks of love to Elmire: "L'a-
mour qui nous attache aux beautés éternelles / N'étouffe pas en nous
l'amour des temporelles" [A passion for the beauties which are eternal
does not preclude a temporal love] (3.3.933–34). Molière plays on the
polyvalence of the term "temporelles," which refers both to a dimension
of existence as described by the church and to the finitude that lies at
the conceptual pole opposite eternity. This semantic play on the representation of time highlights Tartuffe's temporal rhetoric, through which
he aims to convince Elmire that her current conversation with him is
occurring at a privileged moment:

> J'en suis ravi de même, et sans doute il m'est doux,
> Madame, de me voir seul à seul avec vous:
> C'est une occasion qu'au Ciel j'ai demandée,
> Sans que jusqu'à cette heure il me l'ait accordée.
>
> (3.3.899–902)

[I too am delighted. I need hardly say how pleased I am to find myself alone
with you. It's an opportunity which I have besought Heaven to accord me—
vainly until this moment.]

By relating his immediate circumstances to the diachrony of a life's itinerary, Tartuffe sounds a tone of urgency in an effort to make advances toward Elmire.

To develop further the expression of his impatience, Tartuffe describes the inception of his affection for Elmire as a privileged single instant, a kind of time he would like to relive. He recalls the moment after he first noticed the charms and the beauty of Orgon's wife: "Dès que j'en vis briller la splendeur plus qu'humaine, / De mon intérieur vous fûtes souveraine" [From the first moment that I beheld its more than mortal splendours you have ruled supreme in my affection] (3.3.973–74). An evocation of the temporal dynamics of interior experience plays a part in this language of seduction. Elmire remains unmoved by Tartuffe's overtures, and the revelation that Damis has been listening to this entire conversation seems to place the impostor in a desperate situation.

With diabolical presence of mind, Tartuffe relies on a hyperbolic rhetoric of micro-time in order to sway the malleable mind and heart of Orgon: "Chaque instant de ma vie est chargé de souillures" [not a moment of my life but is sullied with some foul deed] (3.6.1077). This disingenuously self-abasing statement achieves its desired effect when Orgon responds, expressing his desire to minimize delay before marrying his daughter to Tartuffe: "[J]e vais me hâter de lui donner ma fille, / Pour confondre l'orgueil de toute ma famille" [I'll hasten his marriage with my daughter and confound the pride of the whole family] (3.6.1125–26). In part by using a particular rhetoric of time, Tartuffe accomplishes the temporal-strategic objectives of accelerating plans for his marriage to Mariane and of gaining more time to spend in Elmire's company: "Non, en dépit de tous, vous la fréquenterez. / Faire enrager le monde est ma plus grande joie, / Et je veux qu'à toute heure avec elle on vous voie" [No! you *shall* see her in spite of them all. Nothing gives me greater joy than to annoy them. You shall appear with her constantly] (3.7.1172–74). Tartuffe gains the permission to devote all of his time to the seduction of Elmire, and it is the master of the household, the official controller of time for the family, who creates for him this advantageous schedule of unwittingly enforced courtship. Tartuffe has capitalized on one of the key ironies structuring family life in Orgon's home. While Orgon ostensibly controls time for his household, he is the character who has the least developed understanding of time and timing. In this context Orgon is the comical opposite of Louis XIV, who not only has the official charge of setting the tempo for his court and kingdom but also, throughout the "Plaisirs de l'île enchantée," displays a stunning ability to perform his sovereign duties. By stark contrast, Orgon's incompetence as time lord to his family constitutes a power void, the kind of vacuum that Tartuffe seeks out and occupies with particular interest.

Seeing that a schedule for seduction has been set, Tartuffe pursues Elmire with an obtrusive vigor: "Quoi? vous voulez aller avec cette vitesse?" [Why must you go so fast?] (4.5.1453). She remarks on the urgency of his efforts: "Et vous ne donnez pas le temps de respirer?" [Won't you even allow me a breathing space?] (4.5.1472). In order to hasten the pursuit of his goals, Tartuffe imposes a time constraint with his "efforts pressants." Elmire reacts by buying time through the request that Tartuffe scan the house to make sure no one is nearby: "[S]ortez, je vous prie, un moment, / Et partout là dehors voyez exactement" [All the same, do go out a moment, please, and have a good look round] (4.5.1527–28). Tartuffe's aggressiveness in the temporal playing field has led Elmire to create changes in space, asking Tartuffe to exit the room and trying to bring Orgon out from under the table that conceals him.

Elmire's strategic resistances to Tartuffe's use of temporal rhetoric and time pressures aid in finally provoking Orgon's intervention, which turns out, characteristically, to be too little and too late. Orgon tries to gain strategic advantage by interrupting Tartuffe and calling for his immediate expulsion: "Mon dessein . . . [Orgon] Ces discours ne sont plus de saison: / Il faut, tout sur-le-champ, sortir de la maison" [My intention . . . That sort of talk won't do now. You must leave the house forthwith] (4.7.1555–56). Orgon's rhetoric of time in demanding a minimum of delay before Tartuffe's departure proves to be without effect, as Tartuffe claims to have a legal prerogative to evict Orgon, based on the possession of the private documents of a former "frondeur" and friend of Orgon and on the fact that Orgon has signed his house over to him (5.4.1753–57). Regardless of her own savvy in the midst of a difficult situation, Elmire's tactical maneuvers appear to end in vain due to prior mistakes made by her husband.

## Strategic Timing

The member of the household who is most efficient at using time strategically to counter the efforts of Tartuffe is Dorine. When Mariane, distraught over the prospects for her betrothal, asks for her advice— "Dis-nous quels ressorts il faut mettre en usage"—Dorine has a plan ready: "Nous en ferons agir de toutes les façons" [Tell us what we are to do. . . . We'll try everything we can] (2.4.794–95). Missing in the translation, the terms "ressorts," "usage," and "ferons agir" suggest a mechanistic conception of the ensuing strategizing. The use of these terms recalls the descriptions of the machines put into operation during the "Plaisirs de l'île enchantée." Similarly to the events of the fête, Dorine's plans take shape through an acute time-consciousness: "En attrapant du temps, à tout on remédie. / Tantôt vous payerez de quelque maladie, / Qui viendra tout à coup et voudra des délais" [If we can only gain time we may set everything right. You can complain of a sudden illness that will necessitate delay] (2.4.801–3). Thinking and strategizing in Mariane's best interests, Dorine proposes changes in schedule as tactics for redirecting the wedding arrangements.

Dorine's awareness of the importance of microdiachronies of the relative present for the purposes of strategic action corresponds to a sensitivity to subjective chronologies of interior experience, the very domain in which Tartuffe has displayed such skill. In the first act, her sympathy for the ailing Elmire provides a comic foil for Orgon's blind interest in Tartuffe:

> La nuit se passa tout entière
> Sans qu'elle pût fermer un moment la paupière;
> Des chaleurs l'empêchaient de pouvoir sommeiller,
> Et jusqu'au jour près d'elle il nous fallut veiller.
>
> (1.4.240–43)

[She never closed her eyes all through the night. She was too feverish to sleep and we had to sit up with her until morning.]

The temporal indications sketching out Elmire's night of illness produce a chronology of subjective experience that is intended to arouse sympathy in Dorine's interlocutor, Orgon, who dumbly repeats: "Et Tartuffe?" [And Tartuffe?] (1.4.245) Dorine's awareness of time structures of interiority operates in the domain of the emotions as well. Her call for action to foil the plan of marrying Mariane to Tartuffe finds justification in sympathy for the trying rhythms of Mariane's sentimental experience:

> Et l'accord que son père a conclu pour ce soir
> La fait, à tous moments, entrer en désespoir.
> Il va venir. Joignons nos efforts, je vous prie,
> Et tâchons d'ébranler, de force ou d'industrie,
> Ce malheureux dessein qui nous a tous troublés.
>
> (4.2.1271–75)

[The betrothal her father has arranged for this evening has reduced her to despair. Here he comes. I beseech you, give us your help. Let us try by hook or crook to frustrate this wretched scheme which is worrying us all.]

Within a time frame of anticipation established by "ce soir," Dorine situates all of the moments of Mariane's despair. The "industrie" that Dorine summons describes a pragmatic mode of thinking and action that includes calculated uses of time, always strategic tools in her impatient time-consciousness.

Dorine urges Valère to minimize delay in his efforts to alter Mariane's current situation: "Sortez, et sans tarder employez vos amis, / Pour vous faire tenir ce qu'on vous a promis" [Off you go and get all your friends to use their influence with her father to stand by his promise] (2.4.811–12). Valère will prove to be an effective and time-conscious ally for Orgon's family. Near the conclusion of *Le Tartuffe*, Valère enters onto the scene announcing the recent results of Tartuffe's treacherous accusations and stressing the necessity of immediate action in the current circumstances: "Avec regret, Monsieur, je viens vous affliger; / Mais je m'y vois contraint par le pressant danger" [I'm very sorry to bring you bad news, sir, but I'm obliged to do so because you are in most urgent danger] (5.6.1827–28). Involved, as he was at the beginning of the second act's fourth scene, in processes of communication outside of Orgon's household, Valère tells Orgon that a friend "me vient d'envoyer un avis" [sent me intelligence, in confidence] (5.6.1833). This recent past of information transmission takes a more specific form when Valère addresses the content of the message in question: "Le fourbe qui longtemps a pu vous imposer / Depuis une heure a su vous accuser" [The scoundrel, who has so long imposed upon you, denounced you to the King an hour ago] (5.6.1835–36). Having convinced his audience of the urgency of the situation by locating its temporal parameters in a recent past, Valère stresses the importance of effective time-management: "Le moindre amusement vous peut être fatal" [The slightest delay may be fatal to you] (5.6.1848). He insists on acting immediately: "Ne perdons point de temps" [We must lose no time] (5.6.1851). In attempting to gain Orgon's approval and to rescue Mariane from an undesirable marriage, Valère acts both as Orgon's watch and alarm clock in the play's penultimate scene.

Tartuffe remains one step ahead of the family, however, and opens the final scene by heading them off at the pass: "Tout beau, Monsieur, tout beau, ne courez point si vite" [Gently, sir, gently, don't run so fast] (5.7.1861). It would seem that yet again Tartuffe is prepared to turn the family's temporal strategies back on them, as he has done in preceding scenes, but in this final scene a reversal takes place. When Tartuffe demands that the "Exempt" accomplish his legal duties, this representative of the sovereign remarks first on the timing of the announcement he makes:

> Oui, c'est trop demeurer sans doute à l'accomplir:
> Votre bouche à propos m'invite à le remplir;
> Et pour l'exécuter, suivez-moi tout à l'heure
> Dans la prison qu'on doit vous donner pour demeure.
>
> (5.7.1899–1902)

[Yes. I have indeed waited too long already and you do well to recall me to my duty. In fulfilment of my instructions I command you to accompany me forthwith to the prison in which you are to be lodged.]

No longer delaying the accomplishment of this official task, the "Exempt" demands that Tartuffe follow him "tout à l'heure," for his imminent incarceration. In this statement power relations between Tartuffe and Orgon are reversed through a rhetoric of time. The immediacy of the impact of these legal disciplinary measures turns strategic uses of time back onto Tartuffe and for the benefit of Orgon, thus inverting the situation cited above in which Tartuffe deflected Orgon's failed temporal tactics back onto him, to Orgon's utter dismay (4.7).

In the play's concluding scene, Orgon's prior failed attempt to turn time against Tartuffe is finally vindicated. The strategic use of time and the verbal expression of this use mediate the reversal of power accomplished by a representative of the prince in the last scene. That a reflection on time is involved in this dramatically privileged moment attests to the centrality of representations of time in *Le Tartuffe*. Along with the spatial question of who can stay and who must leave the house, Molière repeatedly raises the corresponding question of who can use moments of time in the relative present to greatest advantage. In the battle over domestic space, time is also of the essence, and it is through the help of temporally aware allies that Orgon finally manages to take time back from Tartuffe and resume the orderly daily chronology of bourgeois life.

## Early Modern Time-Consciousness: Tartuffe in Context

An acute consciousness of time pervades dialogues between Molière's characters in *Le Tartuffe* and contributes to the overall atmosphere of temporal awareness that played so significant a role in the

"Plaisirs de l'île enchantée." Placing *Le Tartuffe* in the historical context of its first performance at this fête links textual and theatrical time structures to a series of ceremonial representations of time: the coat of arms worn by the prince de Marsillac, the actors representing the hours of the day on Apollo's chariot, and the careful timing of fireworks displays, to mention but a few of the examples discussed above.

What did all of this symbolic and pragmatic attention to time mean? What can a study of "Les Plaisirs de l'île enchantée" reveal about ways of thinking time in the first decade of Louis XIV's reign? To try to answer these very broad and complex questions, it is necessary to analyze a variety of forms of cultural production relevant to the construction of temporal concepts at Versailles. For the fête of 1664, Molière's plays clearly constitute an important piece of the puzzle. The ways that time is represented in Molière—as a kind of substance for strategic manipulation and as a structural marker for dramatic action—provide an interpretive context for the modes of temporal conceptualization that the fête proposed, both in its overall organization and as a part of its spectacles and processions. In an opposite and complementary direction, the proceedings of the festival suggest angles of approach to texts and performances that emerged as part of the events.

The cultural history of chronometry before and during Louis XIV's reign provides a framework for understanding the significance of quantifying approaches to time, in social life, in administrative efforts of Louis XIV and his ministers, and in new modes of subjective formation. For indicators of the temporal construction of subject and society under Louis XIV, I have looked to the cultural history of court life and more specifically to practices of scheduling in the organization of daily proceedings at Versailles. These practices of everyday ceremony developed in continuity with highly symbolic activities recorded as part of the king's new home's famous fêtes.

Perhaps the most significant result of the new time structures elaborated at Versailles was the establishment of Louis XIV's authority near the beginning of his reign. The Sun King clearly saw that success in the temporal playing field was esthetically, epistemologically, and pragmatically indispensable for political success. The pursuit of precision timekeeping and the rigorous codification of social existence at Versailles were part of an effort toward more effective control of the king's realm. The significance of the issue of temporal control in *Le Tartuffe* points to an implicit commentary in Molière's play on this effort toward spatiotemporal domination of the court and the emerging nation. Along with the emphasis on intersubjective dynamics of time and political uses of time, Molière's characters also evoke the new subjective temporalities that came into existence alongside new forms of social life and administration. The early modern subject's experience of time was situated at the border between increasingly centralized strategies of organization and control, on the one hand, and the new private experience of daily life that the new institutions rendered possible, on the other.

*Le Tartuffe* can be seen as an exploration of some of the possibilities and indeed the dangers of new domains of individual temporal experience. While a character like Dorine reveals the hope and the possibility that anyone can keep apace with the newly rapid temporal and communicational dynamics of daily life, the treacherous gossips in Orgon's neighborhood, Madame Pernelle, and Tartuffe himself point to the dangers inherent in the epistemological shifts that marked the 1660s and 1670s in France. The greatest protection against the harrowing prospect of a world of rapidly proliferating (mis)information and strategic, subjective manipulation of time was, of course, a rational and clement sovereign in complete control of time in his realm. In order to protect his subjects from potential misuses of new temporal structures of experience, the early modern king had to do the Tartuffes one better, controlling not only the tempo of external social reality but also the most intimate sphere of individual life. As is suggested in the conclusion of *Le Tartuffe*, the monarch could even see inside his subjects:

> Nous vivons sous un Prince ennemi de la fraude,
> Un Prince dont les yeux se font jour dans les cœurs,
> Et que ne peut tromper tout l'art des imposteurs.
> D'un fin discernement sa grande âme pourvue
> Sur les choses toujours jette une droite vue
>
> (5.7.1906–10)

[We live under the rule of a prince inimical to fraud, a monarch who can read men's hearts, whom no impostor's art deceives. The keen discernment of that lofty mind at all times sees things in their true perspective.]

The king's perpetual access to the hearts and minds of his subjects guarantees that the temporal dynamics of intersubjective strategizing will never spin out of control. Thus Tartuffe sounds a warning of things to come but does not threaten to destroy the social order from within the most intimate space of the subject. As the king controlled each minute increment of time during the proceedings of the "Plaisirs de l'île enchantée," he implicitly invited his court to participate in a similar microtemporal vigilance, a significant mark of a new era and a new kind of thinking.

The subjective experience of public and private life in the second half of the seventeenth century involved an unprecedented kind of awareness and valorization of microdiachronies of the everyday. Situated within a complex interweaving of temporalities both ancient and modern, both Parmenidean and Heraclitean, centered alternatively on notions of eternity or immediacy, the relative-present time frame of individual life grew in significance during the initial decades of Louis XIV's reign. This temporal perspective and its articulation in thinking practices and in writing mark the beginnings of a new era for the ideation of time in occidental culture. While scientific advances and patterns of social and political organization reveal indications of this newly predominant temporality, subjective experiences of this kind of time offer perhaps the most intriguing glimpses into the epistemological shift that marked the second half of the seventeenth century. One of the most skilled writers to give voice to this experience of time, Mme de Sévigné, will be the object of the following chapter, a study that frames an individual temporal exploration of language within the administrative structure of daily life—the postal system—that made this practice of thought and writing possible.

# 3

## Time, Postal Practices, and Daily Life
## in Mme de Sévigné's Letters

*It is natural to use the present tense, because we live in her presence. We are*
*very little conscious of a disturbing medium between us—that she is living,*
*after all, by means of written words. But now and then with the sound of her*
*voice in our ears and its rhythm rising and falling within us, we become*
*aware, with some sudden phrase, about spring, about a country neighbour,*
*something struck off in a flash, that we are, of course, being addressed by one*
*of the great mistresses of the art of speech.*

—Virginia Woolf, *The Death of the Moth*

MME DE SÉVIGNÉ WAS A MARQUISE, A MOTHER, A FRIEND TO MME DE
Lafayette and La Rochefoucauld, and an occasional visitor at Louis
XIV's court, but she is remembered principally as a great writer of letters. Her voluminous correspondence occupies a long-standing position
in the French literary canon, while differing generically from the seventeenth century's great works of theater, poetry, and prose. Unlike other
masterpieces of the "Grand Siècle," an era of punctilious esthetic codification, Sévigné's writings reveal a close relation to the material conditions and circumstances of their production, to their author's daily life.
Perhaps the most personal of the French classical era's correspondences, Sévigné's letters constitute at the same time one of this tradition's most artful and evocative epistolary works. The marquise's letters
at once develop an esthetic of writing, a sustained meditation on facts
of human existence, and an account of everyday experiences.

The diurnal, realistic nature of the letters sets Sévigné apart from
epistolary rhetoricians like Jean-Louis Guez de Balzac (1594–1654),
for whom letter-writing provided a forum for painstakingly composed
essays. Sévigné's spontaneity distinguishes her letters also from salon
writing. Virtuosic practitioners of preciosity like Madeleine de Scudéry
and Vincent Voiture (1598–1648) wrote letters that either debated intellectual and linguistic issues of the day (in the case of Scudéry) or

elaborated lavish formulations of emotion and personal experience in ornate sentences (in the case of Voiture). Neither the argumentation of Balzac, the inquiries of Scudéry, nor the flourishes of Voiture made use of the potential for the letter to serve as a diary, as Mme de Sévigné did for much of her life.[1] While these three authors wrote letters with explicitly artistic intent, we cannot know whether Sévigné aimed to be the literary figure she would eventually become. The unanswerable question of authorly intention contributes to the originality of Sévigné's texts, their simultaneously esthetic and documentary quality. Whether the marquise was aware of it or not, she before any other epistolary writer explored the realistic potential of the personal letter as a diurnal form of literature.[2]

In this chapter, I argue that the dual literary and historical character of the Sévigné correspondence lends the reading of these texts to an interdisciplinary approach, including analysis of documents taken from postal history on the one hand, and of narrative prose on the other.[3] Both the marquise's experiences as she recounted them and her thoughts as she expressed them factored into her daily life, an existence structured in time by the activities of receiving and sending mail.

In February 1671, Sévigné's daughter Françoise-Marguerite comtesse de Grignan (1646–1705) left Paris for Provence to live with her husband, thus becoming separated from her mother definitively. The departure of Mme de Grignan spurred the marquise to write hundreds of letters: 68% of Sévigné's letters, or 764 out of 1,120, are addressed to her daughter.[4] It goes almost without saying that postal services had become a central concern of her life. In July 1671, Sévigné marveled at the improvements that had been undertaken in the institution that made her long-distance communication possible:

> Je suis en fantaisie d'admirer l'honnêteté de ces messieurs les postillons, qui sont incessamment sur les chemins pour porter et reporter nos lettres. Enfin, il n'y a jour dans la semaine qu'ils n'en portent quelqu'une à vous et à moi; il y en a toujours et à toutes les heures par la campagne. Les honnêtes gens! qu'ils sont obligeants! et que c'est une belle invention que la poste.
>
> (7.12.71, 1:293–94)

> [I am bent on admiring the goodness and decency of these postal messengers, who are incessantly on the roads, carrying our letters about. Not a day goes by that they are not carrying one letter or another to you and to me; they are out and about at all times, at all hours. These kind men! they are so helpful! and what a lovely invention the postal system is.]

France's postal system, newly centralized, was indeed a kind of "belle invention" of Louis XIV's régime. Michel Le Tellier marquis de Louvois (1639–91), newly appointed *Surintendant général des postes* [General Postal Superintendent] as of 1668, had the mails running more smoothly and worked at expanding them to serve more users at the time Sévigné was beginning her correspondence with Mme de Grignan in Provence. Increasingly precise postal schedules placed a structure on daily life that Sévigné described throughout her letters. Postal timetables motivated Mme de Sévigné to pay a new kind of attention to time, to focus persistently on the minutes and hours of daily existence.

Sévigné's approach to the experience and measure of time, evident in her present-oriented style, had much in common with the practicality of administrative measures taken under Louis XIV to make institutions run more efficiently. Louvois oversaw a thorough reform process that brought greater precision to postal schedules as France's mails became a centralized organization, a "Ferme des postes" in close connection with the country's symbolic and administrative center at Versailles. Time-management was a privileged focus of reform in postal operations under Louvois, an efficient and loyal servant of the crown who had proven himself as Louis XIV's minister of war. He had an eye for effectiveness and promptness in action, and saw to it that the mails would serve the Sun King both more efficiently and to greater financial benefit.

Whereas during the Renaissance mail service was limited and letters could take days or weeks to get from sender to recipient, Sévigné's postal reality was marked in time by *ordinaires*, regular, usually biweekly deliveries of mail that connected Paris to the provinces on a consistent schedule.[5] The temporal cycle of regular mailing structured the marquise's epistolary activity. In an ambivalent state of excitement with what the mails offered and frustration with the limits of their rapidity, Sévigné produced enormous quantities of letters. Her epistolary production was thus inextricably tied to the development of a centralized postal institution in France, whose operation was a condition of the correspondence's possibility. To understand Sévigné and to appreciate the conditions under which her literary activity became possible, we must examine how the *Surintendance générale des postes* took shape at the time when the marquise was doing some of her best writing. A correspondence like Sévigné's cannot be adequately described without a study of the procedural and material dynamics, the practical epistemology of how this body of texts came into being. The study of the French postal system that follows sketches out the mode of thinking time that was evident in the postal institutions that contributed to structuring Sévigné's writing and daily life.

## AN IMPATIENT ADMINISTRATION: POSTAL REFORM UNDER LOUVOIS

> *Faut-il que pour gagner sa vie*
> *Un malheureux se hâte à crever son tombeau [?]*
> . . .
> *Vous qui pouvant aller plus doux*
> *Etes ennemis de votre aise,*
> *Riches Seigneurs, défaites-vous*
> *D'une coutume si mauvaise:*
> *Apprenez à vous ménager.*
>
> —Anonymous, "Burlesque contre la poste"

### The Ferme: *From Feudalism to Centralization*

The royal treasury, sapped by reckless spending at home and by the War of Devolution with Spain (1667–68), was in dire need of replenishment when Louvois took charge of the mails. The new superintendent's administration would go to unprecedented lengths to make the postal institution a source of quick funds for the state. While the use of a postal system for royal political objectives dates back to Louis XI and the exploitation of the mails for revenue to Cardinal Richelieu, never had France seen its postal service take the centralized institutional form that Louvois gave it.[6] Louvois applied to the postal system an idea that can be traced back to the thirteenth century. King Philippe le Bel, when he was in need of money, procured sums from wealthy nobles, whom he would designate as "Fermiers." These "Fermiers," having attained a position of political privilege by helping the king, then paid themselves back by taxing the populace.[7]

Through a royal decree of 15 and 19 March 1672, Louvois exploited the postal system for Louis XIV's immediate benefit by transforming the mails into a "Ferme générale."[8] The Pajot-Rouillé family, a bloc of financiers, agreed to augment Louis XIV's treasury by the sum of 2,700,000 livres, and delegated the title of "fermier général" to Lazare Patin, who acted as their representative.[9] Revenues from the mails were to flow into the "Ferme," which functioned as an organ of Louvois's *Surintendance générale des Postes*. With this new form of administration for the postal system, the state had opted, in its financial exigency, for immediate access to funds, while delegating authority for collection of postal taxes to the "Fermier."

In the early 1670s, aiming to connect the mails financially to the "Ferme générale," Louvois's administration pursued a more immediate objective: eradicating the system of "offices" which, since 1630, had granted authority over individual postal bureaus to regional "Maîtres de Courriers."[10] In doing away with the old system of provincial post-masters, Louvois executed a kind of administrative temporal subterfuge that unexpectedly abbreviated the duration of the *maîtres'* authority: "The Superintendent called on 30 July 1669 for an ordinance summoning the postmasters of the kingdom and of foreign countries and all the officers working under them to bring within fifteen days of the signing of the ordinance the original documents certifying their employment. Should they fail to do this, they were to be replaced."[11] Thus began the process that would relieve the *maîtres* of their powers, which had been intended to last, according to a law passed in 1662, until 1674—two years longer than Louis XIV and Louvois would eventually allow.

Working toward a postal monopoly, the administration rendered irrelevant the laws that had been signed and accepted a decade earlier: by 1672, the government had control over practically all operations in the local postal bureaus. With the "decree of 19 March 1672 . . . the *Fermier* acquired . . . the authority to choose 'whomever he wished' to execute henceforth the duties of the dispossessed officers."[12] Eugène Vaillé underlines the importance of the elimination of intermediaries between the state and the local workings of the mails. A postal monopoly could attain its full potential only if the central motivating force of the monopoly, the king and his ministers, maintained direct control over as many aspects as possible of the organization's functioning. Such direct access also ensured the swift and certain passage of revenues from local bureaus, at the political margins of the state, to the *Ferme*, an entity tied to the central government: "Simultaneously fiscal and corporate at its origin, . . . the postal system ended up almost completely centralizing its operations in the hands of the *Fermier général*, once the intermediaries between central power and local personnel (appointed directly by the *Ferme*) had been eliminated."[13] Through a homogenization of personnel that was designed to ensure smooth and rapid passage of funds from postal bureaus to the *Ferme*, the state fundamentally changed the workings of the mails.

Understandably, the system of "offices," after having been in place for forty-two years, did not immediately disappear without a trace. At times it was more advantageous for the new administration to leave things the way they were, if the situation in question assured the proper functioning of the postal bureau. Vaillé characterizes the *Ferme*, in its ititial years, as a "transitional system where here and there old practices survived, but which whenever possible made room for new, directly appointed officers."[14] Complications in the passage from the system of *Offices* to the *Ferme* reveal a specific modality of the more global transition, between feudalism and centralization, that France was undergoing during the seventeenth century. As William Beik points out, this transition cannot be adequately explained by a "repression view" of Louis XIV's régime, according to which measures imposed from above would have transformed society immediately and with little or no resistance from the king's subjects.[15] More realistically, Beik argues, processes of cooperation and bonds of common interest between government representatives and regional officials factored heavily in the advances made under Louis XIV's régime. The Baron Ernouf extols Lazare Patin's ability to integrate regional practices into a centralized system of administration: "It was no easy matter to establish a kind of relative unity in this confused interweaving of customs and provincial routines, to bring together and discipline all the local agents who could be utilized in the new system of centralization and to make sure all the others would cooperate."[16] Patin went to great lengths to bend previously established customs to newly conceived administrative norms, without provoking outright rebellion.

Significant as Patin's intermediary role may have been, however, the ultimate authority over what changes would be made in the postal system belonged to Louvois, who carefully oversaw the new system in its minutest details:

> If the *Fermier général,* or at least his financial backers, had in principle all the authority necessary to ensure the regular and productive functioning of the enterprise, this authority was always exercised under the shadow of the *Surintendant* and the latter did not tend to let his role diminish in importance. He considered the functionaries of the *Ferme* as just so many employees under his direct command, and he intervened at all hours in the minutest details of procedure with considerable fervor for his mission.[17]

In his ability to maintain simultaneously a global view of his entire administration as well as a scrupulous eye for detail, Louvois used techniques of government described by Louis XIV. In his memoirs, the king discussed his own tireless work habits and detailed practices of bookkeeping, which allowed him to intervene at any moment in particular administrative matters and kept him constantly one step ahead of his subordinates. As a means of educating the future dauphin, Louis XIV described his own work habits and ways of dealing with ministers as follows:

> Encore qu'il y ait en toutes sortes d'affaires un certain détail où nos occupations et notre dignité même ne nous permettent pas de descendre ordinairement, je fis dessein après que j'aurais choisi mes ministres, d'y entrer quelquefois avec chacun d'eux, et quand il s'y attendrait le moins, afin qu'il comprît que j'en pourrais faire autant sur d'autres sujets et à toutes les heures.[18]

> [Even though in all kinds of business dealings there is a certain degree of detail to which our other responsibilities and even our dignity do not let us stoop ordinarily, I decided that after I had chosen my ministers, I would occasionally enter into points of detail with each of them, and precisely when they would least expect it, so that they might understand that I could do likewise on other issues and at all hours.]

Louis XIV did not content himself with choosing loyal subordinates; he constantly tested them, "à toutes les heures," in order to reassert his own authority. The king reinforced his power by timing his interventions in detailed matters of government in such a way as to throw his subjects off-balance. He combined an overall, systematic readiness to discuss detailed matters with an inexorable impatience in the instant of professional interaction. In perfect accordance with these temporal tactics of government, Louvois appears to have been a demanding superior, insistent on working quickly in a rapidly growing organization.

The *Ferme*'s more solid administrative center allowed the system to expand at its margins. Numerous new relays were established along postal routes under Louvois: "In July 1669, 48 such establishments were set up in various areas."[19] By 1675 a user of the French postal system could find out departure and arrival times for mail in many French cities, and even a number of cities outside the kingdom, in the *Liste alphabétique des villes et lieux . . . où les Couriers des Postes de France portent les Lettres et Paquets, et les jours et heures de leur départ* [Alphabetical list of towns and places . . . where the postal messengers of France carry letters and packages, and the days and times of their departures].[20] The list contains 579 of these "villes et lieux." Degrees of temporal precision vary in this series of postal schedules. For example, the entry for Auvergne tells only that the mail leaves "Les Lundis, Mercredis et Vendredis au soir" [Mondays, Wednesdays, and Fridays in the evening], while in

Montereau one knew that mail departed "Les Dimanches, Mardis et
Jeudis à 10 heures précises du matin" [Sundays, Tuesdays, and Thursdays at exactly ten in the morning]. At certain places, like Bolbec, one
knew both arrival and departure times: "Tous les jours à midi, et arrive
tous les matins à 7h" [Every day at noon, and arrives every morning at
seven]. Many of the towns' and cities' entries only give days of departure, and some entries give no information whatsoever. All of these differences indicate that the scheduling of postal activity was evolving in
1675, and that an effort was being made to determine at precisely what
times mail came and went and to inform users of the mail throughout
France of these schedules. An increasingly regularized, efficient system,
based in part on an exacting use of time, thus served a growing public
throughout France during the late 1660s and through the 1670s.

*Temporal Organization of Work and the Quest for Speed*

Many of the steps taken to reform the postal service under Louvois
took speed as the main criterion for the proper functioning of the system. The administration avidly pursued a goal described in Louvois's
correspondence as "le bien et accélération des dépêches de Sa Majesté"
[the good and the acceleration of His Majesty's dispatches].[21] That
"bien" and "accélération" are thus juxtaposed sheds light on the postal
superintendent's conceptions and objectives. Delays were to be eradi-
cated or at least minimized. While time lag inheres in any form of postal
communication—Sévigné's correspondence amply testifies to this—the
minimization of time lag as a systematic goal of reform marks Louvois's
administration as a factor in an emerging, present-oriented epistemology of time. The history of postal reform thus reveals that the measure
and use of hours and minutes began to take on more importance in
seventeenth-century time conceptions.

Evidence of an administrative focus on time-measurement exists even
from the time before Louvois's appointment as *Surintendant général.* In
1666 the king's messengers had encountered significant delays on their
way into Spain, in the customs bureaus of the border town of Bayonne.
In May of that year, Louis XIV considered that this situation was
causing

préjudice . . . au service de Sa Majesté et à celui du public. En jugeant important d'y remédier au plus tôt, Sa Majesté a défendu et défend très expressément aux commis des bureaux . . . de Bayonne, et tout autour d'arrêter

les courriers ordinaires d'Espagne pour Flandres, et de Flandres pour Espagne . . . plus d'une heure en chaque bureau.[22]

[difficulties . . . for the service of His Majesty and of the public. Considering it important to rectify this as soon as possible, His Majesty has forbidden and expressly forbids all postal officers in the bureaus . . . in and around Bayonne to stop the ordinary mail dispatches, from Spain to Flanders, and from Flanders to Spain . . . for more than one hour in each bureau.]

Concern for the speed of transport took the form of a specific temporal restriction on official activity. The legal language used to compose this document relied on a measurement of time to create the provisions that would accelerate the activity of the king's messengers.

Under Louvois, postal administrators continued watching the clock, around the clock. In an effort to make efficient use of all hours of the day and night for postal activity, the government required that the *maîtres de poste* at different relay points along postal routes be prepared to receive messengers at any time. Customarily, mail carriers arriving in the middle of the night had to wait until morning to continue their route with fresh horses. The administration deemed unacceptable the delays that couriers had thus incurred: "The edict of 7 February 1669 . . . ordered the postmasters to provide horses for ordinary messengers at any time of day or night and forbade them formally from delaying them for any reason whatsoever."[23] For Louvois and Louis XIV, late-night hours were as important as daytime hours for the adequate functioning of the postal system. Disregarding conventional conceptions of scheduling, Louvois's administration measured and controlled activity in time according to an overriding criterion of speed in the transmission of mail.

Messengers traveling at night and needing to go through a certain town or city would often find the gates closed, with no one there to let them pass. Waiting until morning resulted in a significant delay. An ordinance of 8 January 1669 rectified the problem:

Sa Majesté ordonne et enjoint très expressément aux gouverneurs desdites villes . . . et à ceux qui y commandent . . . de faire ouvrir les portes desdites villes et bourgs auxdits Couriers ordinaires, . . . à quelque heure de nuit qu'ils s'y présentent, sans y apporter ni permettre qu'il y soit apporté aucun délai.[24]

[His Majesty expressly commands the governors of the aforementioned towns . . . and those in command there . . . to have the gates of the towns

and villages opened for the ordinary messengers, . . . no matter at what time
of night they present themselves, without causing or allowing any delay.]

The exercise of royal authority extended to all towns and cities of
France, thus permitting mail carriers to demand access, at any hour of
the night, to spaces that had formerly been closed off, by reason of a
particular convention in scheduling. Conceptions of appropriate times
for certain kinds of activity, namely the opening of the gates, were rede-
fined according to the imperatives of rapidity in postal delivery. The
postal administration acted on a conception of time that was simultaneously more fluid and more rigid than previously operative notions of
scheduling. This flexible understanding of time took the entire contin-
uum of day and night as potentially productive time, whereas tradi-
tional practices had sharply separated day from night and limited work
in postal bureaus and at city gates to daytime hours. The postal reformers' view of time was more rigid than common wisdom in that it selected
units of use-time from leisure time and demanded a constant readiness
to undertake specific procedures in these new blocs of work-time. This
placed new stress on the *maîtres de poste* and the town governors who
had to be prepared to receive messengers at all hours.

While postal reform placed certain new pressures on servants of the
state, the system catered to government officials' need for quick mail
delivery. In a letter addressed to a number of governors on 19 December 1668, Louvois affirmed that their letters would enjoy a special privilege in the process of sorting and delivering to be carried out in their
local postal bureaus, "celles du Roi ou de messieurs les Ministres une
demi-heure avant celles du public" [those of the king of his ministers
half an hour before those of the public].[25] The ministers had demanded
even more, expecting their official mail to be delivered to their homes.
While the postal system did accord the privilege of temporal priority to
official mail, home delivery remained out of the question. It would have
taken local employees far too long to ensure that the mail of ministers
arrived at their homes, while if operations remained in the central bureaus, workers could sort, prioritize, and make mail available within the
time frame prescribed by the administration.

Rouillé, a secretary who worked closely with Louvois, complained to
the superintendent on 29 April 1674 that a certain governor, the
marquis de Ferté, was insisting on home delivery, and that his demands
threatened to overburden the local post office and disrupt scheduling:
"[D]'aller défaire les paquets chez MM. les Gouverneurs comme ils
prétendent, c'est bien le moyen de mettre tout à confusion, étant à la

merci d'un chacun et l'on perd du temps" [Going to open packages at the homes of the governors like they want us to do is just a good way to generate confusion, being at the mercy of each individual, and to waste time].[26] Louvois responded immediately, reiterating to all concerned that such practices must be abandoned. Accelerating the process of government by half an hour was seen as a desirable goal; catering to the demands of ministers at the expense of the overall rapidity of postal operations was deemed excessive.

In Louvois's administration, the interests of local governors and ministers lost out to the demand for the speedy and efficient functioning of the mails that was taken to be an institutional priority. Louis XIV and Louvois himself, however, did not hesitate to make use of the postal system for their personal needs and even pleasures:

> An ordinance of 15 February 1669 shows that Louis XIV was accustomed to using the postal system to procure fresh fruits and vegetables—such as new green peas, small oranges, etc.—from the Midi region for his table. . . . As per the aforementioned ordinance, Louvois reminded the postmasters of the Lyon route that they were expected to speed up the transport of these items, "above and beyond the usual weight of the cargo."[27]

In order to ensure that the king would have fresh fruit and vegetables for his banquets, the administration disregarded restrictions on the weight of cargo normally permitted for mail carriers. The notion of the freshness of these items, transported over postal routes from the south of France to the king's kitchens, gives a picturesque indication of the rapidity with which the postal system was expected to operate. Louvois had a particular taste for partridges, "perdrix rouges d'Anjou" [red partridges of Anjou], and insisted on having fresh ones delivered to him regularly by way of the mail. Once he even ordered a batch of live birds to be delivered by this method.[28] Thus, while celerity often constituted a criterion for the most pragmatic administrative calculations in postal reform, Louis XIV's and Louvois's valuation of rapidity played a role also in satisfying finer tastes. In this instance, speed appears to have been a commodity reserved for the powerful and privileged. While cooperation existed between the central government and its provincial ministers, those who were in the positions of highest authority placed strict limits on the nature of the privileges that would be accorded to government officials while making rather striking exceptions for themselves.

By contrast, temporal restrictions on the activities of postal workers became increasingly rigorous as they were applied to lower echelons of the institutional hierarchy. The messengers traveling postal routes had to devote every hour, minute, second, and moment of their activity to the swiftest possible transport of the mail in their bags, or "melons," as they were called. On 24 February 1676, in a letter to Rouillé, Louvois insisted that the couriers adhere strictly to regulations: once they were mounted and on their way they must not stop for any reason whatsoever, nor might they accept mail anywhere along their route.[29] The administration situated the messenger's path within a tightly restricted space of utter temporal economy. Once one had entered this space, every moment of activity was made to contribute to the advancement of the task. Procedure dictated the necessity of uninterrupted travel, at maximum speed, and thus imposed a temporal form of discipline on messengers.

The time of departure as well as that preceding it came under regulation as strict as that controlling time spent en route. An ordinance of 9 January 1677 indicated precisely the hours of the day during which postal employees had to collect mail, assemble the "melons," and send the mounted messenger on his way:

Le temps y étant, de faire monter à cheval ledit courrier devant 2 heures sans que (les directeurs) puissent, pour quel prétexte que ce soit, mettre dans lesdits melons aucunes lettres arrivant à la poste après la susdite heure de midi, à la réserve de celles de service qu'on recevra jusques au départ dudit courrier . . . à moins qu'en ayant reçu l'ordre du Roi, je puisse le leur donner par écrit.[30]

[Allowing time so that the aforementioned messenger may mount his horse before two o'clock. At this time the directors of the bureaus may not for any reason add letters arriving after the aforementioned hour of noon to the mailbags, with the exception of letters coming directly from the service, which can be received up to the departure of the aforementioned courier . . . except if, having received a direct order from the king, I can transmit it to them in writing.]

Mailboxes, which were emptied precisely at noon, and mail bags, which were prepared starting at noon, became sealed spaces, inaccessible even to the directors of the postal bureaus, once midday had struck. Every second of time between twelve and two o'clock had to go toward preparations for the optimally efficient transport of mail: "The objective was to end up with regular transport in the minimum of time established by the regulations. Louvois personally strove to avoid even the slightest delay."[31] Under his administration, the desire for rapidity in the functioning of the postal service took the form of a legal language that aimed to optimize the performance of postal employees by measuring the time of their activity and by rigorously channeling specific quantities of time to certain tasks.

The measurement of weight, along with the measurement of time, factored into the equation for rapidity. Horses could only carry a certain amount before their burdens would slow their gallop. An ordinance of 6 April 1669 established standards for what the couriers were permitted to carry, while placing precise temporal restrictions on the activity of weighing their loads: "The postmaster was authorized to acquire scales in order to weigh mailings, without being allowed to delay the courier by more than half a quarter-hour."[32] In this regulation, one procedure aiming at the optimization of the messenger's speed encountered another. The possibility that the horse's burden might slow it down combined with the possibility that the *maître de poste* might take too much time in evaluating the weight imposed on the horse. The result of these two threats of delay coming together was the stipulation of this "demi-quart d'heure," this 7 ½ minutes, identified and prescribed in the language of official procedure. This ordinance reveals the concerted chronometrical precision, in the constraining of couriers' activity, that furthered the administrative quest for rapidity.

*Time, Discipline, and Postal Monopoly*

Ever conscious of structuring time to maximize efficiency, Louvois initiated punitive practices to ensure the punctual preparation and departure of messengers and their properly organized cargo: "The employees 'who must equip the messengers' had to have prepared their dispatches at the specified hour, and Louvois approved that those not arriving at the correct time for this work be fined."[33] The application of penalties to the late arrival of postal workers aimed to highlight the importance of the specific hour of the day that the administration had designated for the activity of preparing the couriers' cargo. As was the government's general policy, the same expectations applied, whether during the day or, as in the following example, at night: "Identical measures regulated the departure of messengers at ten o'clock at night and at midnight. . . . In the event of any infraction of these orders, the directors of the bureau of Paris 'would be relieved of their duties and others appointed by me in their place.'"[34] From "commis" to "directeurs," all employees of the postal system under Louvois worked under specifically designated and strongly enforced time constraints.

When, in 1680, Louvois, fearing a delay in operations, had prohibited messengers from transporting goods for money, some couriers slowed their pace by way of protest. The reaction of the *Surintendant* was decisive: Louvois "gave . . . instructions, in Paris and in Lyon, so that the first messenger arriving an hour late be immediately releived of his duties."[35] In the thinking of the administration, tardiness merited punishment because the temporal negligence of the employee in question unnecessarily reduced the speed with which the postal system was intended to operate. This criterion for the proper functioning of the mails was becoming increasingly inflexible, as state power took the form of systematic time-management.

In 1670, Louvois accomplished the government's monopolization of the mails by placing strict temporal limits on the activities of messengers not in the employ of the government:

Sa Majesté étant en son Conseil, a fait très-expresses inhibitions et défenses à tous rouliers, voituriers, muletiers, piétons, et maîtres des coches, tant par eau que par terre, de porter dans leurs voyages aucunes lettres et paquets de lettres de quelque sorte et nature que ce soit . . . le tout à peine de cinq cent livres d'amende, et de confiscation des chevaux et équipages qui sera encourue à la premiere contravention. Ordonne en outre Sa Majesté qu'aux fins de ladite Requête, les Messagers des Provinces de Lyonnois et Dauphiné seront assignés au Conseil: Et cependant leur a fait très-expresses inhibitions et défenses sur les mêmes peines, et notamment à ceux de Lyon et Grenoble de marcher la nuit, pour faire aussi grande diligence que la Poste; ains d'aller à journées réglées entre deux soleils, sans relayer.[36]

[His Majesty being in his Council has expressly forbidden all carriage drivers, mule drivers, and pedestrians, on land or on water, from carrying any letters or packages of whatever nature . . . in the case of infraction all horses will be confiscated and a fine of 500 livres assessed. His Majesty also orders that for this request the messengers from the provinces of the Lyonnais and the Dauphiné be assigned to the Council: and meanwhile His Majesty has expressly forbidden, with the same penalties for infraction, especially those of Lyon and Grenoble from working during the night with the aim of achieving the same speed of transport as the postal system. Rather, they must work in ordered days, between the two suns, without establishing relays.]

Nocturnal dispatches by private messengers incurred the same punishments as the illicit transport of letters which only the state's mails could legally deliver. Monopolization had a central temporal element, as the administration prohibited private couriers from accomplishing "aussi grande diligence que la Poste" by limiting the time available for their activity to "journées réglées entre deux soleils." The temporal capacity for round-the-clock rapidity in postal delivery thus belonged to the government alone. Any infraction would warrant punishment.

The insertion of disciplinary measures into the process of postal reform corresponded to uses of the mails that aided in penal procedures. Article X of an "Arrêt du Conseil d'Etat du Roi, concernant le transport des marchandises" [Edict of the State Council of the King, concerning the transport of merchandise] stipulated that "[l]es Messagers à l'exclusion de tous les autres, se chargeront de la conduite des Prisonniers, et du port de tous Procès Civils et Criminels" [messengers to the exclusion of all others will be charged with the transport of prisoners and of the documentation of all civil and criminal trials].[37] Thus the king's messengers, while being subjected to disciplinary routines as part of Louvois's postal reforms, also were expected to carry out disciplinary measures as representatives of the state. As the historian Yves-Marie Bercé has shown, couriers of the Bordeaux region executed these duties with particular concern for defending themselves in case of attack and for sufficiently constraining the prisoners:

> Messengers had to be elite horsemen, furnished with the best horses, armed to the teeth and able to get out of an ambush. . . . They at times had to transport prisoners transferred from one jurisdiction to another or condemned to death by a local court and taking their appeal to the Parliament. In order to control the prisoners, they tied their hands and feet, the ropes on the feet passing under the belly of the horse.[38]

The prisoner tied to a horse and traveling a postal route was situated at the intersection between a system of communication and the practices of discipline required by the government that controlled that system.[39] As we have seen, Louvois's administration used time as a tool of discipline in regularizing the schedules of postal activity and demanding punctual performances from employees.

The early modern postal monopoly came into being through a dynamics of time and power, a practical epistemology based on the rational use and measure of time. Practices of centralized scheduling placed constraints on postal employees and solidified the government's role in serving as messenger to all corners of France. The obligatory interaction between individuals and a state-run institution newly structured the rhythms of early modern daily life. As Michel Foucault has shown, the experience of the modern subject is determined to a significant extent by patterns of procedural constraint. For postal workers under Louvois, structured time played a role in determining the nature of work and in disciplining the individual. The administrative approach to time that wrought more rigid work schedules grounded itself in utilitarian concepts. The conception of time as a resource which could be broken down quantitatively and arranged in pursuit of procedural efficiency pervaded reforms under Louis XIV and deeply affected the daily lives of both postal workers and users of the system.

While Foucault highlights the importance of detailed time-consciousness in operations of institutional organization, the work of Michel de Certeau describes the tactics by which subjects inhabiting social and institutional power networks trace their own paths and patterns of activity.[40] In contrast to the programmed time of practices of control, de Certeau identifies a more inconsistent, unpredictable temporality: "Accidental time appears only as the night that creates accident and lacuna within the area of production. It is a lapse in the system, its diabolical adversary."[41] Simultaneously with the "modern mutation of time into controlable space," then, the historian can examine the "daily practices, based on a relation to opportunity, that is to say to accidental time, practices that are scattered all along the line of duration."[42] Improvisational thinking and opportunistic action answer, from within the sphere of private activity, to the means of control that structure the public arena.

Denis Richet points out that, while institutional imperatives exerted increasing control over private lives in the seventeenth century, those who were affected by these administrative measures never ceased putting up their own "real resistances to orders coming from centralized power."[43] As Chartier has shown, while individuals took on an "esprit des institutions" [institutional state of mind] in their public activities, conversely the broadening field of institutional organization served to shore up a private sphere of experience (see chapter 1). The centralization of the postal system under Louvois made possible a new kind of private epistolary experience and a new, practical attention to minutes and hours of time. As I will show in the next section, Mme de Sévigné stands as an example of this early modern time-consciousness and epistolary subjectivity. The marquise's reactions to her dependence on the postal system, her strategic manipulation of procedures to her own benefit, and her reflections on time in her reliance on the mails, all serve to open up a strong subjective dimension in the history of the postal system, an individual perspective on sending and receiving letters that evokes numerous aspects of daily life under Louis XIV.

## POSTAL AND PERSONAL PRACTICES IN MME DE SÉVIGNÉ

*En réalité, Sévigné se fiche de l'éternité, c'est le temps qui l'intéresse, lui seul; le temps qui écrit, souverain, rapide, lent, microscopique, les «petits événements enchaînés et entraînés les uns dans les autres pour en venir là».*
— Philippe Sollers, *Le Monde*

### Time and Mail: Mme de Sévigné's Everyday Life

Mme de Sévigné lived a kind of time that was closely congruent to the workings of the postal system. In one particularly revealing instance, Sévigné associated her most immediate sense of time's passage—the biological rhythm of her heartbeat—with the anticipated arrival of news by mail: "On ne sera pas longtemps sans apprendre de grandes nouvelles; le cœur bat en attendant" [We won't be long without hearing major news; my heart beats fast as I wait] (6.2.72, 1:525). The time increments corresponding to the most visceral experience of life charted the anticipatory temporal course that the marquise traveled, between a dissatisfying present and a desired near future. In another letter to her daughter Sévigné expressed her radical existential dependence on the mail by referring to the rhythm of her breathing: "Dès que j'ai reçu une lettre, j'en voudrais tout à l'heure une autre; je ne respire que d'en recevoir" [As soon as I have received a letter, I'd like another one right away; they are my life's breath] (2.18.71, 1:161). No matter how quickly news arrived, it could and should have arrived more quickly. All was well if a letter came, but things would have been better if another had come immediately afterward, and then another.

The marquise's insatiability for mail made her a highly critical user of the evolving French postal system. As early as 1652, Sévigné complained about a postal mishap to her friend and mentor Gilles Ménage (1613–92): "Il y a eu un désordre à notre poste de Vitré, qui certainement est cause que je n'ai pas reçu vos dernières lettres. . . . [J]e ne fais simplement que me plaindre de l'infidélité de nos courriers et me loue si fort de votre tendresse et de votre amitié" [There was a problem with our post office at Vitré, and this must be the reason why I did not receive your last letters. . . . All I can do is complain about the unfaithfulness of our messengers and rejoice in your tenderness and your friendship] (8.19.52, 1:18). Sévigné used the contrast between an unfaithful postal system and a faithful friend to emphasize her affection for the latter. Though the "poste de Vitré" had not served her in a concrete sense, the messengers furthered Sévigné's rhetorical objectives by occupying the affective pole that lay opposite, in the antithesis she constructed, to the letter-writer's "tendresse" for Ménage.[44] The marquise reacted to postal delay by representing this very inconvenience in her letter, in such a way as to solidify her friendship with Ménage in the act of communication. She used language creatively in order to capitalize, within an economy of epistolary relationships, on the otherwise adverse effects of postal delay.

Sévigné was not only frustrated by the time lags that resulted from unexpected errors of postal bureaus; she expressed dissatisfaction with the time intervals separating regular, biweekly deliveries of mail: "Je trouve comme vous, ma bonne, et peut-être plus que vous, qu'il y a loin d'un ordinaire à l'autre. Ce temps, qui me fâche quelquefois de courir si vite, s'arrête tout court" [I find, just as you do, my dear, and maybe even more, that there is a long time from one *ordinaire* to another. This time, that angers me sometimes by going by so fast, suddenly stops dead in its tracks] (6.19.75, 1:736). Her affective dependence on mail in her daily life led Mme de Sévigné to reflect on the way that her subjective disposition to life's rhythms structured her experience of time. In another letter to her daughter, Sévigné summed up her relationship to the mails with a verbal play on postal operations, a rather ingenious pun: "[J]'attends vendredi de vos lettres avec mon impatience ordinaire" [Friday I will wait for your letters with my ordinary impatience] (11.25.71, 1:383). At her provincial home in Les Rochers, Friday marked the arrival of an "ordinaire," a regular delivery of mail from Paris.[45] Each "ordinaire" inspired impatience in the marquise, who was always awaiting one or more missives from her daughter. That her anxiousness became a matter of habit, an ordinary experience of dealing with the "ordinaires," indicates not just the existential significance but also the quotidian nature of the marquise's dependence on the mails. Paradoxically, the more mundane this need became, the more significant a place it grew to occupy in her subjective self-construction. Her use of wordplay to express the experience of postal dependency indicates that Sévigné's response to her epistolary frustrations was a literary one, a way of reacting to her institutionally mediated predicament through exploratory use of language.

In late autumn 1675, the temporary elimination, due to bad weather, of one of the week's "ordinaires" provoked strong reactions in Sévigné's writing:

Je n'ai point reçu de vos lettres, ma fille; c'est une grande tristesse. Dubut me mande que cela vient du mauvais temps et que le courrier de Provence n'arrive plus assez tôt pour que votre paquet soit mis avec celui de Bretagne. Je ne crois point cela, et je m'imagine que votre rhume est augmenté, que vous avez la fièvre et que vous n'avez pas voulu me faire écrire par un autre. Voilà, ma chère Comtesse, de quelle couleur sont les pensées que l'on a ici. (11.20.75, 2:168)

[My daughter, I didn't get any of your letters; what a great sadness. Dubut tells me that it's because of the bad weather and because the mailing from Provence no longer arrives early enough to be dispatched with the one from Brittany. I don't believe this at all, and I imagine that your cold has gotten worse, that you have a fever and that you didn't want to have someone else write for you. My dear countess, these are the colors of the thoughts we have here.]

The marquise rejected the concrete reason—the slow passage of mail from Provence to Paris—for explaining why news of her daughter's health had not reached her in Brittany and adopted a purely subjective stance. In a typically Sévignéan moment, postal delay intensified maternal worry. Sévigné revealed her awareness of this emotional dynamic by juxtaposing her *maître d'hôtel*'s explanation to her own imagined account of the situation. She poeticized this latter view by giving these "pensées" a specific "couleur." This image recalls a letter from 1671 in which Sévigné described her "pensées qui ne sont que gris-brun . . . [et qui] deviennent tout à fait noires" [thoughts that are just gray-brown . . . only to fade to black] (6.14.71, 1:272). The color of the worried mother's thoughts in 1675 must have reflected the gray skies that foretold the approach of winter and of the conditions that delayed transmission of mail from Provence to Paris, and then to Brittany.

Sévigné personified the gap in her winter postal schedule by referring to the missing *ordinaire* as "ce jour de poste à qui je fais la mine" [this day of mailings that makes me pout] (12.29.75, 2:202). The time unit, this "jour de poste," took on a human form, became a "qui," in the marquise's subjective, poeticizing experience of time. This familiar span of daily existence became a rather recalcitrant life's companion, a kind of beloved but sluggish relative. Indeed, time often takes the form of a veritable literary character in the correspondence, as in the case of the postal disorder of autumn-winter 1675, which provoked, in one instance, a remarkable literary effusiveness:

Si on pouvait avoir un peu de patience, on épargnerait bien du chagrin; le temps en ôte autant qu'il en donne. Vous savez que nous le trouvons un vrai [brouillon], mettant, remettant, rangeant, dérangeant, imprimant, effaçant, approchant, éloignant, et rendant toutes choses bonnes et mauvaises, et quasi toujours méconnaissables. Il n'y a que notre amitié que le temps respecte et respectera toujours. Mais où suis-je, ma fille? Voici un étrange égarement, car je veux dire simplement que la poste me retient vos lettres un ordinaire, parce qu'elle arrive trop tard à Paris, et qu'elle me les rend au double le courrier d'après; c'est donc pour cela que je me suis extravaguée, comme vous voyez. Qu'importe? En vérité, il faut un peu, entre bons amis, laisser trotter les plumes comme elles veulent; la mienne a toujours la bride sur le cou. (11.24.75, 2:170)

[With just a little patience, one could avoid much grief; time relieves us of as much of it as it gives us. You know that we find it to be an agent of confusion, placing, replacing, arranging, rearranging, printing, erasing, coming close, moving farther away, and making all things good and bad, and pretty much always unrecognizable. Only our friendship remains, which time respects and will always respect. But where am I now, my daughter? Now there's a strange digression for you, for I simply want to say that the post office is keeping your letters from me for one more *ordinaire*, because they arrive too late in Paris, and that I get a double dose in the following delivery; it's for this reason that I'm going off the deep end, as you can see. But who cares? Truly, between good friends, we have to let our pens trot along as they wish; mine always has its bridle on its neck.]

A meditation on time, on its alternately constructive and destructive, globally disorienting effects, opens Mme de Sévigné's letter to her daughter. It soon becomes clear that the reflection on temporality has been motivated by the specific postal predicament in which one of the week's *ordinaires* from Provence has been removed from the mailing schedule. Sévigné's frustration with this situation appears in the vocabulary of disorientation that runs through her examination of the effects of time: "chagrin," "brouillon," "dérangeant," "méconnaissables," "où suis-je," "étrange égarement," "extravaguée." Time lag in correspondence thus produces troubling experiences, but the representation of these very experiences in language takes part in a writing process, whose vitality and spontaneity Sévigné emphasizes in concluding the paragraph. Her pen, frequently a personified object, seems to run along ("trotter") on its own, "la bride sur le cou," in composing the marquise's letters. The temporality of postal frustration, one of life's tribulations for Sévigné, serves here to populate the letters with figural presences and provides a pretext for improvisational writing.

Mme de Sévigné's daily interaction with the postal system yielded a literary practice that allowed her to react to the concrete realities of postal procedure with inventive writing techniques. Through her consistent references to the material processes that made her epistolary communication possible, Sévigné practiced what Bernard Bray considers a new kind of realism: "[L]'épistolière intègre l'échafaudage à l'édifice de sa correspondance" [the letter-writer integrates the scaffolding into the structure of her correspondence].[46] While imbuing her letters with the modernity of realistic detail, the marquise also transformed concrete realities by reacting to them, as we have seen, with techniques of literary figuration: antithesis, personification of postal practices and of time itself, wordplay, metaphorical evocation of emotions in reaction to postal delays, a reflection on the subjective experience of postal time lags, and figurative portrayals of the very writing process that gave voice to Sévigné's imagination.

While Sévigné undoubtedly represented time and mail in her own unique way, this subject matter was certainly not of her own invention. Formulations of a strong desire for more mail and comments on sending and receiving were a commonplace in epistolary literature of the seventeenth century. Voiture, for example, used the self-reflexive *incipit* as a place for ornate declarations of affection and devotion: "Madame, j'ai reçu avec votre lettre la plus grande joie que j'aie eue depuis que vous n'êtes plus ici. Si vous vous souvenez avec combien d'amitié et d'esprit sont écrites toutes celles que vous me faites l'honneur de m'envoyer, vous n'en douterez pas et vous n'auriez pas l'opinion que vous avez de ma négligence, si la fortune n'avait fait perdre la dernière que je vous ai écrite" [Madame, I received with your letter the greatest joy that I have had since you are no longer here. If you remember with how much friendship and ingeniousness you have written all of those which you do me the honor of sending me, you will not doubt it, and you would not have the opinion you have of my negligence, if fortune had not made us lose the last one I wrote you].[47] Letters, in Voiture's self-referential stance, contain and produce human thoughts and emotions, poeticized in the terms "joie," "amitié," and "esprit." Acts of sending mail at particular times have the quasi-moral repercussions designated by "honneur" and "négligence." From the joys of receiving Mlle de Rambouillet's much-awaited missives to the regret of having lost a mailing to chance, letter-writing constitutes a precious drama for Voiture, whose epistolary self-awareness provided a pretext for complex forays of style.

Sévigné reveals Voiture's influence on her own writing when she similarly foregrounds emotional experiences in the drama of letter-writing: "Ma bonne, je vous l'avoue, je suis très fâchée que mes lettres soient perdues. Mais savez-vous de quoi je serais encore plus fâchée? ce serait de perdre les vôtres. J'ai passé par là, c'est une des plus cruelles choses du monde" [My dear, I admit to you, I am quite disappointed that my letters have been lost. But do you know what would pain me even more? It would be to lose yours. I've been there, it's one of the cruelest things in the world] (4.13.72, 1:476). The relative degrees of value placed on one's own mail and the letters of one's correspondent produce a clearer contrast in Sévigné than among the circuitous litotes of Voiture, however. Further in this same letter, Sévigné goes from emotionally expressive writing to a more practical approach by concentrating on the actual procedures through which her mailings have been disrupted: "Je ne comprends point comme cette lettre du 25 a été perdue. Quand je les envoie le soir, je réponds de mes laquais; on les met très fidèlement avec toutes les autres" [I don't understand at all how this letter of the 25th could have been lost. When I send them in the evening, I count on my servants; they're quite faithfully placed with all the others]. The marquise not only reflects on her own epistolary successes and miscommunications and their stated emotional impact; she then recounts her dealings with "laquais" and postal workers and how these activities fit into daily routines. Writerly meditations on the epistolary process intermingle in Sévigné with practically oriented descriptions of administrative and material processes.

While she wrote imaginatively and thought deeply, Sévigné also had a penchant for procedures. In order to increase the efficiency with which the mails served her, the marquise enlisted specific postal employees to handle her personal correspondence. The first of these assistants was named Dubois: "Je crois . . . que mes ordres sont bons; j'aurai pour le moins tous les vendredis de vos lettres. Mon petit ami de la poste est fort affectionné; il s'appelle M. Dubois, ne l'oubliez pas. Quand vous serez à Grignan, et qu'il faudra changer d'adresse, vous n'aurez qu'à lui mander" [I think . . . my orders will be carried out; I will at least have your letters every Friday. My little friend at the post office is a dear; his name is M. Dubois, don't forget it. When you are at Grignan and you have to change your address, all you'll have to do is let him know] (5.18.71, 1:256). As this letter to Mme de Grignan indicates, Dubois served as an intermediary between Sévigné and her daughter. Since all mail went through Paris by means of bi-weekly *ordinaires* at the time Sévigné wrote, the marquise focused her efforts to speed up the mail on the country's major relay point in the capital city. When Mme de Sévigné wrote from Brittany, Dubois would receive the letter in Paris, put the Grignan address on the marquise's letter, and include it in the next batch of mail for Provence. With Dubois's help in this forwarding process, Mme de Sévigné avoided missing an *ordinaire* and maximized the potential for rapidity in mail delivery that the postal institution of her time provided.[48]

When things were running smoothly, Sévigné's "petit ami" remained "fort affectionné." When problems arose, a tone of annoyance would enter the correspondence:

> Mon petit ami de la poste ne se trouva point hier à l'arrivée du courrier, de sorte que mon laquais ne rapporta point mes lettres. . . . Ce retardement me déplaît beaucoup. Mon petit . . . ami m'en demande excuse, mais je ne lui pardonne point. En attendant, ma bonne, je m'en vais causer avec vous. (5.23.72, 1:516)

> [My little friend at the post office was not there yesterday when the mail got there, so that my servant didn't bring me any letters. . . . This delay displeases me to no end. My little . . . friend asks me to pardon him, but I will not. In the meantime, my dear, I shall chat with you.]

This time Sévigné concentrated on the process of receiving mail, which had been slown down by the untimely absence of Dubois. The "laquais," Sévigné's first intermediary, was unable to bring more mail to the marquise on that day, but the material obstacle to communication served as a pretext for an epistolary "causerie." Her ambivalent relation to the postal system never ceased to serve as a narrative motor.

A few years later, Mme de Sévigné expressed satisfaction with the services of a new "petit ami": "Je trouve que vous recevez mes lettres fort promptement; car j'ai fait un nouvel ami à la poste, plus fidèle que M. Dubois, qui nous servira très bien" [I find that you are receiving my letters quite promptly, for I have made a new friend at the post office, more faithful than M. Dubois, and who will serve us well] (7.3.75, 1:746). With Dubois having gone off to war in Holland, a new postal employee, named Riaux, began looking after the letters between Sévigné and her daughter.[49] The marquise's satisfaction with her new postal assistant's performance arose from her perception that her letters were traveling quickly, "promptement." The rapidity of transmission and the minimization of time lags remained Sévigné's main points of focus in using the postal system. If this service did not function efficiently enough for her, the marquise took steps to speed up the works: "J'ai été à la poste, ma bonne. Je n'y ai point trouvé de vos lettres. J'ai pris des mesures pour les avoir plus tôt qu'à l'ordinaire" [I have been to the post office, my dear. I didn't find any of your letters there. I took steps to have them earlier than usual] (6.18.77, 2:470). When faced with delays in postal operations, Sévigné used her own initiative in order to make the mail travel as quickly as it could between her and her correspondents.

Irregularities and delays in the functioning of the mails could provoke angry, exclamatory reactions from Mme de Sévigné: "La poste est haïssable" [The postal system is detestable] (5.8.76, 2:288), "Quelle sottise à la poste!" [What a stupid blunder at the post office!] (10.7.76, 2:419). At other moments, she marveled at the possibilities for communication that the postal service provided: "Nous ne pouvons nous lasser d'admirer la diligence et la fidélité de la poste. Enfin je reçois le 18 la lettre du 9. C'est le neuvième jour; c'est tout ce qui se peut souhaiter" [We cannot stop admiring the speed and faithfulness of the postal system. Finally, I receive the letter of the 9th on the 18th. It's the ninth day; it's all we can hope for] (10.20.75, 2:136). Through all of her ambivalence with regard to the functioning of this institution, Sévigné maintained a constant effort to maximize the possibilities for communication that the organization presented: "C'est une belle conversation que celle que l'on fait de deux cents lieues loin. Nous faisons de cela cependant tout ce qu'on peut faire" [Such a lovely conversation, the one we hold from 200 leagues away. We do nonetheless make the most of it] (1.1.76, 2:208). By never missing an *ordinaire*, the marquise did everything in her power to maintain this "belle conversation": "Je vous ai écrit ce matin . . . mais je veux encore écrire ce soir, afin qu'il ne soit pas dit qu'une poste arrive sans vous apporter de mes lettres" [I wrote you this morning . . . but I want to write again tonight, so that no one can say that mail arrives without bringing you some letters from me] (1.15.72, 1:416). Thus while she lived in subjection to the vicissitudes of a newly monopolized postal administration, Mme de Sévigné reacted to her situation of dependence by criticizing this system, by always wanting more from it, and, most importantly, by making the best possible use of what was at her disposal. The daily activity of dispatching and trying to obtain letters as quickly as possible served as an object of narration and as a pretext for the continuation of writing. The Sévigné letters thus reflect realities of everyday life and give indications of the nature of material culture in seventeenth-century France, while at the same time elaborating a lavishly rich and stylistically varied writerly voice. It is in part for these reasons that Sévigné has been admired as a highly eloquent artist of the letter and chronicler of the French classical era.

The documentary quality of the Sévigné correspondence sets it apart from other works of epistolary literature. From heartaches to medical problems, the marquise recounted all aspects of daily life that fell within the domain of her experience. As we have seen in the case of postal routines, practices of the everyday not only serve as objects of documentation but also as objects of literary representation. Focus on daily living motivates stylistic exploration in Sévigné, without one of the two tendencies—documentation or literary narration—subordinating the other. The constant equilibrium between expressiveness and diurnal recording endows the Sévigné letters with an unprecedented kind of early modern realism.

The complex interweaving of personal documentation and literary narration in Sévigné provides a window onto seventeenth-century time conceptions. The increasingly rigid structure of postal operations left a temporal mark on Sévigné's daily life that is discernible, for the twenty-first-century historian of culture, in the marquise's letters. Living in an era of increasingly precise scheduling, both in social life and in administrative practices, the marquise both experienced and tracked closely the time constraints that governed the operation of the French postal system.

In a much less voluntary way, those who worked under Louvois, from messengers to *maîtres de poste*, began adapting to time constraints imposed (not entirely without resistance) from above. Evidence of precise scheduling in postal reforms suggests that, for employees of the French postal system, daily life was taking a more definite shape in time. At the heart of the evolution of institutions lay the development of methods to constrain individual behavior in structuring work. Like cogs in a machine, if individual workers could operate at regular intervals and perform specific tasks at specific times, the whole organization could both expand and improve. It was the sort of transformation that marked the evolution of the French mails under Louvois's brand of proto-Taylorism.

*Temporalities of Constraint, Sociability, and Subjectivity*

The tendency to constrain and control individual behavior played a significant role within early modern institutions, from the lowest echelon of an organization's hierarchy to the highest.[50] The codification of individual behavior that placed such an exacting temporal grid on human experience during the seventeenth century pervaded the lives of the French nobility, a kind of social institution in its own right, and even determined the actions of the Sun King himself. As I argued in chapter 2, no one was more rigorous in disciplining his own activity than Louis XIV, whose meticulously constructed daily schedule added a temporal dimension to the geometrical arrangement of space at Versailles.

For the French nobility, Louis XIV's régime wrought an era of time constraints and extremely precise patterns of sociability. The temporally structured nature of this period renders the late seventeenth century a privileged object for the study of time conceptions. Sévigné's accounts of structured time in social life add a private dimension to the cultural record of seventeenth-century schedules and practices. Her reactions to the rites of conviviality that inflected her life illuminate aspects of everyday experience in a personal and lively narration that closely tracks the passage of time.

It may seem surprising, considering the number of her letters, but the marquise could not always find time to write. Social obligations placed time constraints on epistolary activity when Sévigné received mail and visits simultaneously. Upon arriving in Paris in December 1671, she needed to make a special effort to find time for letter-writing: "J'arrive tout présentement, ma très chère bonne. Je suis chez ma tante, entourée, embrassée, questionnée de toute ma famille et de la sienne; mais je quitte tout pour vous dire bonjour" [I just got here, just now, my very dear daughter. I'm over at my aunt's, surrounded, embraced, questioned by my whole family and by yours; but I leave all that to tell you hello] (12.18.71, 1:393). Faced with a demanding regimen of sociability, the marquise procured for herself a few stolen moments, in order to convey her epistolary "bonjour" to Mme de Grignan. A few days later Sévigné described a situation that rendered her unable to find time for letters: "Un moment après que j'eus envoyé mon paquet le jour que j'arrivai, le petit Dubois m'apporta celui que je croyais égaré. . . . Je n'y pus faire réponse, parce que Mme de Lafayette, Mme de Saint Géran, Mme de Villars, me vinrent embrasser" [A moment after I'd sent my *paquet* the day I arrived, little Dubois brought me the one I had considered lost. . . . I couldn't respond to it, because Mme de Lafayette, Mme de Saint Géran, Mme de Villars, came to embrace me] (12.23.71, 1:395). A moment after having sent a letter, Sévigné received one that had been delayed, then read it, then was incapable of responding, "je n'y pus faire réponse." The visit that interrupted her writing was clearly a pleasant one, considering that it involved Mme de Lafayette, one of Sévigné's close friends. But this social circumstance placed a constraint on Sévigné's postal activity nonetheless: she lost the capacity to continue the epistolary dialogue, the rhythm of which — "le jour que j'arrivai," "un moment après" — she evoked at the beginning of her letter.

Even though the visit may have been perfectly agreeable, it limited the marquise's time for letter-writing.

In her home at Les Rochers, Sévigné reacted strongly when she found herself obligated to keep company that she did not enjoy: "Je crains qu'il ne me vienne des madames, c'est-à-dire de la contrainte" [I'm afraid there are ladies coming, which is to say constraints] (10.2.75, 2:115). The routines of provincial women's society at times imposed exasperating constraints on daily activity. Sévigné commiserated with Mme de Grignan, who also was often subjected to the pressures of social obligation in her home in Provence: "Vous deviez bien me nommer les quatre dames qui vous venaient assassiner. Pour moi, j'ai le temps de me fortifier contre ma méchante compagnie; je la sens venir par un côté, et je m'égare par l'autre" [You should certainly tell me the names of those four ladies who came to assassinate you. As for me, I have time to steel myself against my unpleasant company; I can sense it coming from one direction, so I take my leave in the other] (10.6.75, 2:118). Though ironic in its hyperbole, the term "assassiner" indicates that the marquise experienced unwanted visits as painful impositions on her schedule. The key to escaping such situations, the marquise suggests, is a strategic use of time: "[J]'ai le temps de me fortifier contre ma méchante compagnie." Sévigné found time within the rush of social activity for her own epistolary endeavors, as we have seen, and for the privacy that she needed to maintain her peace of mind. She expressed her love to Mme de Grignan by wanting to give some of these moments of solace to her daughter: "Vous me paraissez accablée de vos *Madames* de Montélimar. Eh, mon Dieu! que ne suis-je là pour écumer votre chambre et vous donner le temps de respirer!" [You seem overwhelmed by your *Madames* of Montélimar. Oh, my God! why can't I be there to hose down your room and give you time to breathe!] (8.15.77, 2:523). Sévigné's wish to provide temporal breathing room for her daughter suggests that, in their milieu, free time could sometimes be difficult to find.

Not only did Mme de Sévigné's sense of private time become more acute when she expressed concern for her daughter's health and well-being; the marquise's own health problems touched off numerous detailed temporal reflections. For example, the highly structured medicinal regimen that Sévigné followed at the spas of Vichy also made her highly aware of her scarce moments of leisure time. The marquise described the strict schedule that determined the activities of patients: "Tout est réglé, tout dîne à midi, tout soupe à sept, tout dort à dix, tout boit à six" [Everything is ordered, we all eat at noon, sup at seven, sleep at ten, take waters at six] (9.7.77, 2:544). The anaphoric repetition of "tout" and the parallel structure of the series of clauses enumerating these routines evoke a monotonous, inexorable rhythm of everyday life. While living according to such exact schedules may have been difficult, the fact that Sévigné was going through this routine in the company of friends seems to have eased the burden: "Je commence la douche aujourd'hui. Je crois qu'elle me sera moins rude que l'année passée, car j'ai devant et après moi Jussac, Termes, Flamarens, chacun sa demi-heure; cela fait une société de misérables qui ne le sont pas trop" [I begin my showers today. I think they will be easier on me than last year, because before and after me I have Jussac, Termes, Flamarens, each of whom gets his half hour; that makes up a company of wretched souls who aren't so wretched for all that] (9.16.77, 2:548). What made this group of bathers a "société" was a common experience of time, "chacun sa demi-heure." Life at Vichy took on its particular character not only from the taking of the waters, but also from the schedules through which these medicinal procedures were applied, from a structured experience of time.

In accordance with her reactions to social obligations, Mme de Sévigné responded to medical time constraints at Vichy by looking for selected moments of solace: "La douche et la sueur sont assurément des états pénibles, mais il y a une certaine demi-heure où l'on se trouve à sec et fraîchement et où l'on boit de l'eau de poulet fraîche: je ne mets point ce temps au rang des plaisirs médiocres; c'est un endroit délicieux" [The showers and the saunas are surely painful states to be in, but there is this certain half-hour when one is all dry and clean and one drinks cool chicken broth: I don't exactly underestimate the pleasure of this time; it's a beautiful place to be] (6.4.76, 2:309). A half-hour of solace in the midst of her rigorous schedule became one of life's most significant pleasures for Sévigné. The subjective appreciation of this time as a "plaisir" and as "délicieux" describes it as a private experience, a moment for comfort that Sévigné viewed in contrast with the "états pénibles" to which her treatments subjected her. Faced with subjection, the marquise sought time for care of the self.

Whether they assumed the form of social rites of provincial women's society or of medicinal regimens, the intersubjective structures of temporal experience occupied a pole in the Sévigné letters opposite to private time. The contrast can be seen clearly in the comparison that the marquise drew between city and country living. Writing from Paris in October 1676, Sévigné opposed the hectic experience of city life to the calm of the rural existence she had temporarily left behind: "J'étais plus à moi en un jour que je n'y suis ici en quinze" [I had more time to myself in one day than I have here in fifteen] (10.16.76, 2:424). The marquise thus set up a dichotomy between the subjective autonomy of country life and the self-alienation that resulted from living in the "tourbillon" (424) of Parisian life. A self-reflexive stability is implied in the expression "être à soi," a subjective coherence that finds its opposite in the experience of dispersion through which one is torn away from oneself for days at a time. Sévigné saw this detachment from herself as an imposition of urban environments. In one instance she was saddened when her daughter was about to leave Grignan "pour aller dans la contrainte des villes" [to go into the constraints of cities] (10.6.75, 2:118). While she valued the information and social opportunities that abounded in the capital city, Sévigné had a limited tolerance for the fast-paced schedules of Parisian life, as her expression of relief at returning to Livry in August 1675 indicates: "[J]'y suis venue ce matin toute seule, fatiguée et lasse de Paris jusqu'au point de n'y pouvoir durer" [I came here this morning all alone, tired of Paris to the point of not being able to last there any longer] (8.21.75, 2:64). The verb "durer" alludes to the temporal elements of city life that have left the marquise "fatiguée et lasse." An experience of subjection to the time of frenetic social activity solicited by way of reaction a desire for a less taxing, more private ("toute seule") kind of time.

Sévigné had no aversion to fast-paced social activities and information-gathering processes: the examples of her news reporting can attest to this. The marquise's quick wit negotiated a mutable actuality with relative ease and captured accounts of recent and current happenings in a lively, temporally nuanced prose. What Sévigné had difficulty dealing with were the time constraints of social convention that placed restrictions and demands on her experience of daily life: "Quelle folie de se contraindre pour des routines de devoirs et d'affaires!" [What insanity, to constrain oneself for routines of obligations and business dealings!] (8.21.75, 2:66). With a kind of negative *carpe diem*, the marquise lamented the distracting effects of official responsibilities: "Les devoirs, les considérations nous font manger de la merluche toute notre vie pour manger du saumon après notre mort" [Obligations and business dealings have us eating dried cod all our lives so that we can have salmon after we are dead] (6.15.76, 2:320). Sévigné feared that the best in life might be passing her by while she occupied herself with "devoirs" and "considérations" instead of concentrating on her immediate present.

The highly structured experience of public existence in Sévigné's times generated the need for a reflection on the temporality of the relative present, on private life. While at times Sévigné experienced the structure of social life as a constraint imposed by forces outside of the individual's control and reacted strongly to these forces and constraints, at other times it may have been the marquise who demanded structured modes of activity, such as organized mailing operations, that served her interests. Further, she may well have imposed a good number of time constraints on others, certainly on her postal assistants and *laquais*, and in all probability on her daughter, who, although she appears to have been a skilled and energetic correspondent, must at times have grown weary of Sévigné's constant demands for mail and news.[51] Just as her rapport with the postal system was ambivalent, Sévigné's perspective on intersubjective constraint versus private freedom was dotted with contradictions. The ambivalence extends to the marquise's views on the institutional power structures that inflected daily life at all points of social hierarchy during the seventeenth century.

*Rhythms of Subjection and Self-affirmation*

Mme de Sévigné implicitly revealed an awareness of the relation between state discipline and the postal system when she ironically thought of sending a letter to her daughter by way of a prisoner convoy: "Hier au soir, je perdis une belle occasion. . . . Je rencontrai la chaîne des galériens qui partait pour Marseille. Ils arriveront dans un mois; rien n'eût été plus sûr que cette voie" [Last evening, I missed a nice opportunity. . . . I met up with a chain of prisoners leaving for Marseille. They'll get there in a month; nothing would have been surer than this route] (4.10.71, 1:216). The nonchalance with which Sévigné saw a "belle occasion" in a carceral operation betrays a point of view detached from the realities of disciplinary procedure. The marquise took in the prisoner convoy with an amused glance and a brief afterthought concerning potential personal uses of this means of communication. Sévigné's perspectives on those subjected to incarceration and capital punishment, her approval of repressive measures taken by the government, have given her the reputation of callousness toward the lower classes.[52]

Sévigné often directed a disdainful aristocratic gaze at the messengers who brought and dispatched her mail. The marquise commented vividly on the physical appearance of one messenger, "cet homme si obligeant, crotté jusqu'au cul, qui m'apportait votre lettre" [this obliging man, spattered in mud up to his ass, who brought me your letter] (12.13.71, 1:391). She seemed to appreciate the difficulties that this "homme si obligeant" must have endured on the postal routes, but she did so while having a little fun at the postal worker's expense. While producing a certain comic effect, the image of the filthy messenger serves a realistic function in the narration by evoking the material processes through which letters were transmitted. When Sévigné received her daughter's letters "de la main crottée de ce postillon," [from the mud-spattered hand of this messenger] the marquise entered into metonymic contact with the postal routes, the material conditions of which mediated the epistolary communication that she carried on with her daughter. Sévigné thus reincorporated elements of the materiality of postal procedure in her imagistic written descriptions: "Notre petit messager crotté vient d'arriver" [Our dirty little messenger just got here] (5.21.76, 2:297). The descriptive element of dirt marked Mme de Grignan's latest letters as recent acquisitions and gave Sévigné's own epistolary activity a sense of immediacy, in the text of the letter that her daughter would be reading several days later. Sévigné used realistic detail to conjure a process of communication based on recent reception of messages and immediate response to them. Thus while adjectives like "petit" and "crotté" apparently connote disdain toward the messengers, the rhetorical functions of these realistic details call our attention to Sévigné's appreciation for the labors of postal workers.

In a moment of utter contentment with the mails, the marquise joined her daughter in applauding the system's efficiency under Louvois:

> Je suis fort aise que vous ayez remarqué, comme moi, la diligence admirable de nos lettres, et le beau procédé de Riaux et de ces autres messieurs si obligeants, qui viennent prendre nos lettres et les portent nuit et jour, en courant de toutes leurs forces pour les faire aller plus promptement. Je vous dis que nous sommes ingrats envers les postillons et même envers M. de Louvois, qui les établit partout avec tant de soin. (10.16.75, 2:130)

> [I am quite pleased that you have noticed, like I have, the admirable speed of our letters, and the fine methods of Riaux and these other obliging gentlemen, who come and take our letters and carry them day and night, running with all their might to get them to go faster. I'll tell you that we are ungrateful toward the messengers and even toward M. de Louvois, who places them everywhere with such care.]

The marquise took notice of the fact that messengers, with all city gates required to open for their passage, labored around the clock. They aimed to optimize the rapidity with which mail traveled, "en courant de toutes leurs forces." Here Sévigné's language suggests the human price at which rapid transmission took place. Depleting their strength through their hurried activity, the couriers guaranteed the quality of postal operations through individual efforts. Sévigné developed an appreciative and optimistic vision of the postal system here, by means of a set of terms that suggest the orderly functioning of the institution and the success of reforms: "diligence admirable," "beau procédé," "promptement," "M. de Louvois, qui établit [les postillons] partout avec soin." By qualifying herself and her daughter as "ingrats," Sévigné called for a greater appreciation, on her daughter's part and in her own thinking, for the postal system's reformers and employees. It was as if singing the praises of the mails might in some way make them operate more swiftly and surely. Sévigné expressed not only her gratitude for specific postal services rendered, but also her hopeful vision of a system that might serve her more faithfully, and that would no longer subject her to the difficult experiences of delay and loss.

Despite the labors of Louvois, potential obstacles to the timely delivery of mail abounded on the postal routes of the 1660s and 1670s. Sévigné frequently complained of lost or delayed mail, sometimes transforming her laments, as in a letter to Bussy in 1675, into imagistic accounts of postal operations: "Quand mes lettres vont comme des tortues par la tranquille voie du messager, et que vous les trouvez dans une cassette de hardes qui sont d'ordinaire deux ou trois mois en chemin, je ne m'étonne pas que vous ayez envie d'être en colère contre moi" [When my letters move like turtles on the tranquil messenger's route, and you find them in a chest of rags that usually take two or three months to get there, I'm not surprised that you want to be angry with me] (4.3.75, 1:708). The excessively slow transmission of mail aroused the anger of Sévigné's correspondent and placed her in an intersubjective position of subjection, as the object of this "colère." The figurative transformation of "lettres" into "tortues" aimed to compensate for the inconvenience of postal disorder with the written accomplishment of a well-placed simile, directed at the literary sensibilities of Sévigné's cousin, as well as his notorious sense of humor. The marquise reacted with creative language to her experiences of subjection, to the disappointment of an impatient correspondent, and to the vicissitudes of a sometimes unreliable postal service.

When thinking about delayed or lost letters Sévigné at times evoked the muddy stretches of postal routes, dangerous zones for the precarious passage of letters through space:

Vraiment, ma bonne, vous me contez une histoire bien lamentable de vos pauvres lettres perdues. . . . On est gaie, gaillarde, on croit avoir entretenu tous ses bons amis, et il se trouve que toute la peine qu'on a prise, c'est pour être dans un bourbier, dans un précipice. (10.6.75, 2:118)

[Really, my dear, you tell me a sad story of your poor lost letters. . . . We are gay, sprightly, we think we have been conversing with our good friends, and it turns out that the pains we have taken have all wound up in a ditch or a precipice.]

The personification of these "pauvres lettres perdues" makes their disappearance significant in human terms. The "on" representing the letter-writer is the subject of "être dans un bourbier." Along with the image of mail flying over a precipice or sinking into a ditch, Mme de Sévigné constructs the scene of a portion of the writer's subjectivity, of her epistolary pains and intentions, lying prone before the elements. Through the unexpected attributions of a creative language, the writing subject in Sévigné takes on some of the fragility and instability of mailed objects.

Traversed by contradictions, Sévigné's correspondence reveals a complex interrelation between perspectives on time and on the power structures and experiences of private life that generated early modern postal temporalities. At times lamenting the constraints that the highly structured modes of social being of the seventeenth century imposed on her and her daughter's lives, Sévigné at other times welcomed the rigidity of advances in scheduling that improved institutions under Louis XIV. At times showing detachment from the concerns of the masses, at other times expressing sympathy for the hard-working messengers who facilitated the circulation of her life's blood—news and the communication of love and friendship by mail—the marquise tracked the moments of experience and the forces that structured those moments in a language that develops a complex subjectivity, the vicissitudes of which reveal numerous insights on the public and private experience of seventeenth-century time.

*Time, Information, and Subjective Instability*

Sévigné's interaction with the mails often brought about unexpected emotional and cognitive changes. Important news could change the marquise's state of mind from one moment to the next, initiating experiences of subjective instability and dispersion in a restricted time frame of rapid information exchange. On a day shortly after Mme de Grignan had miscarried, Sévigné was expecting news of her daughter's health.

No letter had come from Mme de Grignan and Sévigné grew increasingly worried. The sudden arrival of a letter from her friend d'Hacqueville, telling good news of the daughter's health, produced a massive shift of emotions in a short span of time: "Quel soulagement, ma fille, d'un moment à l'autre! et quel mouvement de passer de l'excès du trouble et de la douleur à une juste et raisonnable tranquillité!" [My daughter, what a relief from one moment to the next! and what a transition, to go from an excess of trouble and sorrow to a right and reasonable tranquility!] (3.1.76, 2:245). Mme de Sévigné marveled at the experiential differences that she could undergo within the temporal framework of her immediate present. A subjectively destabilizing relation to time came into being in this instance through interaction with the postal system.

When describing the moment at which she opened the letter containing news of the birth of Mme de Grignan's son in 1671, Mme de Sévigné recalls being in a feverish emotional state:

En voyant une lettre de M. de Grignan, je me suis doutée que vous étiez accouchée; mais de ne point voir de ces aimables dessus de lettre de votre main, c'était une étrange affaire. Il y en avait pourtant une de vous du 15, mais je la regardais sans la voir, parce que celle de M. de Grignan me troublait la tête. Enfin je l'ai ouverte avec un tremblement extraordinaire, et j'ai trouvé tout ce que je pouvais souhaiter au monde. Que pensez-vous qu'on fasse dans ces excès de joie? (11.29.71, 1:384)

[Seeing a letter from M. de Grignan, I worried that you had given birth; but not to see these lovable markings on the letter in your hand, it was a strange business. There was however one from you from the 15th, but I looked at it without seeing it, because the one from M. de Grignan made my head spin. Finally, I opened it, shaking uncontrollably, and I found there everything in the world I had hoped for. What do you think one can do in this extreme state of joy?]

Looking at a letter from Grignan, but without her daughter's characteristic "dessus de lettre," Sévigné grew confused and concerned: "je me suis doutée," "[cette lettre] me troublait la tête." It was with a "tremblement extraordinaire" that she opened her daughter's letter to find that all was well, and passed from a troubled emotional state to "ces excès de joie." An abrupt affective transition took place within the restricted time frame of a postal encounter—a few glances at the exterior of two missives, followed by the opening and reading of these letters. This experience of profound change in a small span of time led Sévigné to reflect further in the same letter on the brevity of happiness: "Si l'état où je suis durait longtemps, la vie serait trop agréable; mais il faut jouir du bien présent, les chagrins reviennent assez tôt" [If the state I am in were to last long, life would be too pleasant; but we must enjoy the happiness of the present, troubles always come back soon enough]. A subjectively destabilizing experience with the mails thus led to the formulation of this affective *carpe diem*. The marquise reacted to the unpredictability of her immediate present not by wishing to transcend this unstable temporal frame, but by immersing herself utterly in its realities, in order to follow closely the events that mattered to her, and to appreciate the fleeting joys that good news could bring.

While mailed reports of Mme de Grignan's health often created unpredictable emotional moments for Sévigné, the political events that interested the marquise changed rapidly enough to keep her off-balance. Sévigné characterized the year 1671 as a time of informational instability: "Les nouvelles de cette année ne tiennent pas d'un ordinaire à l'autre" [The news this year doesn't stay the same from one *ordinaire* to the next] (2.18.71, 1:163). The rapidly changing news reports coming from the king's armies in Alsace-Lorraine during autumn of 1675 led the marquise to refer to this season as a "temps de nouvelles" [time of news] (9.6.75, 2:94). Near the end of the War of Holland (1672–78), Sévigné described to Bussy-Rabutin the extreme uncertainty in which she and her friends attempted to keep up with current events: "On est à présent dans la plus belle incertitude qu'il est possible; on croit la trêve et la guerre quatre fois en un même jour" [We're at present in the most amazing uncertainty possible; we think there is peace, then war, four times a day] (2.12.78, 2:596). The communal state of mind indicated by "on" transforms the individual experience of political instability into a social condition. Those waiting on news from the front were likely to be subjected to numerous contradictions and informational reversals within a short span of time.

Not only political events but also social relations were fraught with instability in Sévigné's time. The social and political agitation of the Fronde that profoundly shook the ranks of French society at mid-century left its mark on conceptions and constructions of subjectivity in the years that followed. In a letter to Ménage, Mme de Sévigné remarked on how quickly relationships could change in an unstable social world: "[V]oici qui est admirable de vous voir si bien avec toute ma famille. Il y a six mois que cela n'était pas du tout si bien. Je trouve que les changements si prompts ressemblent fort à ceux de la cour" [Now this is admirable, to see you getting along so well with my whole family. Six months ago it wasn't at all this nice. I find that such abrupt changes strongly resemble those of the court] (10.1.51, 1:16). Relations between and among families, friends, and enemies mutated rapidly at mid-century. Alliances shifted, power and privilege changed hands, favor and disfavor often replaced one another in rapid succession. For the nobility, the second half of the seventeenth century thus began with the perception of social and individual instability, of radical disjunctures and unpredictable circumstances. Observing unexpected reconciliations between estranged parties, Sévigné expressed amazement with the mutability of her social world: "Comme tout change d'un moment à l'autre!" [How everything changes from one moment to the next!] (10.2.76, 2:414). Keeping up with recent events, one of the marquise's principal occupations, could prove to be a challenging, demanding endeavor. Staying aware of the changes that took place from one moment to the next required close contact with the time of one's immediate present and considerable commitments of one's personal time.

The anxiousness aroused by postal delays, the subjective instability caused by changing social and political situations, and the time constraints imposed by social conventions all contributed to Mme de Sévigné's experience of subjection to time. All three kinds of temporal phenomena placed stresses on the marquise as she carried on her epistolary dialogues with daughter, cousin, and friends. It was in her letters that Sévigné expressed her reactions to different kinds of time pressure and temporal difficulty: she represented the very situations that challenged her, in a language that reconstructed the temporal dynamics of these circumstances and the subjective perceptions through which the marquise apprehended these dynamics. By closely tracking her experience of time in an unfailingly energized present time of writing, Mme de Sévigné paradoxically overcame the very conditions of her temporal subjection by elaborating a subjective perspective on that same experience.

In the reporting of news, Sévigné similarly asserted herself in the domain of letter-writing as a means of compensating for the feeling of powerlessness and disorientation that came from trying to follow the news, sometimes at home, sometimes in distant lands. By accepting the early modern challenge of keeping up with breaking events and rendering accounts of those events within a new kind of communicational system, Sévigné took the conditions of her own temporal destabilization and turned them into some of her greatest literary and documentary weapons. In the sections that follow, I analyze how Sévigné developed a kind of journalistic writing as a way of orienting herself within an increasingly complex social and political reality and of expressing love and friendship by keeping friends and loved ones informed of events that she held close to heart. Keeping others informed and communicating with them regularly required at times the accomplishment of temporal subterfuges in the writing process. Twisting narrative time for her own purposes, manipulating time through figurative and conceptual constructs, was one of Sévigné's epistolary specialties.

## Time Increments in Sévigné: Writing de provision

Always anxiously awaiting the days of the postal system's *ordinaires*, Mme de Sévigné revealed an unusual sensitivity to the dynamics of time's passage: "J'attends vendredi avec de grandes impatiences; voilà comme je suis à toujours pousser le temps avec l'épaule, et c'est ce que je n'aimais point à faire, et que je n'avais fait de ma vie, trouvant toujours que le temps marche assez sans qu'on le hâte d'aller" [I await Friday with considerable impatience; you see how I am always pushing time with my shoulder, and it's precisely what I never used to like doing, and had never done in my life, finding always that time moves fast enough without our helping it along] (11.11.71, 1:378). A metaphorical temporal construction concretized time as a substance that the marquise tried to manipulate to suit her subjective needs. This figurative way of taking time's measure was supplemented in the marquise's correspondence by a more calculating approach to units of time.

The most extensive method that Sévigné used to keep track of time developed in the epistolary writing process. As Jacques Derrida points out, written texts are made up of temporal gaps: "Within each sign already, in every mark or every stroke, there is distance, the postal system, what is necessary for it to be legible to another."[53] This postal separation inhabiting every act of written communication creates time lags that writing can ignore or take into account, but which it can never escape. Letter-writing, as Janet Altman has shown, tends to highlight temporal dynamics in language constructions, as the writer plays on the temporal complexities that determine her/his intersubjective and communicational situation:

> Haunted by the interlocutor's absence, letter-writers conjure a presence through writing, just as in their narrative they charge even reporting of the past and anticipation of future event with the immediacy of their present state. Letters as both narrative and dialogue, therefore, are the product of

temporal absence, yet they are preoccupied with the compensatory creation of present-ness.[54]

Letters, in their dependence on the material mediation of transmission, have the potential to highlight the internal temporal divisibility of textual constructions. Mme de Sévigné never neglected to explore the problems of time that writing and sending letters presented. While she wrote, her awareness of the dynamics of letter-writing permitted her to illuminate numerous temporal levels within the writing process with considerable accuracy.

A characteristically Sévignéan *incipit* from a letter written to Mme de Grignan in 1671 reveals the inner temporal complexity of the letter: "Ceci est un peu de provision, car je ne vous écrirai que demain. Mais je veux vous écrire présentement ce que je viens d'apprendre" [This is rather provisional, because I will not be writing you until tomorrow. But I want to write to you quite presently about everything I have just learned] (2.12.71, 1:157). The temporal dynamic in these two introductory sentences operates on a number of levels. Sévigné designates her own writing process with the very first word of the letter, "Ceci." Thus the letter begins as a meta-letter, a commentary on the very epistolary activity that Mme de Sévigné is currently undertaking. This "Ceci," this beginning of an excuse for writing on a day when the letter cannot be mailed, opens up an autoreferential function in Mme de Sévigné's narration that supplements the usual referential function of reporting news (in this case, news of a number of minor courtly events). While it appears that "Ceci est un peu de provision" qualifies and thus limits the discourse that Sévigné here elaborates, in another sense, that of the commentary in writing on the writing process itself, the qualification expands the potential of Mme de Sévigné's letter. It divides the discursive practice of letter-writing into different levels of thought about writing and into different levels of temporality.

The term "de provision," modifiying the inchoative "Ceci," inserts the writing process into a temporal frame of anticipation. To write "de provision," for Sévigné, is to write without the immediate intention or capability of sending the letter. Her use of the term "provision" expands on existing definitions in a creative way. The most commonly accepted definition for "provision" refers to an accumulation of goods indispensable for daily life and for security in times of war. This is the first definition given by Furetière: "Amas qu'on fait en temps et lieu des choses nécessaires à la vie, tant pour sa nourriture, que pour sa défense contre les . . . attaques des ennemis" [Accumulation one makes in time and space of things necessary for life, as much for nourishment as for defense against the . . . attacks of enemies]. Richelet, Huguet, and Godefroy all include this principal definition of "provision" as a precautionary act of stocking-up. All of these dictionaries also give a legal meaning for "provision," which is summed up most succinctly by the *Dictionnaire de l'Académie Française*: "Ce que l'on adjuge par avance à une partie, en attendant le jugement définitif" [That which one adjudicates in advance to one party, while awaiting a definitive judgment]. In the time preceding an awaited, definitive judgment, courts may take provisional measures. Stocking up on necessities in times of war, handing down temporary decisions while awaiting a definitive solution: both of these activities take place in a time frame of anticipation, the same kind of forward-looking, pro-visional time that Sévigné experiences when writing one day before the departure of an *ordinaire*. Her use of the term in the specific context of anticipatory letter-writing is innovative, in that it departs from the specific logistical and legal contexts that frame the term in most of its dictionary definitions.

Sévigné's use of "provision" does resonate, however, with two particular seventeenth-century definitions of the term. The first is given by Richelet: "Fourniture de choses nécessaires pour quoi que ce soit" [Furnishing of necessary things for any needs]. This generalized way of viewing "provision" opens up the term for the kind of figurative turn that the marquise would give it. The "choses nécessaires," for Mme de Sévigné, are the words that she accumulates in order to be able to make the most of an upcoming opportunity for communication with her daughter. In using "provision" to refer to texts and ideas, Mme de Sévigné comes close to an unusual definition of "provision" included in Furetière: "Provision se dit figurément en choses morales et spirituelles. Si vous cherchez de l'esprit, de la doctrine, cet homme-là en a bonne *provision* pardevers lui. Cet homme a beaucoup lu, il a grande *provision* de lieux communs, de passages sur cette matière" [*Provision* is used figuratively in moral and intellectual matters. If you are looking for wit and doctrine, that man has a good *provision* of it. This man has read much, he has a great *provision* of commonplaces, of passages on this subject]. Here the term refers to an accumulation of what Pierre Bourdieu would call cultural capital, of wit and knowledge.[55] A new meaning for the word "provision," which referred to discursive abilities and textual knowledge, was thus coming into use in the late seventeenth century. Sévigné was pushing the word in a similar direction, but in her own style. While Sévigné's "[c]eci est un peu de provision" may be related to the definition given by Furetière, the marquise's usage is unique in that it applies specifically and exclusively to letter-writing, to a practice, accomplished in a time frame of anticipation, that highlights the temporal dynamics of epistolary activity.

Writing "de provision" takes place in a static time of nontransmission, a time during which the letter-writer is temporarily isolated in a writing process whose goal of transmission to an intended reader is eventual, though eventual in relative proximity: "[J]e ne vous écrirai que demain." On a purely literal level, Mme de Sévigné contradicts herself by writing that she will not be writing until the next day: she writes in order to say that she is not able to write, due to the limitations imposed by the scheduled departure of the mail. However, if we take into account the multiple meanings of the verb "écrire" which Sévigné evokes, at the moment of inchoation of this text, at the moment when she opens up, in the process of writing, a reflection on the process of writing, we can differentiate between different usages of "écrire."

The use of "écrire" in the future tense, in "je ne vous écrirai que demain," applies a particular performativity to the verb. Tomorrow, Sévigné's epistolary efforts will result in the actual sending of her letter. Though the verb "écrirai," acting indirectly upon "vous," has no direct object, it is nevertheless imbued with a particular kind of transitivity. The transitivity of "écrirai" is not grammatical but etymological/performative. We may recall here that the term "transitive" comes from the Latin *transire*, meaning to move through space. On the thirteenth of February, a Friday, one of the days of the Paris *ordinaire*, Sévigné will write her letter in the sense that her activity will result in the motion of this letter through space, toward the "vous" that designates the missive's intended, beloved recipient.

"Ecrirai" attaches the present moment of writing and reflecting on writing to a near-future time that will put this writing into the material process of transmission. "Ecrirai" has as much to do with addressing the letter and giving it to the postman as it does with putting pen to paper on Friday the thirteenth, on the much-awaited day of the departure of an *ordinaire*, the dispatch of mails that will, barring all bad luck, successfully deliver every letter to its proper destination. In this instance, for the marquise, writing is not writing without mailing. Because she is unable to send her letter on the day when she writes it, Sévigné summons the process of postal transmission in her temporally nuanced use of "écrire." For not being able to bring her letter to the postal bureau on a certain day, she brings representations of postal procedure into her writing on that day.

Mme de Sévigné uses the verb "écrirai" in order to apply a particular performativity to her thoughts on using the postal system in the near future. The appearance of the verb in the infinitive, in the letter's second sentence, brings about different results. Unlike the verb "écrirai" in the first sentence, "écrire" remains an infinitive, in a compound verb construction, with "je veux." The infinitive takes on the added valences of personal desire and authorial intention. The adverb "présentement" gives a sense of urgency to the verb construction, the direct object of which, "ce que je viens d'apprendre," connects the present activity of news reporting to a recent past of information acquisition. Frustrated at not being able to send the news of the day on that day, Sévigné opens up new temporal registers to give her reports a sense of immediacy. Against the uncomfortably distended interval between present and future, she constructs a contracted pairing of the present with the recent past.[56] Just as writing attaches itself to mailing with a use of the future tense, writing joins activities of conversation and information gathering in its proximity to a recent past.

Authorial preoccupations with communication and information project Mme de Sévigné's writing out into the world of postal procedure and social interaction, into domains of activity that do not have any necessary relation to writing. Simultaneously, however, the ways in which Sévigné represents her informational reality bring our attention back to her texts. In the passage cited above, the complexity of the writing process's engagement with the workings of the postal system is reflected in the temporal nuances of the verb "écrire." Sévigné's writing, while opening referentially onto modes of activity that are alien to literary practices, folds back on itself in the same instant, in a textual gesture of literary self-referentiality that plays on the temporal increments constitutive of the writing process itself.

For Sévigné, attention to specific units of time serves purposes that differ greatly from those of Louvois's administration. Nevertheless, the identification of an analytical approach to time in postal reform highlights similar temporal conceptions in Sévigné, to reveal a modernity of literary practice that is not entirely disconnected from practices of time-management in postal operations: both Louvois and Sévigné concerned themselves, each persistently, with the dates and times of mailings, and with how quickly the mail would (and could) travel.

*The Pomponne Letters: Speed of Communication and Ways of Knowing*

The marquise's concern for the rapidity of information transmission became especially pronounced at times when she sent news of recent and current events to friends and loved ones. What follows is a study of a series of letters that exemplify Sévigné's desire for speedy communication. This epistolary sequence dates from before and thus historically foreshadows the procedural accelerations that would be accomplished by Louvois's administration. During the year 1664, Mme de Sévigné kept her exiled friend, Simon Arnauld marquis de Pomponne (1618–99), informed of proceedings in the trial of their mutual friend Nicolas Fouquet, the former Minister of Finance, who had been accused, at his successor Colbert's behest, of abusing his office for personal gain. Showing her affinity to the emerging practice of what is now journalism, the marquise referred to these letters as "mes gazettes" [my gazettes] (11.22.64, 1:60).

Altman identifies "the rise of journalism" along with novelistic innovations as the principal "cultural shifts in modes of printed discourse that took place in the second half of the seventeenth century."[57] She remarks that "news reporting in the early gazettes and newspapers of the seventeenth and eighteenth centuries would frequently borrow the discourse of the letter." The example of Mme de Sévigné makes it clear that this overlap of discursive practices operated in the opposing direction as well: the marquise's letters often take the form, initially in exchanges with Pomponne and later in voluminous letters to Mme de Grignan, of a proto-journalism.

Sévigné's vivid accounts of the Fouquet trial remain valuable documents as well as works of literature.[58] Just as in her early correspondence with Ménage and her cousin Bussy-Rabutin the marquise trained herself in creative uses of language, in the letters to Pomponne she honed the art of reporting current events. This narrative activity required specific language structures that conveyed the mood of the trial and the state of mind of those who followed the proceedings:

> Tout le monde s'intéresse dans cette grande affaire. On ne parle d'autre chose; on raisonne, on tire des conséquences, on compte sur ses doigts; on s'attendrit, on espère, on craint, on peste, on souhaite, on hait, on admire, on est triste, on est accablé; enfin, mon pauvre Monsieur, c'est une chose extraordinaire que l'état où l'on est présentement. (12.17.64, 1:76)

> [Everyone is interested in this great matter. No one talks of anything else; we reason, draw conclusions, count on our fingers; we get emotional, we hope, we fear, we curse, we wish, we hate, we admire, we are sad, we are overwhelmed; in any case, my poor sir, it is an extraordinary state we are in right now.]

This passage of a letter to Pomponne describes a collective state of mind, in a present time of uncertainty and anxiousness. The brevity of the phrases set between commas and semicolons, along with the anaphoric repetition of "on" in combination with a present-tense conjugated verb, represent the abruptness of the cognitive and emotional transitions that the trial's observers were undergoing. Suspended in an anticipatory time frame, between the initiation of accusations against Fouquet and the eventuality of definitive judgment, the marquise viewed the passage of time as an agonizingly slow process: "Je vous assure que ces jours-ci sont bien longs à passer, et que l'incertitude est une épouvantable chose" [I can assure you that these days are long to live through, and that uncertainty is a frightful thing] (12.9.64, 1:70). For those, like Sévigné, who impatiently hoped for a positive outcome, the trial progressed at a snail's pace.

The marquise took notice of the rates at which the litigation unfolded and included this information in the reports she transmitted to Pomponne. She reacted with impatience when time was being wasted:

Le rapporteur a lu, et cette lecture a duré si longtemps qu'il était dix heures et demi quand on a fini. Il a dit: 'Qu'on fasse entrer Fouquet'. . . . Mais il s'est trouvé qu'il n'avait point dit qu'on le fît venir, de sorte qu'il était encore à la Bastille. On l'est donc allé quérir; il est venu à onze heures. . . . Si l'on travaille tous les jours aussi doucement qu'aujourd'hui, le procès durera encore un temps infini. (11.26.64, 1:62–63)

[The reporter read, and this reading lasted so long that it was ten-thirty when he finished. He said 'Bring in Fouquet'. . . . But it turned out that he had not at all sent for him, so that he was still at the Bastille. So he was brought, he came at eleven. . . . If work goes as slowly every day as it is going today, the trial will last forever.]

Once the trial got underway, however, the proceedings accelerated, and Sévigné apprised her friend of this development. The "temps infini" that the marquise had feared had given way to a rapidly developing present situation: "Il y a deux jours que tout le monde croyait que l'on voulait tirer l'affaire de M. Fouquet en longueur; présentement, ce n'est plus la même chose. C'est tout le contraire: on presse extraordinairement les interrogations" [Two days ago everyone thought that they wanted to drag out M. Fouquet's trial; now, it is no longer the same thing. It's the exact opposite: the interrogations are exceedingly hurried] (12.1.64, 1:66). In the first sentence of this passage, an antithetical construction places two legal temporalities on either side of the semicolon: we pass from "Il y a deux jours," "tirer," and "longueur" to "présen-tement" and, in the next sentence, the urgency of "on presse extraordinairement les interrogations." Sévigné followed the rhythms of the legal proceedings closely and evoked these temporalities in her letters to Pomponne.[59] By reproducing some of the trial's time struc-tures the marquise kept her exiled friend informed, in a way that placed him close to events, by sharing with him the rhythms of their unfolding.

In order to keep Pomponne up to speed, Sévigné took measures to minimize time lags in the transport of letters from Paris to Frênes, where her friend was living out his exile:

Je vous écrirai tous les soirs, mais je n'enverrai ma lettre que le samedi au soir ou le dimanche, qui vous rendra compte du jeudi, vendredi et samedi; et il faudrait que l'on pût vous en faire tenir encore une, le jeudi, qui vous apprendrait le lundi, mardi et mercredi. Et ainsi, les lettres n'attendraient point longtemps chez vous. (11.26.64, 1:63)

[I will write you every evening, but I will only send my letter Saturday eve-ning or Sunday, and it will tell you about Thursday, Friday, and Saturday; and we'd have to get one to you Thursdays that would inform you about Monday, Tuesday, and Wednesday. That way, letters would not long be de-layed in getting to you.]

Twice a week the marquise arranged to have a mailing, containing three days' worth of news, delivered to Pomponne. Sévigné's meticulous at-tention to the temporality of legal procedures was complemented by a practical focus on the rapidity with which her reports of the Fouquet trial would reach Frênes. Thus the process of epistolary news reporting included not only rhetorical descriptions of anxious states of mind, not only a precise vocabulary of time, but also a strategic deployment of messengers and a concern for the temporality of her friend's acquisition of information through the mail.

The marquise associated the speed of her letters' transmission with her hopes for a clement sentence:

Je . . . disais [à Mme du Plessis] . . . que si nous avions un arrêt tel que nous le souhaitons, le comble de ma joie était de penser que je vous enverrais un homme à cheval, à toute bride, qui vous apprendrait cette agréable nouvelle, et que le plaisir d'imaginer celui que je vous ferais, rendrait le mien entière-ment complet. (12.9.64, 1:71)

[I . . . was telling Mme du Plessis . . . that if we had a sentence like we were hoping for, the height of my joy was thinking that I would send you a man on horseback, going as fast as he could, and informing you of this wonderful news, and that the pleasure of imagining what I would provide for you would render my own pleasure complete.]

A central element, indeed "le comble" of the happiness that good news would give the marquise resided in the thought that she would relay this news quickly to her friend, by means of "un homme à cheval, à toute bride." In 1664, well before Louvois's successful monopolization of the mails, Mme de Sévigné delighted in imagining the use of a swift and sure private courier. She mentioned using this means of communication two days later: "Vous aurez peut-être encore une de mes lettres, et si nous avons de bonnes nouvelles, je vous les manderai par un homme exprès à toute bride" [You might get another one of my letters, and if we have good news, I will send it to you by a special messenger, as fast as the horse can go] (12.11.64, 1:73). Once again, if news came it would travel "à toute bride," the fastest possible way. Thoughts of the rapidity of information transmission were intimately intertwined with hopes for the mild sentencing of a friend. Sévigné accorded equal importance to both the referential content of news and to the processes by which the news would be communicated in time. The marquise expressed sympathy for Fouquet, a friend in trouble, through her concern for swift communication with another friend, the exiled Pomponne, who was in need of information.

While focusing on the rhythms of the hearings and the rates of transmission of her written reports, Sévigné also reflected on the temporality of her friends' thought processes. As a way of expressing her friendship for Pomponne, the marquise placed great importance on the act of communication by which she finally informed him of Fouquet's sentence. Worried initially that her courier might not have traveled swiftly enough to be the first to announce the news, Sévigné later delighted in knowing that she had indeed been the first to tell Pomponne that Fouquet would not be executed:

Je mourais de peur qu'un autre que moi vous eût donné le plaisir d'apprendre la bonne nouvelle. Mon courrier n'avait pas fait une grande diligence; il avait dit en partant qu'il n'irait coucher qu'à Livry. Enfin il est arrivé le premier, à ce qu'il m'a dit. Mon Dieu, que cette nouvelle vous a été sensible et douce, et que les moments qui délivrent tout d'un coup le cœur et l'esprit d'une si terrible peine font sentir un inconcevable plaisir! (12.21.64, 1:78)

[I was scared to death that someone besides myself would give you the pleasure of learning the good news. My messenger had not made very good time; he had said in leaving that he would only sleep over in Livry. Well, at least he got there first, from what he told me. My God, how sweet this news must have been to you, and how the moments that suddenly deliver the heart from such terrible pain can create such an inconceivable pleasure!]

Though the messenger had spent the night at Livry, only halfway between Paris and Frênes, he still managed to make it to Pomponne's residence the next day before anyone else could give Sévigné's friend the news.[60] The marquise imagined Pomponne's emotional reaction to her letter: "Mon Dieu, que cette nouvelle vous a été sensible et douce." She gave her conception of this feeling of relief a temporal specificity by identifying the "moments qui délivrent tout d'un coup le cœur et l'esprit." Sévigné's narration represented the affective and cognitive time increments of a personally significant act of information acquisition: the moment at which Pomponne received the set of facts and the way of knowing them that the marquise had wished to transmit.[61] This mode of knowledge, similarly to the one which will be discussed in the section that follows, took shape in Sévigné's textual time structures and allowed the reader of the marquise's letters to follow events as closely and vicariously as possible.

### The Vatel Incident and Sévigné's Rhetoric of Time

After Mme de Grignan left for Provence in February 1671, her mother went to considerable lengths to keep her informed of social and political events in and around Paris. One of Sévigné's laments over lost mail revealed the mother's desire to impart a knowledge of recent and current happenings to her daughter: "Je suis fâchée que vous ayez perdu un de mes paquets; comme ils sont pleins de nouvelles, cela vous dérange, et vous ôte du train de ce qui se passe" [I am really sorry that you lost one of my *paquets*; since they are full of news, that inconveniences you and removes you from the rush of what is going on] (7.3.72, 1:546). Mme de Sévigné always closely observed and highly valued this "train de ce qui se passe," this perpetual process of influx and transmission of information that formed her knowledge of the world around her. She wanted her daughter to stay within this cognitive mode. The postal flaw that removed ("ôte") Mme de Grignan from this way of knowing produced an undesirable disruption, "cela vous dérange." The opposite of "déranger," the verb "ranger," denotes an effort to place things or thoughts in an orderly arrangement. The informational thinking processes which Mme de Sévigné wished to cultivate in her daughter constituted a cognitive order based on the rapid acquisition and transmission of knowledge. In relating recent and current events, the marquise aimed to impart as much information in as little time as possible, in order to share a specific way of knowing, ordered in time.

A letter to Mme de Grignan from 24 April 1671 contains one of the most notable examples of Mme de Sévigné's literary news reporting. On this day the prince de Condé gave a sumptuous party at his residence in Chantilly for Louis XIV, entertaining the king with fireworks, games, hunts, and elaborate meals. Condé's particularly perfectionistic *maître d'hôtel*, a man named Vatel, became enraged when an order of seafood had not arrived at the appointed time for its preparation. Believing, erroneously, that the event had been ruined and that he would be humiliated, he ran himself through with his sword. The "fruits de mer" arrived shortly afterward and the party went on, though not without at least some discussion of this tragic suicide.

In her reports of these events, Mme de Sévigné shows her own predisposition to anxious anticipation in the acquisition and transmission of letters. Sévigné initiates her report on the king's visit to Chantilly by prognosticating the arrival of more information about the event: "Sa Majesté y arriva hier au soir; elle y est aujourd'hui. D'Hacqueville y est allé; il vous fera une relation à son retour. Pour moi, j'en attends une petite ce soir, que je vous enverrai avec cette lettre, que j'écris le matin avant que d'aller en *Bavardin*; je ferai mon paquet au faubourg" [His Majesty arrived yesterday evening; he is here today. D'Hacqueville went there; he will give you an account upon his return. As for me, I am waiting for a little news this evening that I will send you with this letter, which I am writing in the morning before going to the chat session; I will make my *paquet* in the *faubourg*] (4.24.71, 1:232). Navigating a relative-present time, from a recent past to a near future, Mme de Sévigné inscribes the processes of acquisition and transmission of information within a rapid succession of political, social, and private epistolary events. At the conclusion of this morning section of the 24 April letter to Mme de Grignan, Sévigné evokes the final moments of the process of mailing her letter as instrumental to the reporting of news from Chantilly: "Tantôt je vous manderai des nouvelles en fermant mon paquet" [Soon I will send you some news in closing my *paquet*] (2:234). The present participle inserts the act of information transmission into the material process of closing the "paquet," a process that can take only minutes and seconds. It is as if the news were arriving just under the wire and were all the more interesting for its recent acquisition and hurried transmission. Through a particular rhetoric of temporality, Sévigné thus sets an informational stage for the arrival of the news that will leave for Grignan thereupon, with the Friday evening *ordinaire.*

On the evening of 24 April, Sévigné appends onto her letter what Longino calls "the news-break" concerning the Vatel incident.[62] Mme de Sévigné writes from the residence of La Rochefoucauld:

> Je fais donc ici mon paquet. J'avais dessein de vous conter que le Roi arriva hier au soir à Chantilly. Il courut un cerf au clair de la lune; les lanternes firent des merveilles. . . . Enfin le soir, le souper, le jeu, tout alla à merveille. Le temps qu'il a fait aujourd'hui nous faisait espérer une suite digne d'un si agréable commencement. Mais voici ce que j'apprends en entrant ici, dont je ne puis me remettre, et qui fait que je ne sais plus ce que je vous mande : c'est qu'enfin Vatel . . . s'est poignardé. (1:234)

> [Alright, I am putting together my *paquet* here. I had intended to tell you that the king arrived here at Chantilly in the evening. He hunted a deer in the moonlight; the lanterns were marvelous. . . . Well, in the evening, the supper, the games, everything went splendidly. Today's weather made us hope for a fitting continuation to such an agreeable beginning. But here is what I learned as I arrived here, from which I cannot recover, and which makes me unable to understand what I am writing to you: it's that Vatel has stabbed himself.]

The initial descriptions constructing this passage accomplish a specific narrational intention: "J'avais dessein de vous conter." Sévigné's use of the imperfect "avais" suggests that another purpose has subsequently come to determine what will be told in the letter. Before this latter object of narration comes explicitly into play, an enumeration of the activities enjoyed by the king and his entourage establishes an orderly timeline of leisurely pursuits: "tout alla à merveille." This time frame opens onto a placid meteorological temporality of larger scope but similar form: all participants hope for a linear "suite" of good weather that will follow the current trend.

At this point Sévigné's narration effects an abrupt transition, with "[m]ais," a conjunction used here for a decidedly disjunctive purpose. The present participle of the adverbial group "en entrant" indicates precisely when Mme de Sévigné learned of Vatel's death. She has received the report that she had been anticipating, but the suddenness with which the news has reached her, combined with the shocking nature of the news, has a cognitively disorienting effect: "[J]e ne sais plus ce que je vous mande." From the calm temporality of kingly enjoyments and meteorological good fortune, Sévigné's narration abruptly enters the frenetic and subjectively destabilizing time of information acquisition and transmission. Vatel's sword, like a premonitory Baudelairean second hand, has pierced the idyllic timeline of courtly pleasures at Chantilly.[63]

Of course, Sévigné's narrative throws kingly transcendence of time and material obstacles sharply into question before even evoking the games, fireworks, feasts, and fantastic nocturnal deerhunts; indeed, even before problematizing the narrational purpose ("J'avais dessein de vous conter") which relates these leisure activities. The very first sentence of the passage brings the reader's attention directly to the materiality of epistolary communication: "Je fais donc ici mon paquet." Sévigné frames the letter she is finishing within the object, the "paquet," the form of which corresponds to the strictures of postal procedure. This close attention to the details of the letter-sending process casts the descriptions that follow in a realistic narrational mode that emphasizes not transcendence of time but rather temporal immanence. Sévigné specifies the moments at which she receives, processes, and transmits news. She plays the role, in her own narration, of an immediate observer of recent events, someone caught up in the rush of arriving news, susceptible to the experiences of disorientation and shock that sudden revelations can bring about. Her narration remains concertedly close to the points of time at which decisive informational dynamics play themselves out and highlights them, often to considerable dramatic effect.

In order to give a sense of urgency to her reports, Mme de Sévigné assumed a stance of subjection to the flood of recent, shocking events. This subjection took the form of a disoriented state of mind: "Je ne sais plus ce que je vous mande." When she transmitted news of the death of her friend the Abbé Bayard in 1677, Sévigné claimed to be in a similarly foggy cognitive mode: "J'admire, ma bonne, que j'aie pu vous écrire tout ceci, ayant sur le cœur la tristesse et la surprise de la mort subite et terrible du pauvre abbé Bayard. Je crois rêver en l'écrivant; ce fut la première chose que je trouvai dans une lettre de d'Hacqueville qui m'attendait ici" [I can't believe, my dear, that I could have written you all this, having in my heart the sadness and the surprise of the sudden and terrible death of poor Abbé Bayard. I think I'm dreaming while writing this; it was the first thing I found in a letter from d'Hacqueville that was waiting for me here] (10.4.77, 2:561). Sudden and saddening news, received through the mail, seemed to threaten the marquise's very ability to write. She managed nonetheless to compose a substantial letter on 4 October 1677, including plans for her family's upcoming move to the Hôtel de Carnavalet and inquiries regarding Mme de Grignan's health. Mme de Sévigné portrayed herself in a position of subjection to events so that her reports of these events would have maximum expressive impact and a sense of urgency in time, based on the recent acquisition and transmission of information. Sévigné implied, in her descriptions of tragic events, that it can at times be difficult to live in a world of information. The rapidity of communication in time, which she so often desired, could in certain instances take a considerable subjective toll. The process itself of reporting these events, however, provided a means for subjective affirmation in the written construction of the reports. Paradoxically, Sévigné used the very material limitations of the processes of information acquisition and transmission that were available to her in order to track as many moments as possible of her social existence and to share this relatively present subjective temporality with friends and loved ones. Through satisfaction and dissatisfaction with time, through manipulation and close observation of time, Mme de Sévigné used her extraordinary stylistic ability to create multifarious new forms of temporal subjectivity.

*Epilogue: The Mother's Watch*

In an attempt to find the ultimate expression of love for her daughter, Mme de Sévigné wrote: "Une belle et sûre marque de la légère disposition que j'ai à ne vous pas haïr, c'est que je voudrais vous pouvoir écrire douze fois le jour" [A sure mark of the slight disposition I have not to despise you is that I would like to be able to write to you twelve times a day] (12.30.71, 1:404). To say "I have a slight disposition not to despise you" in order to convey the message "I love you" is to use a figure of classical rhetoric, in this case a litotes. The marquise wrote this flowery circumlocution to express affection to Mme de Grignan via thoughts on time and mail. The twelve imagined letters were to convey a regular dosage of maternal love for all twelve hours of the day. Sévigné's maternal "disposition," her subjective attitude toward her daughter, had the face of a clock. Just as the ineffable dynamics of love find figurative expression in this remarkable sentence, so does time, the most intangible of concepts.

That the Sévigné correspondence translates so many complexities of the subjective experience of time attests to the literary quality of the marquise's letters. In these texts, language is a medium for experimentation, an object that the marquise shapes with figures of rhetoric like litotes, metaphor, simile, metonymy, personification, hyperbole, antithesis, and anaphora. Critical debates over whether or not Madame de Sévigné had authorial intentions should not prevent us from approaching her letters as literature and analyzing them according to literary strategies and structures. An appreciation of the esthetic richness of Sévigné's letters is indispensable for the study of time in her writing and daily life. The use of literary/critical interpretations of Sévigné's letters in this chapter reflects the conviction that the study of early modern representations of time requires such readings.

Approaching the letters as literature in no way reduces their value as documents that record particular ways of knowing during a historical period characterized by large-scale institutional reform. The state-run postal system increasingly became a part of daily life for Sévigné in the 1660s and 1670s. Her experience of the rhythms of institutional interaction complements historical data on postal reform by opening up a subjective dimension in our conception of everyday life in France during the late seventeenth century. The marquise's personal experience of time, as observed in her correspondence, developed in close structural proximity with postal schedules, which were becoming more precise with the advances of postal reform under Louvois.

No matter how thoroughly Louvois managed to improve the mails, however, they could never work regularly enough to please Sévigné, for whom the days between *ordinaires* inevitably seemed eternal. She was a demanding user of the postal system, one who took practical measures, like enlisting her "petits amis de la poste," to minimize delays in her own communication with friends and family. Acting in parallel with modern processes of institutional reform, the marquise had in common with the Louvois administration an analytical approach to time. While Louvois viewed time in specific units in order to give precise structure to postal procedures, Sévigné used her awareness of temporal increments to construct detailed narrations, describing moments of information acquisition and transmission. Like the *Surintendant général des Postes*, Sévigné in her own way meticulously measured the rapidity with which news traveled.

The marquise's focus on rates of transmission made her letters open onto the material processes of epistolary communication. In the opposing direction, the ways in which Sévigné represented time and mail reincorporated postal procedures within a system of textual prerogatives and elaborated a new literary practice of institutional realism. She also practiced a proto-journalism. In her news reports, Sévigné developed a rhetoric of time that gave a sense of immediacy to the events that she wished to recount to her readers. These textual time structures imparted specific ways of knowing, mostly about current events, to daughter and friends. Sévigné's literary writing—her institutional realism and her rhetoric of time—reflects a particular *episteme* or intellectual spirit of the 1660s and 1670s, a period marked by increasing information and accelerated administrative processes, by abrupt changes and a growing perception of time constraints.

In her accounts of epistolary communication and information-gathering processes, Sévigné suggested that a world full of rapidly changing information could be difficult to inhabit. The fast rhythms of this emerging reality exerted stresses on the subjects who lived according to its norms. The Louvois administration placed very specific time constraints on the employees of the communications system that made increased circulation of information possible. As we have seen, Sévigné was highly sensitive to time pressures in her own life and reacted to these stresses by representing them in writing. Disorientation in the midst of floods of news and exasperation in the face of constricting schedules cast Sévigné's narrating subject in a position of subjection, to time and to her times.

This subjective attitude was of the marquise's own making—it was also another of her many narrational strategies. This stance permitted her to recount the events and communication processes that were central to her life. Through a creative, constantly experimental use of language, Sévigné confronted the challenges that her world presented.

In her remarks on time constraints in social life, the marquise both documented and commented on a characteristic of seventeenth-century daily life that has been studied, by historians such as Michel Foucault, Norbert Elias, and Jacques Levron, but which remains to be described in further detail. The moments and minutes of daily life constitute a domain of human experience that can seem difficult to discern with any precision, but which is nevertheless partially accessible in documents of cultural history and in works of literature.

An irreducible hybrid of literary narration and personal documentation, the Sévigné correspondence constitutes a precious resource for insights into how conceptions of time changed during the seventeenth century in France. The letters give voice to private experiences while at the same time opening onto the aspects of material culture—namely, postal procedures—that made this body of texts possible. In order fully to describe seventeenth-century time, an object of study with both objectively measurable and ineffably subjective dimensions, the historian must draw on both historical documentation and esthetic production.

The Sévigné letters provide avenues for research in both of these directions.

The clearer, more precise structures of everyday life that came into being in the seventeenth century ushered in a new temporal epistemology, oriented toward hours, minutes, and moments of human experience. In these terms, to be modern is to take into account not only the deep temporalities inherent in history, memory, and notions of eternity, but also the rhythms of daily life. These latter temporal dynamics increasingly became discernible in the seventeenth century, as individuals more frequently referred to temporal standards, such as postal schedules, news reports, and timepieces.

Mme de Sévigné once expressed to Mme de Grignan her delight with the accuracy of a new watch: "Cette montre que vous m'avez donnée, qui allait toujours trop tôt ou trop tard d'une heure ou deux, est devenue si parfaitement juste qu'elle ne quitte pas d'un moment la pendule" [This watch you gave me, that always went an hour or two fast or slow, has become so perfectly accurate that it never strays from the clock's time for even a moment] (7.15.71, 1:297).[64] As was the case for her observations of the postal system, Sévigné approached procedures of time-measurement critically and took pleasure in chronometrical precision. Her consistent temporal awareness throughout the letters takes extensive stock of her present-oriented reality, thus standing as an early example of modern time-consciousness. The literary quality of the letters evokes aspects of lived time that can only be discerned from within the domain of subjective experience. Whether she intended to or not, Sévigné left a legacy of brilliant, temporally nuanced narrations that remain to be studied in all their depth. The enigma of Sévigné's authorly intentions contributes to the uniqueness of her writings, which open onto postal history as readily as they lend themselves to literary interpretations of subjective experience. The richness and scope of these letters point to the possibility for further explorations, in a simultaneously historical and literary practice of French cultural studies, of Sévigné's times and of time itself.

# 4

# Time and Information In and Around
## *La Princesse de Clèves*:
## Anteriority, Communication, Interiority

*[T]hree issues [are] central to the problem of fictional time: the question of how temporal settings within narratives may be related to the outside world of clock- and calendar-time, the question of how time-concepts shared within a culture may influence expectations about the writing and reading of fiction, and above all the question of how narratives shape the phenomenal time experienced by their readers.*

— Paul K. Alkon, *Defoe and Fictional Time*

## ANNOUNCEMENTS, DEBATES, CRITICISMS

### *Anticipating* La Princesse de Clèves

MADAME DE LAFAYETTE'S *LA PRINCESSE DE CLÈVES* WAS AN OBJECT OF considerable discussion and speculation long before March 1678, when the novel first appeared in print. Prior to becoming a popular success and eventually a recognized masterpiece, this novel was initially the object of a kind of literary newsbreak, in the pages of *Le Mercure galant*, a periodical that printed poetry and prose, reported news, and sponsored debates. Seen in its contemporary context, *La Princesse de Clèves* was above all a literary work surrounded by discourses of anticipation and reaction, a work conditioned by the temporal dynamics of its publicity and reception.[1] The public emergence of this work followed rhythms of readerly expectation and engagement that were determined by carefully timed circulation of talk about the novel and by the dissemination of readers' written comments on the fictional princess. By posing questions about the novel in the *Mercure*, the editor of this early modern literary magazine, Jean Donneau de Visé (1638–1710), sparked considerable interest in Lafayette's protagonist, a new kind of literary character.

A temporal study of the publication of *La Princesse de Clèves* necessarily includes the analysis of the process by which this novel became known to the public, in an anticipatory time frame. One of the distinguishing temporal characteristics of Lafayette's novel is the atmosphere of anticipation and speculation on the novel that preceded its actual appearance in print. Two months before the work became publicly known, a short tale strikingly similar to *La Princesse de Clèves* had appeared in the January issue of the *Mercure*. This story, entitled "La Vertu malheureuse" [Unhappy Virtue], tells of a young woman whose affection for a charming marquis threatens to divert her from the obligation of devotion to a suitor whom her father has chosen for her. The internal conflict, between an involuntary and potentially adulterous predilection, on the one hand, and a sense of duty and commitment to husband and family on the other, drives the young woman to confess her dangerous longings to her husband. The confession scene in "La vertu malheureuse" takes place in a wooded pavilion, near which the marquis eavesdrops on the conversation.

The similarities between the wife's dramatic confession in "La Vertu malheureuse" and the avowal scene in the *Princesse de Clèves* (in which Lafayette's protagonist confesses to her husband her love for another man without naming the object of this illicit affection) establish clearly the importance of "La vertu malheureuse" as a precursor to Lafayette's novel. The initial published appearance of a prototype for Lafayette's famous confession episode can thus be considered "a veritable conditioning of the public."[2] This readership would then discuss the avowal scene, in an exchange of letters published by the *Mercure galant* in newly introduced supplementary issues called "Extraordinaires."[3] "La vertu malheureuse" had appeared in this publication and implicitly announced a literary event and prepared a readerly discussion. In so doing, it established the importance, for Lafayette's novel, of a time frame of anticipation.

*La Princesse de Clèves* was first discernible in print between the lines of the story that sketched out one of the novel's major scenes and sounded some of the work's central themes. Lafayette's novel thus first appeared in a near-future time of potential publication. The work was, in the first instance, a virtual novel. "La Vertu malheureuse" pointed toward *La Princesse de Clèves* as an imminent event of publication. However, the anticipatory story could only hold the significance of an announcement in a pre-established context: readers could not perceive such a projection without some prior knowledge of the existence of *La Princesse de Clèves*. As Monique Vincent points out, such knowledge was indeed in circulation well before the publication of this "famous novel that, as its contemporaries attest, was publicly known before its publication."[4] Mme de Sévigné mentioned the novel to her daughter as early as 16 March 1672: "Je suis au désespoir que vous ayez eu *Bajazet* par d'autres que par moi. C'est ce chien de Barbin qui me hait, parce que je ne fais pas des *Princesses de Clèves et de Montpensier*" [I am in utter despair that you received *Bajazet* from someone besides me. It's that dog Barbin who hates me, because I do not compose *Princesses of Clèves and of Montpensier*] (1:459). It would stand to reason that one of Lafayette's closest friends would have known of the existence of her unpublished work in progress. Evidence of the novel's existence can be found from as early as 1671.[5]

The time frame in which this text appeared becomes complicated, then, at another level, a second anteriority, by the conversations announcing the upcoming publication of a new and extraordinary work of literature: "Surrounding the book, even preceding it, a rumor is born:—the anticipation, the desire of the book leads one to believe that the relation between the reader and the text necessarily includes a representation of this text that would be anterior to its reading."[6] Preceding the *Princesse de Clèves* was "La Vertu malheureuse," a representation in miniature of the novel to come. In anticipation of this anticipation, rumors about a new novel circulated and sparked interest in potential readers.

The discourses, both unpublished and published, through which readers announced and anticipated *La Princesse de Clèves* served a strategic purpose for Jean Donneau de Visé, though the extent to which he orchestrated these pre-readings would be difficult to ascertain. Suffice it to say that the *Mercure's* editor capitalized on a rapidly developing situation. The result of the growing interest in Lafayette's soon-to-be-published novel prepared the epistolary discussions in which avid readers of the *Mercure galant* would exchange opinions regarding the avowal scene and other aspects of *La Princesse de Clèves*. Equally important for the novel as the temporality of announcement and eager awaiting, then, is the time of strategic anticipation. A publicity campaign before the novel's publication created the necessary conditions for an extended readerly discussion in an increasingly popular periodical publication, one of the first of its kind.

In the March 1678 issue of the *Mercure galant*, Donneau de Visé evoked the suspense that had surrounded the novel's projected publication as he announced its appearance to his fictional interlocutor: "Vous trouvez *la Duchesse* [sic] *de Clèves* dans mon paquet. Vous savez depuis quel temps et avec quelle favorable préoccupation tout le monde l'attendait. Elle a rempli cette attente et je suis certain que je ne pouvais procurer une lecture plus agréable" [You will find *The Duchess of Clèves* in this mailing. You already know for how long and with what a favorable predisposition everyone has awaited it. It has fulfilled these expectations, and I am certain that I could not have found a more pleasant read] (198). The first criterion Donneau de Visé gave for evaluating the novel's quality was the fact that the work had "rempli cette attente" in providing a "lecture agréable." Even at the moment when the novel could be bought, picked up, and read, when there was no longer any need to speculate about it, Donneau de Visé still found it necessary to link the value of the work to the anticipation that had preceded its publication. Even up to the last moment, then, Donneau de Visé publicized Lafayette's novel by making use of the temporal strategy of anticipation.

While the editor of the *Mercure galant* rhetorically invoked the atmosphere of suspense that had preceded the appearance of *La Princesse de Clèves*, in the same March issue of the *Mercure*, Fontenelle (1657–1757) (calling himself the "Géomètre de Guyenne") expressed caution regarding speculation on an unreleased work of literature:

[J]'ai attendu la *Princesse de Clèves* dans cette belle neutralité que je garde pour tous les ouvrages dont je n'ai point jugé par moi-même. . . . [L]a renommée publiait son mérite dans nos provinces longtemps avant qu'on l'y vît paraître, et en prévenant les uns en sa faveur, elle en avait donné des impressions désavantageuses aux autres, car il y a toujours des gens qui se préparent avec une maligne joie à critiquer ces ouvrages que l'on a tant vantés par avance. (57)

[I awaited *The Princess of Clèves* in the perfect neutrality that I maintain for all works that I have not judged on my own. . . . The forces of renown had already publicized its merits in our provinces long before it appeared there in print, and, predisposing some in the work's favor, it had given unfavorable impressions to others, for there are always people who prepare themselves with a malicious glee to criticize the works that have been praised in advance.]

In contrast with the ideal of a "belle neutralité," the disorderly forces of "renommée" could produce equally dubious positive and negative impressions about the novel in the minds of those who anxiously anticipated the possibility of lauding or criticizing the work. In a cool, rational tone, this reader explained that he would only pass judgment on works that he had read: "Pour moi j'ai attendu à juger de *La Princesse de Clèves* que je l'eusse lue" [As for myself, I waited to evaluate *The Princess of Clèves* until I had first read it] (58). Fontenelle's use of the verb "attendre," in this passage and in the one cited above, differs strikingly from the use Donneau de Visé makes of the verb ("Vous savez depuis quel temps et avec quelle favorable préoccupation tout le monde l'attendait"). While Donneau de Visé's imperfect describes a generalized condition of eager anticipation in a reading public, Fontenelle's circuitous subjunctive refers to an individual reader's patience and restraint. Donneau de Visé invoked a charged atmosphere of suspense; the "Géomètre de Guyenne" called for calm, calculated suspension of opinion. While for Donneau de Visé an anticipatory time frame facilitated publicity, for Fontenelle the ambiguities of this temporality threatened to produce misinformation and uninformed opinions.

If Fontenelle claimed to remain utterly impartial with regard to *La Princesse de Clèves* before the novel's publication, the two critics to whom book-length analyses of Lafayette's work were attributed in the following year, Jean-Baptiste-Henri du Trousset de Valincour (1653–1730) and the Abbé Jean-Antoine de Charnes (1641–1728), both admitted that their readerly opinions were affected by the discourses in circulation before the novel's publication. One of the fictional discussants in Charnes's *Conversations sur la critique de "La Princesse de Clèves"* showed an unequivocal determination to approve of the novel, on the basis of positive assessments from reputable sources: "J'admirais cet homme [l'auteur supposé], et je ne pus m'empêcher de dire qu'on en serait bientôt éclairci, puisqu'il devait paraître dans peu de jours: mais que j'étais persuadée par avance, que cet ouvrage ayant été approuvé par des personnes très-éclairées et très-capables d'en juger, ne pouvait être qu'excellent" [I admired this man (the supposed author), and I could not stop myself from saying that we would soon be informed of his identity, since he was to appear in a few days: but that I was persuaded in advance that, this work having been approved by some very enlightened and capable readers, it had to be excellent].[7] This reader had allowed herself to be "persuadée par avance" in regard to a work that "ne pouvait être qu'excellent." The discourses surrounding Lafayette's novel prior to its publication exerted considerable persuasive power on this reader, who was only a potential reader at the time she was forming the opinions that she described. From a time frame posterior to the publishing and reading of the novel, Charnes's character represented an anticipatory temporality by using a combination of imperfects and infinitives: "devait paraître . . . ne pouvait être." Through the fictional characters to whom he gave voice in his *Conversations*, Charnes discussed a recent work by designating a slightly less recent anteriority of hermeneutical predispositions to the work. The activity of literary analysis thus took place in a constricted time frame, based on a relative present of discussion, a recent past of reading, and an immediate anteriority of anticipated reading.

In his *Lettres à Madame la marquise \*\*\* sur le sujet de "La Princesse de Clèves,"* Valincour was much less certain of the novel's quality than Charnes. When describing his eagerness to receive the new work, however, Valincour invoked the same atmosphere of curiosity that both Donneau de Visé and Charnes seemed to relish:

> Jamais ouvrage ne m'a donné plus de curiosité. . . . [L]'on peut dire qu'il est peu de livres qui aient, après l'impression, une approbation aussi générale que l'a eue celui-ci, avant même que d'avoir été vu du public.
> Ce me fut une très grande mortification de me voir éloigné de Paris dans le temps qu'on le publia, et de ne l'avoir que des derniers; mais enfin je trouvai moyen de l'avoir, et je le lus avec toute l'avidité et l'attention possible.[8]

> [Never has a work given me more curiosity. . . . One might say that there are few books that enjoy, after their printing, approval as widespread as this one has had, before even being seen by the public.
> I was quite mortified to find myself at a remove from Paris during the time when it was published, and to be among the last to have it; but finally I found a way to get it, and I read it with all the eagerness and attention possible.]

Valincour presented himself as a latecomer to the debate surrounding *La Princesse de Clèves*. Having been absent at the crucial time of publication, this critic struggled to obtain the work and read it with sufficient energy to get himself back up to speed. From anxious anticipation of the novel, to the time when the work was published, Valincour's description of the temporality of his initial encounters with *La Princesse de Clèves* placed his readerly and critical activity (not entirely without irony) in a time frame of tardiness: he was one of the last to gain access to the text in question.

Anticipation as the temporal paradigm for readerly approaches to *La Princesse de Clèves* quickly changed to reaction, as readers of the novel and of the *Mercure galant* developed opinions on the work's plot and themes in a series of animated exchanges of ideas. This is not to say that anticipatory temporality lost its significance for Lafayette's novel once it was published. To the contrary, as the passages quoted above from Donneau de Visé, Charnes, and Valincour show, the curiosity and suspense that talk of the novel had generated before the work's publication continued to inform readers' opinions and reactions. As I discuss later in this chapter, anticipation, both as an emotional state of eager awaiting and as a time-conscious stance for strategic action, factored significantly into the events recounted in *La Princesse de Clèves*. A distinguishing temporal characteristic of Lafayette's novel, often considered to be the first modern novel, is its existence, prior to this work's actual publication, as an object of discussion and as a virtual intertext for an annunciatory story, "La Vertu malheureuse."

A novel that represented premeditative temporal structures in a tightly woven combination of near-future and recent-past events thus came into being through similarly compacted temporal dynamics of publicity and publication. These temporal homologies between publication processes and plot developments render Lafayette's literary work inseparable from the history of its publication. Time structures in each of these domains mutually illuminate each other; it is the purpose of this chapter to contextualize readings of passages in the novel with a study of publishing practices and readers' reactions that were contemporary with the novel's appearance before its seventeenth-century reading public.

*Reactions to* La Princesse de Clèves

The animated discussions that followed the publication of *La Princesse de Clèves* constitute the analogue, in a posterior time frame, of the anticipatory interest that had preceded the work's appearance in print. Critics and readers of Lafayette revealed different conceptions of time in interpretive activities and reading practices that in their own right followed various temporal dynamics. The remarks on time made by the readers of Lafayette and of the *Mercure* show that a significant component of responses to *La Princesse de Clèves* consisted of readerly time-consciousness. Donneau de Visé set the tone and initiated the rhythm that his readers' exchanges would follow by publishing a provocative "Question galante" [a kind of a riddle] for his audience to ponder.

Donneau de Visé introduced the question concerning *La Princesse de Clèves* by referring to the interest that had been aroused by the *Mercure*'s previous query: "Comme je ne doute point que les spirituelles réponses qu'on a faites sur la Question galante ne vous aient donné beaucoup de plaisir, j'en vais proposer une autre que la *Princesse de Clèves* a peut-être déjà fait agiter" [Since I have no doubt that the lively responses that have been made to the *Question galante* have given you much pleasure, I would like to propose another that the *Princess of Clèves* has perhaps already stirred up] (April 1678, 298). The editor does not claim here to be introducing anything new; rather, he contributes the "Question galante" to an ongoing discussion about Lafayette's novel, in which the issues to be raised might already be an object of debate, or interpretive agitation.

Having admitted the possibility that the issue might have been raised already, Donneau de Visé proceeds to inquire whether a wife in the princess's position should conceal or reveal to her husband her feelings for another man. The question itself was a reaction to the novel, and more specifically to the avowal scene, in which the princess's judgment must have struck the questioner as unusual. According to Maurice Laugaa, not only does the question provoke replies; the "mode of the riddle . . . predetermines the responses."[9] But did the question actually precede discussions that might already have been taking place? Did readers anticipate Donneau de Visé's query, or did the "Question galante" determine the nature of the epistolary exchanges that would follow? The answer lies somewhere in-between, difficult to discern in the compacted temporality of successive events of publication and critical deliberation. Though it cannot be answered, simply raising the question of the "Question" reveals the dense dynamics of time, a combination of reactions and anticipations, through which the debate over *La Princesse de Clèves* developed.

Discerning the temporal complexity of this seventeenth-century readerly discussion requires detailed focus on a limited span of time, because the debate was rather short-lived. Responses to the "Question galante" were published in the July and October "Extraordinaires," the latter of which contained the conclusion of the conversation. The practice of printing supplementary issues containing readers' opinions was a new one: "It should be remarked that the form of the supplementary, trimestrial issue had been only recently invented at the time (January 1678). The launching of the novel benefited from the launching of the magazine, and vice versa."[10] The initiation of the "Extraordinaire" anticipated the appearance of Lafayette's novel and briefly followed this literary event. From January to October 1678, a significant time period for a reading public awaiting, then digesting a new kind of novel, the *Mercure*, "after having limited itself for over a year to appearing regularly every month, . . . takes on a new significance at this time in order to appear at extraordinary times."[11] Through the timing of anticipation, publication, and discussion of Lafayette's novel, literature had become news in the pages of the *Mercure galant*.

As readers not only read *La Princesse de Clèves* but also strove to stay informed of developments in the debate about the novel, their remarks took on a temporal precision that is revealing in regard to seventeenth-century reading practices. Monique Vincent considers that the letters contained in Donneau de Visé's "Extraordinaires" provide "a direct view of daily reality" and constitute "a precious document for the history of mentalities."[12] Characteristic of the mindset of the *Mercure's* readership was a considerable eagerness to receive the next issue and an awareness of the time of reading. Many of the *Mercure's* readers lived far from Paris and energetically pursued the possibility of following the literary and cultural events taking place in the capital: "These were provincials, so they were readers eager to catch up on fashions developing elsewhere."[13] One reader of the *Mercure* expressed satisfaction with the efficiency and regularity of the periodical's distribution: "Vous saurez par cette lettre, Monsieur, que votre Mercure s'acquitte parfaitement bien de son devoir selon vos intentions, c'est-à-dire qu'il parvient régulièrement jusqu'aux extrémités de la France, pour nous faire part de vos galantes nouveautés" [You will be informed by this letter, Monsieur, that your Mercure perfectly fulfills its duties according to your intentions, that is to say that it regularly reaches even the remote corners of France, in order to inform us of your fine bits of news] (July 1678, 157). Even at the nation's geographical limits, the *Mercure* kept readers informed.

A *Mercure* reader named De Merville described the rapidity with which readers in his community would snatch up Donneau de Visé's publication as it arrived in the mail:

Il n'est pas plutôt arrivé en ce pays-ci, qu'on se l'arrache des mains pour le dévorer. Ensuite on se caballe pour les énigmes. . . . Je suis au nombre de ces impatients lecteurs, et j'attends avec empressement le premier qui viendra pour m'ôter l'inquiétude que me donnent les énigmes du mois de juin. La première m'a fait rêver plus d'un jour. (July 1678, 211)

[As soon as it arrives in this region, we tear it out of one another's hands to devour it. Then we argue about the riddles. . . . I am among these impatient readers, and I eagerly await the first who will relieve me of the anguish that June's riddles have given me. The first one made me think on it for more than a day.]

De Merville evoked a generalized impatience in a circle of readers ("on") who made maximum use of the moments available for reading immediately after the periodical had arrived in their region. Animated discussions ("on se caballe") quickly followed reading. When a particular riddle challenged the reader, he pondered the question for a more extended period of time, which he specified ("plus d'un jour"). If a day constituted the measure for an extensive time of reading and reflection, then quite possibly the acts of reading De Merville described took place in a more constricted timespan—the minutes and hours immediately following the arrival of the *Mercure*.

De Grammont, writing from Richelieu, contrasted his experience of receiving an eagerly awaited *Mercure* to the doldrums of a voyage devoted to business dealings:

> Je terminai [mes affaires] le plus promptement que je pus, afin de venir ici jouïr d'un ciel plus serein, et d'un commerce plus tranquille et plus spirituel. Je n'y fus pas plutôt arrivé, que je trouvai votre Extraordinaire d'avril, qui me consola heureusement de tous les mauvais moments que j'avais passés dans le triste séjour dont je viens de vous parler. (July 1678, 223)

> [I finished my business dealings as promptly as I could, so that I could come here and enjoy a more peaceful sky and more tranquil and mentally stimulating occupations. No sooner had I gotten here, than I found your "Extraordinaire" from April, which happily consoled me for all the bad moments that I had spent in the sad place that I just mentioned.]

As opposed to the hectic rhythms of work at a remote locale, the *Mercure galant*, comfortably perused at home, provided a "commerce plus tranquille et plus spirituel." The "mauvais moments" of undesirable experience that De Grammont had recently undergone faded into the past as this reader found a kind of experiential compensation in the pages of the *Mercure* (the migraine he reports having contracted from pondering the issue's "Enigme" notwithstanding). De Grammont garnered solace from Donneau de Visé's periodical in a set of good moments, designated by verbs in the *passé simple*, indicating distinct events: "trouvai," "consola." He had received the journal immediately upon his return ("Je n'y fus pas plutôt arrivé"). Similarly with the situation recounted by De Merville, the moment of arrival of the periodical is dramatized. The emphasis on the moments of time immediately following the acquisition of the publication suggests that the contents of the *Mercure* were being received as news items and as information. Knowledge, appearing at a particular moment and mediated in the small time increments designated by De Merville and De Grammont, took the initial form of information, before being exchanged in conversation or reviewed in rêverie.

De Merville and De Grammont's letters to the *Mercure* provide glimpses of new temporalities of reading in seventeenth-century France. The rhythms of interior experience that they evoke in describing receipt of Donneau de Visé's publication reflect broad changes in the culture of reading that were integral, as Roger Chartier argues, to the development of early modern modes of thought: "The spread of literacy, the widespread circulation of written materials whether in printed or manuscript form and the increasingly common practice of silent reading, which fostered a solitary and private relation between the reader and his book, were crucial changes, which redrew the boundary between the inner life and life in the community."[14]

The practice of scanning texts in privacy and mulling them over in silence profoundly affected the epistemological changes that ushered in a new era of intellectual life: "This 'privatization' of reading is undeniably one of the major cultural developments of the early modern era."[15] Breaking from the tradition of orality, early modern readers increasingly processed texts through pure cognitive activity, independently from the mediation of enunciation. The result was a quickened mode of thought, because "silent reading was faster, easier, and more immediate in its impact on the inner self." Accelerated ways of knowing included a valorization of ever smaller temporal increments in the acquisition of knowledge by means of written texts.

### Time Conceptions of Lafayette's Critics

Valincour and Charnes developed accounts of eager leisure reading in their critical analyses of Lafayette's novel. At the same time, though they portrayed themselves or the fictional characters holding the interpretive discussion as casual readers, these two critics undertook the serious task of evaluating *La Princesse de Clèves* as a work of literature, according to criteria of historical accuracy, verisimilitude of narrative events, dramatic impact of key scenes, and other considerations. A number of remarks in these critics' texts described temporal structures in Lafayette's novel. Valincour, in assessing rhythms of reading and periods of narrative duration, practiced a kind of critical chronometry through which he imposed his own conceptions of time onto *La Princesse de Clèves*.

Valincour expressed impatience with digressive passages in Lafayette's novel that delayed the further development of plot: "L'esprit, qui s'est fait un plaisir de voir la suite d'une histoire qui lui paraît agréable, se hâte d'aller jusqu'au bout, et souffre avec impatience, et quelquefois même avec dégoût, tout ce qui le retarde dans sa course, et qui lui paraît étranger à ce qu'il cherche" [The mind, which finds pleasure in following a story that seems pleasant to it, hurries to get to the end and reacts impatiently, sometimes even with disgust, to anything that slows it down and that seems foreign to what it seeks] (19). The reading process is portrayed as a "course," a race or a run during which the reader impatiently pursues certain objects of interest and deals reluctantly with obstacles that delay his rate of textual traversal. The terms "suite," "se hâter," "jusqu'au bout," and "course" construct a strictly linear conception of the reading process. Ideally, according to Valincour, one would pass smoothly and swiftly from one end to the other of a simple narrative diachrony. This ideal timeline of readerly efficiency is superimposed onto the novel in Valincour's criticism of it, and the novel, not surprisingly, is found wanting in temporal construction.

The gap or lag between an idealized time of purposeful reading and the digressions, deferrals, and complexities constitutive of Lafayette's narration creates a temporal interval into which the critic's activity inserts itself. Valincour measures the discrepancy between his expectations of time in the novel and the problematic timeline that Lafayette's work presents to him. In one sense, the critic capitalizes on this time lag by using it as a frame of reference for interpretive activity. Seen from another angle, the gap between Valincour's expectations and the actual time structures of *La Princesse de Clèves* serves as an indication of the novel's irreducibility to reductive temporal readings.

Without grasping the full temporal complexity and the originality of *La Princesse de Clèves*, Valincour has recourse to examples from antiquity and invokes Virgil as the ultimate practitioner of succinctness in recounting digressive material.[16] He complains of the "licence que nos écrivains se sont donnée" [liberties that our writers have taken] in relating tales that he considers irrelevant to the narrative matter at hand (21). Valincour's concern for temporal economy in narration leads him to make specific calculations in evaluating the impact of the avowal scene:

> En effet, quel embarras n'est-ce point que d'avoir à faire venir de la Cour Monsieur de Clèves, faire égarer le Duc de Nemours, le faire cacher dans un pavillon, y amener Madame de Clèves et son mari, et tout cela, pour entendre une conversation d'un demi-quart d'heure, que l'on lui eût fort bien fait entendre par tout ailleurs. (46)

[Indeed, is it not confusing to have to bring Monsieur de Clèves from the court, to have the Duc de Nemours lose his way and go and hide in a pavilion, to bring Madame de Clèves and her husband there, and all this so that one may hear a conversation of half a quarter-hour that he could have been made to hear anywhere else.]

In the critic's conception of time, the dramatic impact of the brief confession does not justify the means by which this scene was prepared in the narration. To put this critical assessment in terms set out by Gérard Genette, the functional value of the scene (the dramatic impact, the pathos generated by it) is to be weighed as being lesser than the motivation, or narrative preparation of the scene.[17] In a calculating approach such as Valincour's, the avowal scene and its framing produce a deficit in narrative economy, due to an excess of motivation in relation to function. The hermeneutic quantification leading to this judgment is a temporal one. In contrast to lengthy and elaborate preparatory passages, the confession itself seems unusually brief, taking only "un demi-quart d'heure" according to the critic's watch.

Referring to the scene in which the Prince of Clèves consults with the spy whom he has sent to observe Nemours, Valincour considers the prince's full fifteen minutes of worried silence to be quite excessive. While Clèves may initially misunderstand the situation, suspecting as he does that his wife has been unfaithful, he could not realistically maintain this illusory impression for the period of time that the novel's author designates: "[D]ès que cette préoccupation dure plus d'un quart d'heure, et qu'un homme s'obstine à deviner le contraire de ce que l'on lui veut dire, elle ne se peut plus excuser; elle sort du vraisemblable" [As soon as this preoccupation lasts for more than a quarter of an hour, and a man insists on guessing the contrary of what someone is trying to tell him, it can no longer be excused; it is no longer believable] (263). Valincour envisions a better version of this scene in a theatrical work: "ces sortes de troubles . . . sont bons dans une tragédie où ils ne durent que la longueur d'une scène, et finissent aussitôt" [these kinds of troubles . . . are good in a tragedy, where they only last for the duration of a scene and are then over] (262). In search of criteria for evaluating the prince's actions, Valincour relies on theatrical norms, the time structures of which have scant relevance for Lafayette's innovative, generically unprecedented work of prose fiction. Though Valincour misreads the use of narrative time in this scene, his annoyance with the prince's inertia reveals the critic's awareness of a significant characteristic of Lafayettian characters—their tendency to remain silent for prolonged periods of time in emotionally taxing situations. Valincour has perceived, even in condemning it, the interiority of these quizzical characters, who appear unusually sluggish to him in their words and actions.[18]

In discussing the episode of the Vidame of Chartres's lost letter, Valincour finds it unrealistic that Nemours and the vidame "demeurent tous deux, l'un jusques à minuit, l'autre jusques au lendemain matin, sans rien savoir d'une chose où l'on leur donnait tant de part, et qui était su de tout le monde" [both stay, one until midnight, the other until the following morning, without knowing anything of a matter in which they are thought to be deeply involved, and which was known to everyone] (31). According to an implicit calculation of rates of information transmission in Henri II's court, the vidame and Nemours are deemed inordinately slow in acquiring information that concerns them personally. While perhaps overestimating the rapidity with which news travels in the courtly world Lafayette's novel portrays, Valincour underscores the importance of processes of communication, and more specifically of their timing and rates of operation, for the plot of *La Princesse de Clèves*. Also highlighted, through the negative examples of the ineffectual vidame and duke, is the importance of strategic action based on knowledge of situations.

Nemours's ineptitude for strategy in timing is repeatedly an object of discussion in the *Lettres à Madame la marquise* ***. The otherwise perfectly gallant duke has a tendency to miss opportunities and commit blunders, as he does when catching his scarf in the window of the princess's pavilion: "Il me semble, ne lui en déplaise, qu'il prenait assez mal son temps pour se montrer" [It seems to me, no offense to him, that he picked a bad time to show himself] (68). One can either make good or bad use of the time that is at one's disposal in a particular situation, and according to Valincour Nemours does the latter, in the scenes discussed above and at the moment when the duke neglects a perfect opportunity. When the princess implicitly reproached him for loving another woman, Nemours, according to Valincour's thinking, should have spoken frankly to Madame de Clèves: "Quel temps plus favorable pour témoigner à sa maîtresse la passion qu'il avait pour elle?" [What could be a more favorable moment to tell his lady of the passion he had for her?] (192). Valincour does not consider the fact that such a confession from Nemours would have destroyed all of the suspense that the narration so meticulously builds both before and after the scene in question. Yet, as was the case for the time of interiority and of communication, Valincour's misreadings of Nemours's actions make both this critic and his readers aware of time structures in Lafayette's novel.

Nemours is not the only character Valincour reproaches for missing opportunities. While the ailing Mme de Chartres eventually gives the princess sound advice regarding the dangers of adulterous passions, she provides these insights much too late to be of any practical benefit:

> On ne saurait combattre [ces sortes de sentiments] d'assez bonne heure, pour les vaincre; et souvent même, lorsque l'on les aperçoit dans son cœur, il est déjà trop tard pour les combattre. Madame de Chartres devait avoir donné ses avis à sa fille dès qu'elle aperçut le besoin qu'elle en avait, et non pas les réserver pour un temps où elle n'était plus capable d'en profiter. (154)

> [These kinds of feelings cannot be fought too early, if they are to be quelled; and often, when one notices them in one's heart, it is already too late to fight them. Madame de Chartres should have given her advice to her daughter as soon as she noticed the need that she had for this advice, rather than waiting for a time when she would no longer be able to benefit from it.]

A conception of love as strategy motivates Valincour's emphasis on the necessity of struggling against a nascent amorous inclination "d'assez bonne heure." Keeping one's own emotions under control can often be a matter of timing, especially when longings develop rapidly and threaten to take over one's heart when it is "déjà trop tard pour les combattre." An opportunistic approach to the temporal dynamics of sentimental interiority combines with an emphasis on effective timing in Valincour's assessment of the princess's predicament. The critic then reproaches Mme de Chartres for having reserved her explanations for an infelicitous moment. While developing an increasingly detailed conception of the time of interiority and strategic action in Lafayette's novel, Valincour ignores the dramatic impact of Mme de Chartres's deathbed monologue, the timing of which makes the admonitions and premonitions contained therein resonate throughout the rest of the novel. Valincour only sees that Mme de Chartres has reacted too slowly to her daughter's situation.

At times the princess herself thinks and reacts too sluggishly in Valincour's estimation. Her reflection on Nemours's superficial relations with women and on his incapacity for commitment comes too late to be of any worth: "[C']est la faute toute pure de Madame de Clèves de ne l'avoir pas faite plutôt. Pourquoi ne la faisait-elle pas lorsque Madame de Chartres lui parla tant de Monsieur de Nemours, pour lui faire comprendre qu'il était incapable d'un véritable attachement? C'était là le temps d'y penser" [It is entirely the fault of Madame de Clèves not to have done it earlier. Why did she not do this when Madame de Chartres was talking so much to her about Monsieur de Nemours, in order to let her know that he was incapable of a long-lasting attachment? That was the time to be thinking about this] (202). After criticizing the timing of the character's realization, Valincour identifies ("C'était là") exactly when the appropriate moment would have been for this recognition. The novel is once again at a remove from the interpretive timeline that the critic has superimposed onto the work.

One of the interlocutors offering his opinions in the *Lettres à Madame la marquise* *** points out an appropriate time for the princess's realization of her feelings for Nemours and contrasts an ideal use of this time with the actual events of the novel: "[E]lle attendait bien tard à se dire des choses qui la touchaient si fort. . . . Que ne se les disait-elle pendant les trois jours qu'elle fit la malade pour avoir un prétexte de n'y point aller [au bal]? A quoi songeait-elle durant ce temps-là?" [She waited quite late to tell herself things that touched her so deeply. . . . Why did she not tell herself these things during the three days she was feigning illness so as to have a pretext for not going to the ball? What was she thinking about at that time?] (151). The uncertainty inherent in times of emotional change notwithstanding, the princess should have been perfectly lucid in regard to her growing inclination for Nemours, and she should have timed her realization strategically in order to protect herself against the dangers that she would face. But she does none of this and only displays an emotive and intellectual lethargy that perplexes Valincour and his fictive discussants.

While the princess may err at times on the side of slowness, in another episode her emotions develop too rapidly to be acceptable to Valincour. He was taken aback by the contrast between the princess's cool indifference toward her husband and the visible emotions aroused by her initial encounter with Nemours. The evening of the royal ball at the Louvre, where the princess and the duke first meet, contains too many interior events for Madame de Clèves, whose passion for Nemours develops too rapidly for the critic's time grid: "Quand ce n'eût été que pour la bienséance, j'eusse voulu que la passion de Monsieur de Nemours eût commencé au moins quelques jours avant celle de Madame de Clèves. Cela eût été plus régulier; et Madame de Clèves n'aurait pas eu de peine à le rattraper, puisqu'elle faisait tant de chemin en si peu de temps" [If only to respect *bienséance*, I would have wanted Monsieur de Nemours's passion to begin at least a few days before that of Madame de Clèves. That would have been more regular; and Madame de Clèves would not have had any trouble catching up to him, since she covered so much ground in so little time] (138). In order for the situation to remain acceptable in the context of seventeenth-century codes of social conduct, the duke should have shown his inclination for the princess at least "quelques jours" previous to the princess's first blush. Along with the problem of Nemours's characteristic tardiness, the scene at the royal ball presents to the reader an unusually rapid *inamoramento*. As in the above quotation, elsewhere Valincour uses a slight irony to reproach the novel's author for the heroine's quickness in becoming enamored: "Que ne devait-on point attendre, dans la suite, d'une passion qui avait fait tant de progrès en une soirée?" [What might one not expect, in the rest of the story, of a passion that made such progress in a single evening?] (137). *La Princesse de Clèves* presents the author of the *Lettres à Madame la marquise* *** not only with cumbersome digressions and torpid characters, but also with situations that develop too rapidly. The brevity of the avowal scene and the abrupt death of the Prince of Clèves strike Valincour, usually an impatient reader, as being uncomfortably fast-paced.

One of Valincour's fictional interlocutors evokes as a criterion of critical acuity a reading practice that differs strikingly from the former's stated impatience. It is an erudite discussant who remarks on the strangeness of one of the statements in Mme de Chartres's deathbed speech: "Cela paraît raisonnable, et même fort délicat à ceux qui ne lisent ces choses qu'en courant; mais pour peu que l'on y fasse de réflexion, l'on trouve ce sentiment tout-à-fait étrange" [That seems reasonable, and even quite delicate, to those who only read things rapidly; but one needs to reflect only a little to find this sentiment quite strange] (152–53).[19] In his preface to comments on Mme de Chartres's words, this discussant emphasizes the importance of slow, careful reading, over against the practices of "ceux qui ne lisent ces choses qu'en courant." Valincour, who describes his process of reading as a "course," must fall into this latter category. The impatient reader, for whom narrative events sometimes play themselves out all-too rapidly, may thus include a subtle self-criticism in his often flawed but insightful critical work on *La Princesse de Clèves*.

In contrast to Valincour's haste, Charnes valorizes patient reading practices, such as the one evoked by Damon, one of Charnes's fictional interlocutors. This approach to Lafayette's text can be applied correctively to the readerly impatience as a result of which Valincour had found Lafayette's digressions to be unacceptable. Damon describes his own textual traversal through the metaphor of an unhurried traveler:

Un voyageur qui n'est pas fort pressé, et qui ne va voir une ville que pour se divertir, ou pour satisfaire sa curiosité, s'arrête avec plaisir à considérer les paysages, les belles maisons, et les autres objets agréables qui se trouvent sur sa route: De même quoiqu'on aille à la conclusion de l'histoire de la princesse de Clèves, quand on l'a commencée, on ne laisse pas de se plaire aux ornements dont l'Auteur l'embellit. (52)

[A voyager who is not in a big hurry, and who will only see a city to amuse himself or to satisfy his curiosity, takes pleasure in stopping to take in the landscapes, the beautiful houses, and the other agreeable sights he finds on his route. In the same way, even though one is moving toward the conclusion of the story of The Princess of Clèves, once one has begun it one cannot avoid taking pleasure in the ornamentation with which the author embellishes the story.]

This reader highlights the importance of a plenitude of perception in experiences of travel and reading. While Damon admits that there is a certain anxiousness inherent in the reading process, he maintains that stopping to appreciate objects of description and retelling on the way to the work's conclusion considerably enriches the reader's experience. Charnes also argues for the quality of the digressions contained in *La Princesse de Clèves*, most notably the lengthy introductory passage to the novel: "Je suis assuré que ces trente-six pages ont coûté plus de trente-six heures à l'auteur et ceux qui s'y connaissent s'en sont bien aperçus" [I am sure that these 36 pages cost the author more than 36 hours, and those who know these things have certainly noticed this] (33). Charnes makes implicit reference here to the exasperation with which Valincour had read Lafayette's elaborate historical background narrative. Critics sensitive to the quality of this text, however, can appreciate that the time it takes to read the passage pales in comparison with the time it must have taken the author to compose it. An experiential time of diligent authorship, "trente-six heures," provides an index for literary quality.

Cléante, another of Charnes's characters, describes *La Princesse de Clèves* in material terms in order to measure the relative brevity of the author's digressions. "L'histoire d'Anne de Boulen, par exemple, est renfermée en cinq feuilles qui ne contiennent pas tant de paroles, que ce que le Critique dit sur ce sujet; et renferme de si grandes choses, qu'il n'y a rien de plus considérable dans ce siècle-là" [The story of Anne de Boulen, for example, is enclosed in five pages that do not contain as many words as there are in what the Critic has said on the subject; and includes such great things that there is nothing more considerable in the entire century] (50). The object of the book is evoked as proof of Lafayette's economy of narration. The material paucity of the five pages corresponds to an economy of time in the reading process. The compositional richness of Anne de Boulen's story amply rewards the reader for the time s/he has spent on this digressive narrative.[20]

Just as a limited timespan of reading can provide considerable insights and a plenitude of readerly experience, brief moments of narrative time can hold dramatic intensity equal to or greater than longer plot developments. Charnes reminds us of this kind of temporal density with a quote from Ariosto: "Ainsi une heure ou un instant peuvent faire advenir ce que mille ans ou plus n'avaient pas produit" [Thus an hour or an instant can bring about that which a thousand years or more could not produce] (72). Valincour seems to be aware of the possibility for this kind of compacted time, in a discussion of the mechanics of perception in lovers: "[U]n geste, un regard, un soupir leur fournissent souvent de longues matières de se réjouïr, ou de s'affliger" [A gesture, a look, a sigh often give them great cause for rejoicing or suffering] (140). As we have seen, however, Valincour tends to view the brevity of significant scenes in Lafayette's novel as an inadequacy of plot development. Charnes, meanwhile, maintains awareness of the importance of small spans of time in Lafayette's dense narrative temporality.

The striking brevity of certain episodes in *La Princesse de Clèves* places the novel's characters in difficult positions for strategic action. While Valincour and his interlocutors criticize Lafayette's characters for their slowness to act and react, Charnes points out that these characters do not always have enough time at their disposal to make ideal decisions. In response to Valincour's characterization of Nemours's strategic maneuvers as the betrayal of his friend, the prince, Charnes emphasizes the temporal limitations of Nemours's situation: "Ce que le Critique appelle trahison dans le Duc de Nemours, n'est proprement qu'une ruse que l'amour lui inspira sur le champ, sans qu'il eût le temps d'en délibérer" [What the Critic calls betrayal in the Duc de Nemours is nothing more than a ruse that love inspired in him right then and there, before he had any time to think about it] (244). Charnes recognizes that there is a realism of practical action in *La Princesse de Clèves*, a novel in which characters adopt behaviors according to circumstances, in the midst of which they do not necessarily have time to premeditate the noblest, most generous possible course of action. Time pressures make characters act in the most expedient way possible.[21] The nonheroics of Lafayettian action constitute part of the modernity of the work to which

Charnes's reading is sensitive, and upon which Valincour repeatedly superimposes the time constructs of idealized, heroic action.

"La Vertu malheureuse" announced the importance of nonheroic action for *La Princesse de Clèves*. The protagonist of "La Vertu malheureuse" distinguishes herself, not only by her own fortitude, but also through her vulnerability to the challenging circumstances in which she finds herself: "[I]l est rare de trouver tant de vertu dans des occasions aussi pressantes de ne pas suivre si scrupuleusement ses maximes" [It is rare to find so much virtue amidst so many opportunities not to follow one's maxims so scrupulously] (*Mercure* January 1678, 93). The stage is set for a new kind of (anti)heroine, one who, instead of transcending all obstacles, makes the most of the possibilities for action that are available to her, while revealing a radical susceptibility to the contingency of life's pressures and conditions.

Valincour does not recognize the fallibility of Lafayettian characters as a mark of the modernity of *La Princesse de Clèves*, but rather imposes criteria for fictional action, drawn from heroic romances and texts of antiquity, onto a novel whose innovations sharply and purposefully break from these traditions. Similarly, Valincour places an idealized critical time grid onto the work. The linearity of this time conception cannot account for the temporal complexity of *La Princesse de Clèves*. Nevertheless, Valincour does show considerable awareness of and sensitivity to time structures of strategic action, communication, and interiority. These three aspects of Lafayette's main characters' thoughts, words, and actions constitute the threefold temporal complexity of *La Princesse de Clèves*, which the following section will describe, through close readings of key passages.

## TIMING OF COURTLY MANEUVERS AND PRIVATE THOUGHTS IN *LA PRINCESSE DE CLÈVES*

### *Good and Bad Timing in Courtly Communication*

Though it is preceded by an elaborate historical narrative and thus considerably deferred from the beginning of the novel, Lafayette's protagonist's entry into the social world of Henri II's court takes place with a striking rapidity. The cosmetic charms of Mlle de Chartres have an immediate effect on others: "Il parut alors une beauté à la cour, qui attira les yeux de tout le monde" [At that moment there appeared at court a beauty to whom all eyes were turned].[22] The temporal marker "alors," in combination with the parallel placement of the verbs "parut" and "attira" places emphasis on the immediate effects of the young woman's presence in the court. Because of her status as an heiress from the family of the Vidame of Chartres, Mlle de Chartres has already been the object of personal and political maneuvers, even before her appearance on the courtly scene: "[Q]uoiqu'elle fût dans une extrême jeunesse, l'on avait déjà proposé plusieurs mariages. Mme de Chartres, qui était extrêmement glorieuse, ne trouvait presque rien digne de sa fille; la voyant dans sa seizième année, elle voulut la mener à la cour. Lorsqu'elle arriva, le vidame alla au-devant d'elle" [although she was very young, many propositions of marriage had been made to her. Madame de Chartres, who was extremely proud, found almost nothing worthy of her daughter, and the girl being in her sixteenth year, she was anxious to take her to court. The Vidame went to welcome her on her arrival] (41; 8). The vidame, whose political and private interests are clearly implicated in the social emergence of his niece, at once places himself in a position to admire her beauty. He is clearly aware of the rumors and schemes for potential betrothal that have preceded Mlle de Chartres's entry into court life. Not unlike the novel in which her tale is told, the future princess's actual appearance takes place only after a preliminary circulation of annunciatory discourses.

Mlle de Chartres is thus already involved in court life before she has seen any of its complexities or dangers, though her mother has tried to prepare her through didactic discussions, especially of the perils of "galanterie" (41). Very little time will elapse before Mlle de Chartres has an opportunity to put her education into practice. While Lafayette's narrator delays the appearance of the future princess considerably, a very narrow timespan separates this initial emergence from its consequences. "Le lendemain qu'elle fut arrivée" [the day after her arrival], the narrator specifies, Mlle de Chartres goes to an Italian jeweler's shop and encounters her future husband there: "Comme elle y était, le prince de Clèves y arriva" [The Prince of Clèves happened to come in while she was there] (42; 8). Immediately enamored, the prince stares rather blatantly at the young woman, who as a result "sortit assez promptement" [left very soon]. The prince, for his part, "conçut pour elle dès ce moment une passion et une estime extraordinaires. Il alla le soir chez Madame, sœur du roi" [conceived for her the greatest love and esteem. That evening he called on Madame, the king's sister] (42; 9). In this social meeting place, the prince speaks of this day's encounter with such fervor that Madame arranges for him and the young woman both to visit her on the next day (43; 9).

With Mlle de Chartres just having been informed of her admirer's fondness for her, "[c]e prince entra un moment après" [A moment after, that person appeared] (43; 9). At this instant of the rapidly developing situation, the prince emphasizes, not the depth or intensity of his esteem for Madame's young guest, but rather the timing of the sentiment's inception: "[I]l s'approcha d'elle et il la supplia de se souvenir qu'il avait été le premier à l'admirer" [He went up to her and asked her to remember that he had been the first to admire her]. The prince later assesses the strategic benefits of his good timing: "L'aventure qui était arrivée à M. de Clèves, d'avoir vu le premier Mlle de Chartres, lui paraissait un heureux présage et semblait lui donner quelque avantage sur ses rivaux" [The good fortune of Monsieur de Clèves in being the first to see Mademoiselle de Chartres seemed to him a happy omen, and to promise him some advantage over his rivals] (44; 10). While a strong and, as it will turn out, a sincere and lasting passion do develop in the prince's thoughts and feelings, these powerful emotions do not prevent this savvy courtier from taking stock of his felicitously timed actions nor from planning future ones.

Mme de Chartres, however, has higher hopes for her daughter and exercises her own abilities for tactical action in pursuing a marriage with the highly placed son of the duc de Montpensier. But Diane de Poitiers, an arch enemy of the vidame, easily anticipates and foils this plan: "Mme de Valentinois, ayant été avertie du dessein de ce marriage, l'avait traversé avec tant de soin, et avait tellement prévenu le roi que, lorsque M. d'Anville lui en parla, il lui fit paraître qu'il ne l'approuvait pas" [But Madame de Valentinois had heard of the contemplated marriage and had laid her plans to thwart it; she had been so successful in arousing the king's opposition that when Monsieur d'Anville spoke of it, he showed his disapproval] (47–48; 13). Valentinois's closeness to the king and her ability to use communication networks in anticipation of Chartres's plans allow her to deflect handily the possibility of a marriage that she finds undesirable.

Mme de Chartres's failure provides a perfect opportunity for the prince de Clèves. The duc de Nevers, father to the prince and a close ally of Mme de Valentinois, had opposed plans for asking Mlle de Chartres's hand, but the duke's death leaves his son free to make his own choices. The prince, who is not exactly incapacitated with grief over his father's passing, begins once again to strategize:

> La mort du duc de Nevers, son père, qui arriva alors, le mit dans une entière liberté de suivre son inclination et, sitôt que le temps de la bienséance du

deuil fut passé, il ne songea plus qu'aux moyens d'épouser Mlle de Chartres. Il se trouvait heureux d'en faire la proposition dans un temps où ce qui s'était passé avait éloigné les autres partis et où il était quasi assuré qu'on ne la lui refuserait pas. (49)

[The death of his father, the Duke of Nevers, which happened at that time, left him free to follow his own inclinations, and as soon as the period of mourning had passed, he thought of nothing but marrying Mademoiselle de Chartres. He was glad to make his proposal at a time when circumstances had driven away all rivals and when he felt almost sure that she would not refuse him.] (14)

Lafayette's narrator gives two temporal indications to highlight the fact that the prince acts quickly and with an acute sense of timing. He begins procuring the "moyens" necessary for marrying Mlle de Chartres "sitôt que le temps de la bienséance du deuil fut passé." The wording of this phrase suggests that the prince did not let a moment pass once this time of mourning had expired. As he embarks on his nuptial effort at a felicitous moment ("dans un temps . . ."), the prince reveals his awareness of timing for the project and estimates that he is acting during a propitious time.

Having acquired the first means necessary for achieving his goal—a private conversation with Mlle de Chartres—the prince impatiently interrogates the young woman: "[I]l la pressa de lui faire connaître quels étaient les sentiments qu'elle avait pour lui" [he begged her to let him know how she felt toward him] (49; 14). The prince's approach is both hasteful and obtrusive. These aspects of his behavior are denoted by the verb "presser," one of the definitions of which appears in Furetière as "Poursuivre vivement, tant au combat, qu'à la dispute. . . . On dit aussi, L'affaire *presse;* la saison, le temps *presse;* l'heure *presse.*" [Pursue vigorously, in combat or argument. . . . One can also say, the matter is *pressing;* the season, time, is *pressing;* the hour is *pressing*]. The temporal and combative dimensions of this word's semantics point to the use of time as a constraint in this scene between the prince and Mlle de Chartres. The prince, by both hurrying and pursuing Mlle de Chartres, deploys an economical conception and use of time to achieve the ends he desires. Though he does not get the kind of affective confirmation that he seeks from the nonchalant Mlle de Chartres, the daughter and mother both agree to accept him as suitor and to respond favorably enough to his advances to keep him hopeful that he will win the love of his wife-to-be.

The prince wastes no time making the remaining arrangements: "Dès le lendemain, ce prince fit parler à Mme de Chartres . . . . Les articles furent conclus; on parla au roi, et ce mariage fut su de tout le monde" [The next day, the prince had his offer formally made to Madame de Chartres . . . . The marriage settlement was drawn up, the king was told of it, and the marriage became known to everyone] (50; 14). This episode is remarkable not only for the speed with which the official channels for marriage are traversed; as soon as these measures are taken, the communication network of the court processes and disseminates knowledge of the upcoming marriage with perfect efficiency: "[C]e mariage fut su de tout le monde." In the blink of a reader's eye, awareness of the prince and future princess's plans are public property, encapsulated in a past participle, "su." The combination of the prince's strategic action and courtly society's processes of communication contribute to changing Mlle de Chartres's life in a succession of events whose narration calls the reader's attention to dynamics of strategic timing and temporal precision.

If the marriage through which she was to become princess contained any elaborate ceremonial elements, the reader knows little of them, though Lafayette's strikingly elliptical narration does give some minimal indications regarding the location of the ceremony and the dinner afterward: "Ce mariage s'acheva, la cérémonie s'en fit au Louvre; et le soir, le roi et les reines vinrent souper chez Mme de Chartres avec toute la cour, où ils furent reçus avec une magnificence admirable" [The marriage ceremony took place at the Louvre, and in the evening the king and queen, with all the court, supped at the house of Madame de Chartres, who received them with great splendor] (50; 16). Compared with the ball at which the princess first meets Nemours (the telling of which is itself rather brief), the single sentence that accounts for her marriage appears scant indeed (53–54; 17–18). Marriage is more a legal matter than a personal matter, especially for the princess, whose feelings do not change along with her name (52; 16). The expediency with which the prince brought about this marriage and the speedy way it was publicized highlight the time structures of strategic action and courtly communication. The temporal markers of Lafayette's narration establish the importance of small spans of time for the actions of the novel's characters, in one of the first key episodes for the life's story of the princess. While unable to inspire emotions in the princess's heart, the prince proves skillful in making use of the slight temporal increments that structure the clockwork of court life.

At the beginning of the second part of *La Princesse de Clèves*, the prince tells his wife the story of his friend Sancerre's troubled relationship with

Mme de Tournon. This episode, which foregrounds timing in the prince's capacity for strategic action, opens in a time frame of anticipation: "Un soir qu'il devait y avoir une comédie au Louvre et que l'on n'attendait plus que le roi et Mme de Valentinois pour commencer, l'on vint dire qu'elle s'était trouvée mal, et que le roi ne viendrait pas" [One evening when there was to be a play at the Louvre, and while they were waiting for the king and Madame de Valentinois in order to begin, word was brought that she was ill and that the king would not come] (73; 30). The imperfects "devait" and "attendait" establish, in the past tense of narration, an atmosphere of eager awaiting among the members of the court designated by the first "on." All of the conditions required for the play at the Louvre to get underway are present, except for the attendance of the king and Mme de Valentinois. The anticipation generated by the imperfect verbs is broken by the passé simple "vint," which announces that Mme de Valentinois will be unable to attend the play.

Tensions created by the experience of anticipatory time produce a microdiachrony of communication in Lafayette's narration. No longer awaiting the arrival of the king and his mistress, members of the court immediately begin to speculate on the reasons for this conspicuous absence: "On jugea aisément que le mal de cette duchesse était quelque démêlé avec le roi. Nous savions les jalousies qu'il avait eues du maréchal de Brissac pendant qu'il avait été à la cour" [Every one guessed that the duchess's illness was some quarrel with the king. We knew how jealous he had been of the Marshal of Brissac during his stay at court] (73; 30). The change of the situation, from anticipation to acceptance of the king and duchess's absence, mobilizes the common knowledge designated by the objects of "On jugea" and "Nous savions." The collective subjects of these verbs of cognitive activity evoke the hushed conversations that courtiers are pursuing in reaction to the turn of events that has just been announced. These exchanges are all the more animated for the uncertainty that accompanies the examination of common knowledge: Brissac's prior departure from the court would seem to discount him as a direct cause for the situation in question, such that "nous ne pouvions imaginer le sujet de cette brouillerie" [we could not imagine the cause of this falling-out].

The prince and his friend Sancerre receive information regarding the dispute during their discussion of the matter at hand: "Comme j'en parlais avec Sancerre, M. d'Anville arriva dans la salle et me dit tout bas que le roi était dans une affliction et dans une colère qui faisaient pitié" [While I was talking about it with Sancerre, Monsieur d'Anville came into the hall and whispered to me that the king was in a state of distress and anger most piteous to see] (73; 30). The temporal marker "Comme" serves to locate d'Anville's entry onto the scene in relation to the gossip that is already circulating about Mme de Valentinois's current indisposition, which appears to be the result of a missing ring, a gift the duchess had received from the king a few days prior and, by all appearances, passed on to the maréchal de Brissac. Even more rapidly than Mme de Valentinois's ring changes hands, the story of the king and duchess's dispute passes from one interlocutor to the next in the communication network of courtly society.

Right away the prince shares his newfound knowledge of the reasons behind the disagreement: "Sitôt que M. d'Anville eut achevé de me conter cette nouvelle, je me rapprochai de Sancerre pour la lui apprendre; je la lui dis comme un secret que l'on venait de me confier" [As soon as Monsieur d'Anville had finished, I went up to Sancerre to tell him the news, assuring him that it was a secret that had just been told me] (74; 31). The conclusion of the exchange between d'Anville and Clèves causes the latter to move quickly toward Sancerre and retell what he has heard only seconds before ("un secret que l'on venait de me confiier"). The momentum with which the news negotiates this channel of communication will carry Sancerre into an indiscreet disclosure.

On the morning following the play at the Louvre, the prince goes to visit his sister-in-law "d'assez bonne heure" [rather early] (74; 31). There he finds Mme de Tournon, with whom Sancerre had conversed the previous night: "Sancerre avait été chez elle au sortir de la comédie. Il lui avait appris la brouillerie du roi avec cette duchesse, et Mme de Tournon était venue la conter à ma belle-sœur, sans savoir ou sans faire réflexion que c'était moi qui l'avais apprise à son amant" [Sancerre had seen her when he left the play, and had told her about the king's quarrel with the duchess; this she had come to repeat to my sister-in-law, either not knowing or not remembering that it was I who had told her lover]. Sancerre must have impatiently awaited the chance to tell Mme de Tournon about the king's troubles while sitting through the play. Mme de Tournon behaves almost identically to d'Anville, Clèves, and Sancerre, by first learning ("Il lui avait appris"), then retelling ("conter"). However, in Mme de Tournon's case, supplementary knowledge is required in order for her to deploy her newsworthy awareness effectively: she must be aware, for the sake of the confidentiality of her relationship with Sancerre, that the prince holds a privileged position in the chain of information through which she has been apprised of recent events in the king's chambers, and through which she has passed the news further down the informational chain. But she tells the tale to her friend, the prince's sister-in-law, "sans savoir" and "sans faire réflexion." In a rapidly functioning communication network, Mme de Tournon has acted too quickly, bypassing thought processes that would have served her interests.

The next and final act of retelling in this episode takes place too quickly for Mme de Tournon, who has no tactical recourse once the prince hears d'Anville's tale for the second time: "Sitôt que je m'approchai de ma belle-sœur, elle dit à Mme de Tournon que l'on pouvait me confier ce qu'elle venait de lui dire et, sans attendre la permission de Mme de Tournon, elle me conta mot pour mot tout ce que j'avais dit à Sancerre le soir précédent" [When I came in, my sister-in-law said to Madame de Tournon that I could be trusted with what she had just told her, and without waiting for permission she repeated to me word for word everything I had told Sancerre the previous evening] (74; 31). The speed with which the story is retold to the prince is triply determined in Lafayette's sentence, with "Sitôt," "venait de lui dire," and "sans attendre." The use of the verb construction "venir de" establishes a homology between this last act of retelling and the initial acquisition of the news by the prince, who had told Sancerre of this "secret que l'on venait de me confier." Now the prince hears it again, "mot pour mot." The radical similarity between one retelling and another suggests that the characters who transmit this information do not control the channel of communication through which they learn and share news; the story seems to have a life of its own, as it moves through court society, remaining intact along the way.

No character makes more clearly visible the power of the story and the complexity of its strategic manipulation than Mme de Tournon, who has lost control over the situation in which she finds herself by handling the tale clumsily. The prince, on the other hand, while he controls the circulation of gossip just as little as Mme de Tournon, displays an opportunistic flair in reconstituting the chain of information transmission that has brought the news item back to him when he had been one of the first to disseminate it: "[J]e n'avais dit la chose qu'à Sancerre, il m'avait quitté au sortir de la comédie sans m'en dire la raison; je me souvins de lui avoir ouï extrêmement louer Mme de Tournon" [I had mentioned the matter to no one but Sancerre, who had left me after the play, without saying where he was going; but I remembered hearing him praise Madame de Tournon very warmly] (74; 31). The prince makes use of what is at his disposal in order to gain new knowledge and, as we shall see, power. His opportunism consists not in controlling the movement of information but in recognizing meaningful elements and timing actions effectively in a rapidly developing situation. As de Certeau puts it, "opportunity is 'seized,' not created. It is furnished by serendipity, by *exterior* circumstances in which the knowing glance can recognize the new and favorable ensemble that they will constitute provided that *one more detail* is added."[23] The prince gains advantage, in the first instance, through an act of seeing: "Toutes ces choses m'ouvrirent les yeux" [All these things opened my eyes]. In the next instance, he must add one final detail, he must communicate one more news item in order to turn the situation definitively to his advantage.

Having seen off a flustered Mme de Tournon, the prince goes to speak with his friend: "Je m'en allai à l'heure même trouver Sancerre, je lui fis des reproches et je lui dis que je savais sa passion pour Mme de Tournon, sans lui dire comment je l'avais découvert. Il fut contraint de me l'avouer" [At once I went to see Sancerre; I reproached him, and said that I knew of his passion for Madame de Tournon, but I did not say how I had found it out. He felt obliged to make a complete confession] (74–75; 31). In anticipation of Mme de Tournon's relation of events to her lover, the prince informs Sancerre of his key object of knowledge ("je savais sa passion"). One small fact, that of the transfer of news from Sancerre to Tournon, suffices, if it is used efficiently, to accomplish a strategic objective. The prince's well-timed act of information transmission, accomplished "à l'heure même" and in anticipation of one of the parties on whom he wishes to gain advantage, imposes a time constraint on the other party, Sancerre, that brings about an avowal. This foreshadows the time constraints, imposed on the princess by her husband, that will lead to the more famous avowal scene. In contrast with the wife's "aveu," which leads to the prince's downfall, Sancerre's confession places the prince in a privileged position with regard to the secretive lovers: "[J]e fus ensuite très avant dans leur confidence" [I was from that time fully admitted to their confidence] (75; 32). The prince has transformed a news item into the kind of knowledge through which he can gain power, by means of a tactical anticipation, within the intersubjective economy of Henri II's court.

Readers of *La Princesse de Clèves* may easily develop the impression that the prince is merely an ineffectual character, a virtually cuckolded husband who could never inspire love, who mistakenly believed that his wife had been unfaithful, and who died from the pain of his own failures. While these elements of the prince's experience may remain relevant to our overall impression of him as a literary character, it is nevertheless necessary to recall, as the readings of the two scenes dis-

cussed above show, that the prince displays considerable skill in manipulating situations through an acute sense of timing. That he times his
deployment of knowledge in order to gain power exemplifies the importance of ways of knowing, not exhaustively, but expediently. Relevant
items of information, even if scant in content, can serve strategic purposes within microdiachronies of communication.

"La vertu malheureuse," along with rumors circulating in regard to
the soon-to-be-published *Princesse de Clèves*, established the importance,
for Lafayette's novel, of a temporality of anticipation. As the two episodes discussed above reveal, time frames of anticipation play an important role in Lafayette's narration. The deferred appearance on the
fictional scene of Mlle de Chartres takes place in an atmosphere of
eager awaiting. The event is prepared, like the publication of the work
itself, by preliminary announcements. Similar dynamics of information
transmission are observable in the scene in which courtiers anxiously
await the king and Mme de Valentinois. Framed by the cognitive temporal contractions resulting from anticipation, the circumstances following this scene play themselves out in a dense temporality of rapidly
accumulated events. Similarly, the princess's entry into court life is immediately followed by numerous encounters, resulting in a marriage
that occupies the space of a single sentence in Lafayette's narration. An
intense focus on small time increments pervades the succinct telling of
these episodes.

Valincour's recognition of the significance of speedy communication
in the world of Henri II's court sheds light on the episode in which the
prince and princess's marriage was "su" with such striking rapidity.
This critic's insight also illuminates the situation following the play at
the Louvre, in which a chain of information exchange stretched from
d'Anville to Mme de Tournon, then circularly back to the prince. A ring
and a story passed from hand to hand with an agitation reminiscent of
the reading practices of provincial *Mercure* subscribers, who, according
to De Merville, practically snatched the periodical out of each other's
hands. Rapidity and timing, both in *La Princesse de Clèves* and among its
readers, seemed to be the order of the day.

Although Nemours is reproached by Valincour for being slow-witted,
he shares with the prince an ability to act and react effectively and time-
consciously in the midst of changing circumstances. When confronted
by a challenging query by the dauphine, the duke shows his ability for
immediate response: "S'il eût eu moins de présence d'esprit, il eût été
surpris de cette demande. Mais prenant la parole sans hésiter . . ." [He
would have been embarrassed by this question if he had had less pres-

ence of mind; but he answered without hesitation] (88; 42). He times
his visits to the prince carefully in order to maximize his chances for
seeing the princess: "Il le cherchait même à des heures où il savait bien
qu'il n'y était pas et, sous le prétexte de l'attendre, il demeurait dans
l'antichambre de Mme de Chartres où il y avait toujours plusieurs personnes de qualité" [He even sought him at hours when he knew he was
not in; then he would say that he would wait for him, and used to stay
in the ante-chamber of Madame de Chartres, where were assembled
many persons of quality] (67; 27). Nemours chose a precise moment, in
an attempt to find time alone with the princess, when he "attendit pour
aller chez elle l'heure que tout le monde en sortirait et qu'apparamment
il ne reviendrait plus personne. Il réussit dans son dessein et il arriva
comme les dernières visites en sortaient" [put off his call until every one
should have left and it was unlikely that others would come in. His plan
was successful, and he arrived just as the latest visitors were taking
their departure] (84; 38). Like the prince, Nemours pays close attention
to the timing of his own actions and those of others. This kind of attention to passing moments within an intersubjective economy of action
and communication marks Lafayette's novel as a narrative representation of the conceptual valorization of temporal precision, an epistemological trend marking the second half of the seventeenth century in
France.

Representative of Lafayette's focus on small time increments, the
well-known episode of the vidame's lost letter combines detailed perspectives on the dynamics of communication with skillfully narrated
rhythms of interior experience. When a potentially compromising missive has fallen from the vidame's pocket into the hands of the valet
Chastelart, who passes it on to the dauphine, who gives it to the princess, a series of frenetic events ensues. The vidame, understandably,
hurries to try and find the letter, which he had intended to return to its
author, Mme de Thémines. Because the letter contains proof that he
has been unfaithful to Mme de Thémines and thus doubly unfaithful to
the queen, with whom he was presumably to have an exclusive rapport
of platonic confidence, the circulation of this potential object of gossip
presents grave problems for the vidame. He leaves a dinner party early,
wakes a friend of Chastelart, "quoique l'heure fût extraordinaire" [al-
though it was very late] and goes to consult with Nemours at a time
when "le jour ne commençait qu'à paraître" [at about daybreak]
(101–2; 52). He beseeches Nemours "de ne perdre pas un moment"
[not to lose a moment] (112; 58). With hopes of getting the letter back
or claiming that it belongs to Nemours, the vidame clutches at possible

solutions to his predicament within a highly charged temporality of fast-moving events.

Meanwhile the princess believes that the letter belongs to Nemours and thus that the duke loves another besides her. The affair costs her a sleepless night: "Elle passa la nuit sans faire autre chose que s'affliger et relire la lettre qu'elle avait entre les mains" [She spent the night in self-reproach and in reading over the letter] (100; 51). Claudette Sarlet describes the rhythm of action and the tenor of emotional experience in the episode of the lost letter:

> The torture of jealousy in Madame de Clèves, the vidame's worry, and for Nemours the fear of having angered Madame de Clèves, followed by the pleasure of passing a few hours with her: all of these emotions are highlighted by the feverishness with which each person spends his/her hours, the slightest instant of which counts for a great deal. The reader senses the fever, the haste, the excitement of each character thanks to the chronological indications. It is the rapid succession of events, part of which occur during the night, that gives this episode its dramatic intensity.[24]

As Sarlet points out, the detailed time structures through which Lafayette's narration represents courtly communication and strategic action in the affair of the lost letter also shape the private emotional experiences of characters, and especially Nemours and the princess. The lost letter provides a pretext for the duke and the princess to spend some time together, as they compose a false copy of the letter in order to oblige the dauphine, from whom the queen has demanded to see it (the letter itself has been returned to the relieved vidame by this time). The two would-be lovers spend "de si agréables moments" [such pleasant moments] together and Nemours is "bien aise de faire durer un temps qui lui était si agréable" [only too happy to prolong so pleasant a visit], such that the letter takes quite some time to get finished: "Enfin à peine, à quatre heures, la lettre était-elle achevée" [At last, at four o'clock, the letter was hardly finished] (117–18; 62–63). The princess and duke, after negotiating a hectic time frame of communication and strategic action, each savor every privileged moment of their respective private experiences of complicity with the other.

Once the spell of these agreeable moments is broken, the princess begins to reflect on the rapid transitions of her own emotional states:

> Après qu'on eut envoyé la lettre à Mme la Dauphine, M. de Clèves et M. de Nemours s'en allèrent. Mme de Clèves demeura seule, et sitôt qu'elle ne fut plus soutenue par cette joie que donne la présence de ce qu'on aime,

elle revint comme d'un songe; elle regarda avec étonnement la prodigieuse différence de l'état où elle était le soir d'avec celui où elle se trouvait alors. (118)

[After the letter had been sent to the crown princess, Monsieur de Clèves and Monsieur de Nemours went away. Madame de Clèves was left alone; and as soon as she was deprived of the presence of the man she loved, she seemed to awaken as if from a dream. She considered with surprise the enormous difference between her state of mind the previous evening and the one she then felt.] (*my translation*)

This scene of self-examination is introduced by an indication of its immediate posterity to an act of epistolary communication. With the departure of duke and husband, the princess "demeura seule." The change in her situation immediately solicits private thoughts, as indicated by the temporal marker "sitôt." In the autoreflexive thought process that follows, she is surprised not only by the dramatic changes of heart that she has just undergone, but also by the timing of these changes, the interval between "le soir" and "alors," the paucity of which highlights the profundity of her affective transition. As in the first meeting of the marquis and the "belle" in "La vertu malheureuse," at the conclusion of the lost letter episode in *La Princesse de Clèves*, circumstances pervaded by temporalities of strategic action and communication give way to the observation of rhythms of interior transformation.

As the radical emotive shifts undergone by the princess indicate, the time of interiority can be as agitated as the time of courtly maneuvering. Directing her focus toward the recent past time frame in which she enjoyed some moments of complicity with Nemours, the princess begins to feel guilty for having had thoughts and feelings incompatible with her ideal of marital duty:

Elle trouva qu'il était presque impossible qu'elle pût être contente de sa passion. Mais quand je le pourrais être, disait-elle, qu'en veux-je faire? Veux-je la souffrir? Veux-je y répondre? Veux-je m'engager dans une galanterie? Veux-je manquer à M. de Clèves? Veux-je manquer à moi-même? Et veux-je enfin m'exposer aux cruels repentirs et aux mortelles douleurs que donne l'amour? . . . Toutes mes résolutions sont inutiles; je pensai hier tout ce que je pense aujourd'hui et je fais aujourd'hui tout le contraire de ce que je résolus hier. (119)

[She thought it almost impossible ever to be satisfied with his love. "But even if I could be," she asked herself, "what could I do with it? Do I wish to endure it? Do I want to reciprocate it? Do I wish to begin a love-affair?

Do I wish to fail in my duty to Monsieur de Clèves? Do I wish to fail myself? And do I wish, finally, to expose myself to the cruel repentance and
mortal anguish that are inseparable from love? . . . All my resolutions are
vain; I thought yesterday what I think today, and I act today in direct con-
tradiction to my resolutions of yesterday."] (*my translation*)

As the tag for the princess's discourse, the "disait-elle," recedes in the
narration, a free-indirect style gives an account of this character's troubled thought process. Her strong inclination for Nemours forces her to
raise a series of questions, phrased in brief sentences and challenging in
their content. As the indirect discourse gives a close view of the most
intimate sphere of the princess's thinking, we observe a rapid succession of anxious self-interrogations, and an acute consciousness of
change over time: "[J]e fais aujourd'hui tout le contraire de ce que je
résolus hier." The use of free-indirect discourse in Lafayette's novel is
one decidedly modern characteristic of *La Princesse de Clèves*. Further-
more, part of this narrative innovation involves a particular time-consciousness on the part of both the narrator and the princess. The
rhythms of interior reflection and changes in attitudes and behavior
over brief spans of time constitute key elements of the experience of
court life and of private life in Lafayette's novel. These are some of the
aspects of this social setting that cause the princess the most trauma and
fatigue. Her perspectives on recent and current events place the princess at a point of intersection where public and private spheres of existence are conjoined. Standing at this crossroads, the princess has
recourse to a mode of discourse, confession, that exteriorizes her internal torment and brings us to the heart of what is at stake in this novel.

## Time Constraints, Confession, and Interiority

The princess's reflection on the dangers of her passion leads her to
conclude that she needs time away from Nemours and the court: "[I]l
faut m'en aller à la campagne, quelque bizarre que puisse paraître mon
voyage; et si M. de Clèves s'opiniâtre à l'empêcher ou à en vouloir savoir les raisons, peut-être lui ferai-je le mal, et à moi-même aussi, de les
lui apprendre" [I must go to the country, strange as the trip may seem;
and if Monsieur de Clèves persists in opposing it, or in demanding my
reasons, perhaps I shall do him and myself the wrong of telling them to
him] (119; 64). The princess announces the avowal scene, soon to come
in the story, as the potentially necessary reaction to pressures that her
husband may place on her, whether by trying to prevent her retreat or

by interrogating her in regard to it. When she expresses her desire for this trip to Coulommiers, the prince "lui répondit qu'elle oubliait que les noces des princesses et le tournoi s'allaient faire, et qu'elle n'avait pas trop de temps pour se préparer à y paraître avec la même magnificence que les autres femmes" [told her that she forgot the approaching marriages of the princesses and the tournament, and that she would not have time enough to make her preparations for appearing in due splendor alongside the other ladies] (120; 64). The reason he gives to convince his wife to stay at the court takes the form of a time constraint: she must adhere to a schedule of courtly obligations, which involves the cosmetic preparations necessary for a suitably elegant appearance at the upcoming wedding and tournament. This passage makes clear that the "magnificence" of Henri II's court, evoked from the novel's very beginning, results from hours of individual application. Keeping up appearances in this setting requires time and quasi-vocational devotion. While the princess wishes to avoid the responsibility of appearance, the prince attempts to oblige her to observe it, but when she insists, he gives in.

Once the prince and princess are in Coulommiers, however, the prince once again begins pressuring his wife to reenter court society: "Mais pourquoi ne voulez-vous point revenir à Paris?" [But why don't you wish to return to Paris?] (121; 65). The princess responds by citing the taxing effects of the "tumulte de la cour" [bustle of the court]. Her husband shows no sympathy: "Le repos . . . n'est guère propre pour une personne de votre âge" [Rest . . . is not meant for persons of your age] (*my translation*). When it becomes evident that the princess has some specific reason, besides fatigue, for wishing to be away from Paris, the prince continues his insistent questioning: "Il la pressa longtemps" [He pressured her for a long time] (121; *my translation*). In one last effort to avoid confessing that she loves another, the princess implores her husband: "Ne me contraignez point . . . à vous avouer une chose que je n'ai pas la force de vous avouer" [Don't compel me to confess something which I have often meant to tell you, but had not the strength] (122; 66). The repetition of "avouer" in the subordinate clause intended to specify the object, "chose," of the first "avouer" represents the princess's tactic of deferral. Avowal must remain a word, a sign with no specific referent, if husband and wife are to avoid a conjugal crisis. Because of the prince's persistent curiosity, this pattern cannot be maintained, and the eruption of referentiality in the midst of the sign systems of social convention produces an unprecedented kind of avowal.

The princess confesses her love for an unnamed other as a result of an accumulation of pressures applied by her husband and the courtly world that she wishes to escape. The social obligations and taxing rhythms of life in Paris constitute the temporal dimension of these constraints that drive the princess to seek refuge in their "belle maison à une journée de Paris" [a country-house they were building at a day's journey from Paris] (120; 64). One of the positive characteristics of this house, for the princess, is its separation, not only in space, but also in time, from a hectic social milieu.[25] However, the prince repeatedly reasserts the relevance of the schedules of court life for the princess's own comportment and thus constrains her into her confession, which takes place at the point of contact between the inexorable clockwork of sociability and the idiosyncratic temporality of private experience.

In the circumstances that immediately follow the confession scene, time structures of communication and interiority are illuminated. Just as the avowal became an object of animated debate in the pages of the *Mercure galant*'s "Extraordinaires," the scene is a topic of discussion among several of the characters in the novel itself. Once the princess returns to the court, the dauphine will tell her the story of her own avowal, which has been spread by Nemours to the vidame, who told it to Mme de Martigues, who had recounted the conversation to the dauphine. Thus, shortly after its occurrence, the confession is reincorporated into the communicational dynamics of the very social setting whose scheduling pressures had motivated the avowal in the first place. The private sphere of the princess's most intimate thoughts thus falls prey to the seemingly unstoppable mechanics of the court.

While still in Coulommiers, the princess reflects on what she has just told her husband: "[E]lle regarda ce qu'elle venait de faire" [she looked back over what she had just done] (125; *my translation*). Reviewing the recent past designated by the locution "venait de," she questions whether she has acted wisely: "Elle se demandait pourquoi elle avait fait une chose si hasardeuse" [She asked herself why she had done this perilous thing] (125; 68). A character from Scudéry or La Calprenède, emerging from a battle or a perilous journey, would never pose such a question. The hesitation and confusion that the princess shows in regard to her recent actions underline the heterogeneity and disorderliness of her thought process. This contributes to the realism that frames Lafayettian characters' sentiments and actions. At a considerable remove from the protagonists of heroic romances, these early modern characters struggle repeatedly to take stock of recent situations and to anticipate what is to come, stumbling as if in the dark, in the midst of unprecedentedly complicated circumstances: "Elle passa toute la nuit, pleine d'incertitude, de trouble et de crainte" [She spent the whole

night in uncertainty, anxiety, and fear]. In a sense, the fallibility of Lafayette's main characters consists in their susceptibility to time, in their
self-questioning focus on recent events and hesitant speculation on
near-future ones. The rhythms of these unsure, self-exploratory
thoughts are brought to us with a clarity of intimate narration unprecedented in the French literary tradition.

While the princess agonizes over the confession she has recently
made to her husband, the eavesdropper Nemours, after his initial ela-
tion, goes through similar pangs of self-doubt: "Il s'abandonna d'abord
à cette joie; mais elle ne fut pas longue, quand il fit réflexion que la
même chose qui lui venait d'apprendre qu'il avait touché le cœur de
Mme de Clèves, le devait persuader aussi qu'il n'en recevrait jamais
nulle marque" [He first gave himself up to this joy; but it was not of
long duration, for he reflected that the same thing which showed him
that he had touched the heart of Madame de Clèves, ought to convince
him that he would never receive any token of it] (125; 68–69). The
duke's thought process is sketched out in time, starting with the temporal marker "d'abord," which describes the ephemeral jubilation that
leads to reflections on a recent past and a near future. Between "venait
d'apprendre" and "le devait persuader" lies the agitated time frame of
the duke's current anxious thinking. Many thoughts race through his
mind: "[E]nfin, il se trouva cent fois heureux et malheureux tout ensemble. La nuit le surprit dans la forêt" [in a word, he felt a hundred
times happier and unhappier. Night came upon him in the forest] (126;
69). The fall of night marks the passage of time during the duke's period
of private reflection.

The time that both the duke and the princess spend mulling over the
latter's dramatic confession, along with the peregrinations of Nemours's
account of it in the communication network of courtly society, frame
the famous avowal scene in a posterior temporality. Foreshadowing before the episode was provided by accounts of the princess attempting to
escape the time constraints of court life, to the incomprehension of her
husband. Both anterior and posterior frames for the avowal scene illuminate temporal dynamics of social interaction and of interiority. The
role the confession plays as an object of tentative reflection after the
fact points to the significance of this scene for understanding the time
structures of private, subjective experience in *La Princesse de Clèves*.[26]

The princess's avowal inspires silent contemplation even before it has
become a past event, as is evidenced by the comportment of the prince:
"M. de Clèves était demeuré, pendant tout ce discours, la tête appuyée
sur ses mains, hors de lui-même" [All the time she was speaking, Mon-

sieur de Clèves sat with his head in his hands; he was really beside himself] (122; 66). The prince's meditative pose and emotional agitation cause him to remain silent in the time immediately following his wife's declaration: "[P]ardonnez si, dans les premiers moments d'une affliction aussi violente qu'est la mienne, je ne réponds pas, comme je dois, à un procédé comme le vôtre" [excuse me if in the first moments of a grief so poignant as mine I do not respond as I should to your appeal]. The prince specifies the time frame of immediate posteriority to the confession as the first moments of his affliction. These seconds or perhaps even minutes correspond to an interior experience so overwrought with affective disturbance that the prince is unable to speak. Perhaps Valincour would have disapproved of the prince's sluggishness in responding to his wife and lifting her from her kneeling stance, in the same way he had disapproved of the prince's silence in reaction to his spy's reticence. Both of these moments of inertia point to a particular intensity of private experience, evoked elliptically by a textual gap.[27]

Relations between the princess and Nemours are dotted with significant silences. In their first opportunity for a private conversation, shortly after the princess's return to social life following Mme de Chartres's death, the duke initially finds nothing to say: "Il demeura quelque temps sans pouvoir parler. Mme de Clèves n'était pas moins interdite, de sorte qu'ils gardèrent assez longtemps le silence" [It was some time before he spoke; Madame de Clèves was equally confused, so that they kept a long silence] (84; 38). When words fail Lafayette's characters, a focus on time—in the textual form of the markers "quelque temps" and "assez longtemps"—comes into the narration to supplement their inaction. A similar silence fills the scene of the duke and princess's last private encounter, which takes place at the vidame's residence: "L'on ne peut exprimer ce que sentirent M. de Nemours et Mme de Clèves de se trouver seuls et en état de se parler pour la première fois. Ils demeurèrent quelque temps sans rien dire" [It would be impossible to express the feelings of Monsieur de Nemours and Madame de Clèves when they for the first time found themselves alone and free to talk. They remained for a long time without a word] (169; 100). It is as if, when her protagonist falls silent, Lafayette's narrator reminds the reader that narrative time is passing. The ellipsis in the dialogue recalls the fact that all dialogue and fictional action is subtended by the structures of narrative diachrony. The characters' internal dimension of private thinking and sentiment is also highlighted during these moments of inertia, and thus the renewed focus on the time during which this story is being recounted inflects the experience of interiority that makes up a principal part of the tale. Breakdowns in communication point to the rhythms of interior experience.

In order to describe the temporal dynamics of intimate thoughts and feelings that are elliptically evoked in the moments of silence discussed above, we must look at scenes that more specifically account for these rhythms. Shortly after her final conversation with Nemours, the princess undergoes a series of conflicting emotions, as she questions whether it had been correct for her "d'avoir souffert, pour la première fois de sa vie, qu'on lui dît qu'on était amoureux d'elle, et d'avoir dit elle-même qu'elle aimait" [to permit a man to tell her that he loved her, to confess that she too was in love] (176; 106). The princess's autoreflexive thought process perturbs her to such an extent that "elle ne se connaissait plus. Elle fut étonnée de ce qu'elle avait fait; elle s'en repentit; elle en eut de la joie: tous ses sentiments étaient pleins de trouble et de passion" [she did not recognize herself. She was amazed at what she had done, and repented it bitterly; she was also made happy by it, — she was completely upset by love and agitation]. As she looks back over her recent actions and scans the horizon of options for her life in the near future, the princess undergoes an alienation from herself in the inner regions of her subjectivity.

Torn between desire and remorse, the princess experiences also the tensions of her mind's attachment to past and future time frames: "Elle eût bien voulu se pouvoir dire qu'elle était mal fondée, et dans ses scrupules du passé, et dans ses craintes de l'avenir" [She would have liked to be able to say that she was wrong both in her scruples about the past and in her fears for the future] (177; 106). Past and future, in the private thinking of the princess, take the respective forms of "scrupule" and "crainte." As she assesses her own situation, her mind moves through time, to recent events and potential ramifications.

On the occasion of one of Nemours's unannounced visits, the princess goes through a thought process structured by the anticipatory temporality of "crainte," constitutive of the future-oriented direction of the Lafayettian relative present: "La crainte qu'elle eut qu'il ne lui parlât de sa passion, l'appréhension de lui répondre trop favorablement, l'inquiétude que cette visite pouvait donner à son mari, la peine de lui en rendre compte ou de lui cacher toutes ces choses, se présentèrent en un moment à son esprit" [Her fear that he would mention his love; her appréhension lest she should give him a favorable answer; the anxiety that this visit would give her husband; the difficulty of repeating or concealing everything that happened, — all crowded her mind at once] (149; 85). This highly charged moment in the princess's inner experience, this instant that closely approaches her most immediate experience of time, contains a threefold opening onto a near-future temporality, in the emotions of "crainte," "appréhension," and "inquiétude." In this passage, these nearly simultaneous sentiments take the grammatical position of the plural subject of the verb "se présenter." This semantic composition evokes a present time, the highly complex, temporally heterogeneous "moment" in which these thoughts emerge.

A scene of anticipatory private reflection that spans a longer period of time occurs after a discussion between the prince and princess, during which they have tried to discover how news of the princess's avowal had been transmitted to members of the court. When their discussion leads to no discovery, the prince decides on the course of action that the princess must follow: "[S]urtout il fallait qu'elle allât au Louvre et aux assemblées comme à l'ordinaire" [above all, he urged upon her the necessity of going to the palace and into the world as much as usual] (138; 78). The husband imposes the time constraint of social obligation on his wife, who then prepares herself for her upcoming travails: "Elle se résolut donc de faire un effort sur elle-même; mais elle prit le reste du jour pour s'y préparer et pour s'abandonner à tous les sentiments dont elle était agitée" [she resolved to make a great effort to control herself; but the rest of the day she devoted to preparations and to indulging the feelings that harassed her]. Part of her preparations, like the ones for the marriage and tournament, would require getting dressed and producing for herself a suitably elegant appearance for her imminent social exposure.

In addition to her cosmetic concerns, the princess must make herself emotionally ready for public activities. "[S]'y préparer" may have as much to do with what is inside the princess, her thoughts and feelings, as what appears on the outside. In order to steel herself for challenging social obligations in the midst of affective turmoil, the princess decides to let her troubled emotions — "tous les sentiments dont elle était agitée" — run their course. A private agitation must be controlled before the princess may engage in the public agitation of court life. The interior monologue which relates some of the princess's anticipatory feelings includes a specific fear: "Je serai bientôt regardée de tout le monde comme une personne qui a une folle et violente passion" [soon every one will look upon me as a woman possessed by a mad and violent passion] (138; 79). Combating this fear and readying herself for a difficult appearance before other members of the court, the princess undergoes an extended process of reflection and self-preparation in an anticipatory time frame. In the events represented in Lafayette's novel, interiority thus factors into the temporality of strategic anticipation, by taking the form of self-preserving reactions to the "crainte" that is inspired by thoughts of the near future.

The emotional states brought about by "scrupules" point the princess's thoughts toward the recent past. These reactions may take place in a single moment, immediately after an event, as is the case for the episode in which Nemours falls from horseback: "Mme de Clèves, après être remise de la frayeur qu'elle avait eue, fit bientôt réflexion aux marques qu'elle en avait données" [After Madame de Clèves had recovered from her fright she began to recall the way she had betrayed it] (96; 48). After a conversation with the duc de Guise, the princess's mind is still fixed on Nemours's recent mishap and her potentially compromising reaction to it: "Mme de Clèves, en sortant de la lice, alla chez la reine, l'esprit bien occupé de ce qui s'était passé" [Madame de Clèves at once went to the queen, with her mind intent on what had just happened] (96; 48). While Guise had spoken to her, the princess heard his words as if through a dream, scarcely noticing their provocative nature: "Dans un autre temps elle aurait été offensée qu'il lui eût parlé des sentiments qu'il avait pour elle; mais dans ce moment elle ne sentit que l'affliction de voir qu'il s'était aperçu de ceux qu'elle avait pour M. de Nemours" [At any other time she would have been offended at his speaking of his feelings for her; but at that moment she thought only of her pain at perceiving that he had detected her own for Monsieur de Nemours] (96; 48). As exterior circumstances change and develop, the princess partially ignores them and continues to reflect on her reactions to a key event that has had personal importance for her. This tendency to disregard the external as a result of a persistent focus on interior experience establishes the radical importance of the rhythms of private thoughts for the plot of *La Princesse de Clèves*.

The personal reflections of Lafayette's characters are separated from another realm of external events, those of sixteenth-century French history. Temporal studies of *La Princesse de Clèves* have tended to focus on the historical timeline that serves as a backdrop for the actions of the novel's characters.[28] In contrast with the broader scope of historical study, my analysis has taken as its object the microtemporalities of strategic action, communication, and interiority, in the events, dialogues, and monologues of Lafayette's novel, time structures characteristic of court life in the time of Louis XIV. I have operated on the understanding, then, that *La Princesse de Clèves*, while situated historically in the court of Henri II (1519–59), can be interpreted also within the historical context of the 1670s, when the work was first discussed and published.[29] The rapid rhythms of action and the animated, often disjunctive temporalities of characters' participation in and reactions to events represent a particular way of knowing about the world. I am arguing that *La Princesse de Clèves* reflects an increasing emphasis that was being placed, in seventeenth-century France, on the rates at which knowledge could be acquired and on how quickly and efficiently this information could be put to use or communicated to others.

As literature became news, in the pages of Donneau de Visé's *Mercure galant*, the importance of accelerated processes of knowledge acquisition and transmission was evident in early modern proto-journalistic practices. Readers of the *Mercure*, who gave accounts of their discussions and reading practices, revealed acute time-consciousness and informational acquisitiveness. The similarity between the processes by which Lafayette's novel was anticipated, disseminated, and discussed on the one hand, and plot elements of strategic anticipation, communication, and interiority within the novel on the other, establishes a close relationship between *La Princesse de Clèves* and the discourses surrounding the work's publication. Part of the significance of Lafayette's novel's appearance as an early modern literary event lay in the fact that the literary work was implicated in practices of information acquisition and transmission that served publicity interests.

On a more theoretical level, the princess and other characters prepare the way for modern literary subjectivity. In the anticipatory strategic actions of Lafayette's characters, one critic sees the "audacious conduct, with carefully calculated risk, that announces the imaginative comportment of Stendhalian heroes."[30] It could be argued as well that the novel's plotlines of rapidly shifting power networks, mapped out on channels of epistolary and verbal communication, pointed in the direction the novel would take toward *Les Liaisons dangereuses* in the eighteenth century. Perhaps the most intriguing legacy of Lafayette and the most radical literary innovation accomplished by *La Princesse de Clèves*, the novel's discourses of interiority, with their heterogeneous and agitated temporalities, initiated reflections on subjectivity and its self-reflexive ambivalences that continue to find narrative expression to the present day.

Lafayette's princess stands as an intriguing representative of the early modern subject, open to and cognizant of new spheres of personal temporal experience while at the same time constrained by the external forces of social life. The court as it is constructed in *La Princesse de Clèves* operates as a kind of clockwork or timetable, both imposing time structures on the individuals caught up in its functioning and providing zones of private activity in the interstices of its required activities. The princess's final withdrawal from the court, perhaps the most puzzling of the fictional events in Lafayette's novel, opens onto a void that points to the quintessential paradox of early modern time: the new and private forms of its understanding that went hand in hand with and were partially a result of new patterns of structured time imposed by government and collective life. Both a victory and a defeat, the princess's final exit from the narrative silently affirms the significance, in the face of growing public time pressures, of the new time of the individual, the time of personal choice and private experience.

# Epilogue

*The process of assimilating real historical time and space in literature has a complicated and erratic history, as does the articulation of actual historical persons in such a time and space. Isolated aspects of time and space, however—those available in a given historical stage of human development—have been assimilated, and corresponding generic techniques have been devised for reflecting and artistically processing such appropriated aspects of reality.*
— M. M. Bakhtin, *The Dialogic Imagination*

EVERY CULTURE AND ERA OF HUMAN HISTORY HAS ITS OWN WAYS OF knowing time. Particular modes of understanding temporality characterize civilizations, in terms of their construction of knowledge, their predominant structures of daily life, and their generic forms of temporal representation. In our own times, as we begin the twenty-first century, the conceptualization and experience of time has become increasingly dependent on processes of communication and on the dissemination of information. Along with the accelerated temporal dynamics characteristic of the information age, present-day subjects have to reckon with the schedules of work and family life and the time structures of organized social life, influenced more and more strongly by technologies of transportation, information, and consumerism. In contrast to all of these forms of collective or public time, private time can be tracked by watching the clock over a lunch hour, eyeing the calendar during a vacation, or feeling the familiar duration of a favorite musical composition or film. Even though the temporalities of social organization have become highly complex, precise, and demanding, the individual subject continues to assert itself in seeking, living, and representing alternative temporalities.

In order better to understand the temporal challenges faced by the individual in a particular sociocultural setting, it is illuminating to look at ways in which subjects and societies have experienced and constructed time in the past. I have argued in this book that France in the seventeenth century constitutes a key moment of change for the social and subjective ideation of time. Technological advances like the pendu-

185

lum clock and the watch furnished with a spiral spring regulator provided new opportunities for chronometry, initially in scientific endeavor. The technologies available to the scientific community then increasingly influenced administrative activity, social life, and eventually even private life, as the audible analysis of duration made possible by early modern timepieces created new avenues for self-tracking. Alongside the first manifestations of the epistemology of temporal quantity and the science of structuring work, new domains of individual experience came into existence, sometimes as a form of resistance to the constraints of public life and sometimes as a kind of paradoxical complement to the scheduling of the collectivity, through which the government was able to assume public functions that created the very possibility of private life and private time.

The subject's feeling and understanding of time in seventeenth-century France found artistic expression most notably in literary works. In authors like Molière, Sévigné, and Lafayette (among others), figurative language, description, dialogue, and narration give nuanced accounts of the early modern understanding of time. From strategic timing in action to interior modes of temporal reflection, the literary temporalities of the authors studied here elaborate a highly complex relative present, within which individuals grapple with recent-past and near-future time frames in order to gain an understanding of their world. At times triumphing over and against temporal structures imposed from without, at other times overwhelmed by the difficulty of living in a world of rapidly changing temporalities, these literary subjects manifest many of the temporal dynamics that newly came to structure their age, and they speak for their age through their ways of knowing and living with time.

What can we learn from the literature and culture of seventeenth-century France as we try in our own lives to come to terms with the nature of twenty-first-century temporalities? The first lesson that can be drawn from the study of time in other periods and cultures is clearly that of heterochrony, or the fact that time takes many and varied forms, according to the historically localized modes of its ideation and representation. In a sense, the greatest danger posed by structured time in social and individual life is the potential misapprehension of a perfectly natural, normal, self-evident temporality, an inescapable pace of living common to all. The assumption that life's rhythm can only be and has always been *métro, boulot, dodo* [subway, job, nighty-night] constitutes a kind of temporal cognitive fossilization to which the activity of critical cultural history can offer corrective insights. The relativization of time concepts that necessarily arises from studying changes in the understanding of time through history disallows the kind of monolithic thinking of time that can produce conceptual-temporal fossilization.

The epistemological shifts in the understanding of time that took place in the wake of Huygensian chronometry are a prime example of how the study of cultural history makes us rethink assumptions we may have about fundamental aspects of our own contemporary lives. At the origins of precision timekeeping we can catch glimpses of its other, a more fluid understanding of time that is entirely independent of the steady ticking of quantification. The tension between the two tendencies in temporal understanding poses an irreducible question, that of the nature of time itself, and brings us back to some of the underlying assumptions we have about what time is and how it inflects our daily lives. Like St. Augustine, when we begin asking ourselves what exactly time is for us, we begin to see how difficult it is to arrive at an answer. That very difficulty, however, is the greatest protection we have against the subjective stasis caused by the implicit acceptance of time structures imposed by the collectivity.

When we are confronted by the aporia of philosophical speculation on time, we can seek interpretive possibilities in works of literature, for figurative, textual representation constitutes one of the most suggestive and detailed ways of knowing time available to us. The subject formations that we find there may, like Mme de Sévigné, offer us insight, solace, and inspiration as we come to terms with a relative present that threatens to disorient us severely but within which we must maintain a clear sense of who we are and what matters to us. The highly complex and varied language of the marquise allows us to glimpse time in some of its most ineffable manifestations and to deepen our understanding of its representation and conceptualization. Mme de Lafayette's dramatizations of tightly wound practices and events in social life offer critical perspectives on the structure of organized life and the challenges the individual faces there. With Molière, we follow patterns of sociability and communication in carefully constructed dialogues that reveal, in finely tuned dynamics of utterance, how time structures of speech and action can be used and abused in the familiar arena of the household. All of these works reveal aspects of the sociohistorical developments — for the purposes of this study, those pertaining to the measurement and understanding of time — that frame their composition, production, and publication, while at the same time suggesting new ways of knowing public and private time, through the drama, performed and/or recounted, of individuals in tension with the society that surrounds them.

One of the main battlegrounds on which this drama plays itself out is the face of a clock or watch.

The struggle to know and manage time in our daily lives requires a recognition of the historical fact that time has never been the same and has always taken forms whose justifications are grounded in specific prerogatives. Leading up to the high industrial era of the nineteenth century, temporal structures of social life were motivated and justified increasingly by an economics of production. While the Taylorist understanding of time is still very much with us today, the more mercurial dynamics of cybernetic information transmission exert an influence at present that may be just as powerful. What must not be forgotten within the epistemological shift of our times is that we face perhaps the most harrowing temporality that humankind has ever had to confront — the race against time and against the forces of environmental destruction that we have unleashed on our world. A digital display like the one in the Baltimore aquarium, which shows acres of South American rainforest disappearing with the passing seconds of a patron's visit, may be the most important kind of clock for our times, one that we may wish to watch with greater attention even than the clock ominously sounding the end of our lunch hour. As the twenty-first century will no doubt reveal, the greatest challenge of a heterochronous understanding of our world will be to learn from past ages in examining our own relative present, so that we may still have a fighting chance, as did the innovators of the early modern world, at a productive future.[1]

# Notes

## INTRODUCTION

1. Saint Augustine, *The Confessions*, 295.

2. See Paul Ricœur, *Temps et récit*, for an elegantly phrased argument for the temporal evocativeness and specificity of literature. See also Stuart Sherman, *Telling Time: Clocks, Diaries, and English Diurnal Form, 1660–1785*, ix–x, for a compelling etymological discussion of the relation between the words "tell" and "toll," as for a bell in a clock tower.

3. Sherman, *Telling Time*, 3.

4. Ibid., 87.

5. Ibid., ix–x.

6. Ricœur, *Temps et récit*, 21. Unless otherwise indicated, all translations are my own.

7. Ibid., 13.

8. Williams, *Marxism and Literature*, 132–33. A discussion of Williams's idea appears, in the context of temporalities of early modern experience, in Sherman, *Telling Time*, 25–26.

9. Sherman's difficulty is in connecting the diurnal, the marking of dates in prose, to the experience of smaller temporalities like hours, minutes, and seconds, key aspects of the new temporalities he describes through his analyses of diurnal writing.

10. Sherman, *Telling Time*, 21.

11. Thompson, "Time, Work-Discipline, and Industrial Capitalism," 93–94.

12. Chartier, ed., *A History of Private Life. III*, 361.

13. Ariès, "Introduction" in *A History of Private Life. III*, 9.

14. Gordon analyzes the unregulated spaces of social life within which individuals under Louis XIV found opportunities for self-actualization and sociability (*Citizens Without Sovereignty*, 7–8).

15. Chartier, ed., *A History of Private Life. III*, 400.

16. Ibid., 399.

17. The present study follows Stuart Sherman's concise definition of temporality as "a way of conceiving time, using it, inhabiting it" (*Telling Time*, x).

18. Sherman, *Telling Time*, 5, 87.

19. Ibid.

20. Ibid., 4.

21. Ibid., 11.

22. Michel Foucault, *Discipline and Punish*, 165.

23. Ibid., 157.

24. Ibid., 139.

25. Ibid., 140.

26. Ibid., 154.
27. Ibid., 139.
28. Sherman, *Telling Time*, 28.
29. Ricœur, *Temps et récit*, 13.

# CHAPTER 1

1. Belmont, *La Montre*, 37–38.
2. Chapiro, *La Montre française*, 7.
3. More specifically, early watches were worn around the neck. In the seventeenth century, pocket watches came into being and remained the predominant mode of personal timekeeping, eventually giving way to the wristwatch (and quartz technology) that holds preeminence to the present day.
4. Defossez, *Les Savants du XVIIe siècle et la mesure du temps*, 329.
5. Bruton, *The History of Clocks and Watches*, 110.
6. Quoted in Bedini, *The Pulse of Time*, 24.
7. The famous legend has it that Galileo first conceived of the pendulum as a chronometrical instrument when observing a lamp swinging in an arch of the cathedral of Pisa. In 1581 or 1582, he timed the swings of the lamps against his pulse (Macey, *Clocks and the Cosmos*, 26). "Galileo's lamp," installed in the cathedral in 1587, is still a tourist attraction in Pisa (Sobel, *Galileo's Daughter*, 358 n).
8. Quoted in Cardinal, *La montre*, 30.
9. Perrault, *Parallèle des Anciens et des Modernes*, 72. Spelling of quotations from seventeenth-century sources has been modernized throughout.
10. Ibid., 86–87.
11. Landes, *Revolution in Time*, 108.
12. Ames, *Colbert, Mercantilism, and the French Quest for Asian Trade*, 53.
13. Murat, *Colbert*, 269. See also Dessert, *La Royale*.
14. Murat, *Colbert*, 273.
15. The excitement was indeed mainly Colbert's. Louis XIV was notoriously indifferent, in the early stages, to the navy, visiting his first ship only in 1681. French men unfortunate enough to be sent out as prisoners on a *galère* or Africans sold into the growing slave trade, undoubtedly the most odious aspect of expansionism under Colbert, stood to lose their lives and families in the dangerous gamble of sea travel.
16. Macey, *Clocks and the Cosmos*, 28.
17. Huygens would spend his career embroiled in similar contests of primacy. In the end, it appears as though he had to expend as much energy substantiating his claims as he did perfecting the devices for which he is now generally recognized. The difficulties and acrimonious competition that Huygens encountered during every stage of his career highlight the intense interest that technicians and political figures alike shared in the science of time-measurement.
18. Hahn, *The Anatomy of a Scientific Institution*, 10.
19. *Journal des savants*, 11 February 1675, 68–69.
20. See Sobel, *Longitude*.
21. Brown, *Jean Domenique Cassini and his World Map of 1696*, 26–27.
22. Thrower, *Maps and Civilization*, 92.
23. Sobel, *Longitude*, 24–25.

24. Brown, *Jean Domenique Cassini and his World Map of 1696*, 18.

25. Ibid., 37.

26. France would officially recognize Greenwich Mean Time only in 1911 (Sobel, *Longitude*, 168). For a discussion of French resistance to Greenwich Mean Time in the nineteenth century, see Blaise, *Time Lord*, 196–213.

27. Brown, *Jean Domenique Cassini and his World Map of 1696*, 26.

28. The full title, printed around the outside border of the circular map, reads *Planisphère terrestre où sont marquées les Longitudes de divers Lieux de la Terre, trouvées par les observations des Eclipses des Satellites de Jupiter*. The original versions of this map, in two different stages, or states, are located at the *Bibliothèque Nationale de France* (BN Ge.DD.2987 and Ge.C.8479) for state 1 and the Clements and Yale University Library for state 2. A smaller-scale reproduction of the map was published by Jean-Baptiste Nolin in 1696, by which time cartographical publishing and mapmaking were flourishing in France:

> With two notable exceptions—Oronce Fine and Guillaume Postel—early French cartographical activity had ranked well below that of the Italians, Germans or the Dutch. However, from the beginning of the seventeenth century Paris developed as one of the most important secondary publishing centres outside of the Netherlands. Nearly all the standard Dutch atlases were issued with French text and co-publications of editions, and of individual maps, is not infrequently found (Shirley, *The Mapping of the World*, XXXIX).

29. Shirley, *The Mapping of the World*, 573.

30. Zumthor, *La Mesure du monde*, 333. Dorling and Fairbairn locate the transition before Cassini in the work of one of France's most famous mapmakers, Nicolas Sanson:

> Early seventeenth-century mapping, especially at small scales, but even for large-scale maps used as working documents, had been highly decorative with considerable embellishment on the map face in the form of heraldic devices such as coats of arms, sketches and portraits, swirling and detailed title boxes and pictures of heavenly cherubs. The reformation in cartography, however, supplanted this pictorial tradition. The new cartography in France, introduced by its first official cartographer, Nicolas Sanson (1600–1667), also relied less on scholarly compilation of written descriptions and more on instruments and measurement. (Dorling and Fairbairn, *Mapping*, 18)

31. Brotton, *Trading Territories*, 153–79.

32. Improvements in accuracy by the end of the seventeenth century were considerable. Mercator's projections, for example, distort the surface area of land masses to such an extent that "two-thirds of the earth's surface appears to lie in high latitudes" (Harley, "Maps, Knowledge and Power," 290). Cartography in the sixteenth and seventeenth centuries still had a long way to go, both in calculating and in visually representing longitude.

33. Harley, "Maps, Knowledge and Power," 279.

34. Ibid., 300.

35. See Crosby, *The Measure of Reality*, for an account of the increasing conceptual significance of quantification in medieval and early modern Europe.

36. Cardinal, *La montre*, 70.

37. It was also during this period that the circular shape for watches became the predominant one, supplanting the wide variety of shapes that came before.

38. Chapiro, *La Montre française*, 50. A number of *oignons* can be seen in the perma-

nent collection of the Louvre, among the "Objets d'art, XVIIe." See Cardinal, *Les Montres du Musée du Louvre*, cat. nos. 54–59, 62–69. As Catherine Cardinal points out, the *oignons* were mostly made of copper or silver. Few were made in gold, due to the frugality that pervaded artisanal works by the end of the seventeenth century, a time when many objects made of precious metals were melted down. In the Louvre catalog, Cardinal cites this reason for the rarity of *oignons* in the present day (Cardinal, *Les Montres du Musée du Louvre*, 68). Some examples, like one signed Champclou, labeled "Paris, milieu XVIIe," have metal cases with elaborate engraved floral designs. Others have cases of studded Moroccan leather. A horologer named Dagneau of Grenoble produced a number of *oignons*. One signed Martinot features a portrait of Louis XIV in profile. N° 54 in the catalog is by Nicolas Gribelin, Paris, *Montre "oignon,"* gold and gilded copper, enamel, Moroccan leather, diameter 5.9 cm, thickness 4.4 cm, dated end of seventeenth century.

Some examples of *oignons* can also be seen at the *Musée international d'horlogerie*, La Chaux-de-fonds, Switzerland: see the *Collections du Musée international d'Horlogerie*. For an extensive listing of early clock and watchmakers, see the *Dictionnaire des horlogers français*.

39. "Watches without the spiral spring were crude instruments for mesuring time; the best among them were still off by fifteen minutes a day. The invention of the spiral spring, like that of the pendulum, considerably improved watches, the precision of which could approach a margin of error of one minute a day with the mechanism as it was constructed in the seventeenth century" (Defossez, *Les Savants du XVIIe siècle et la mesure du temps*, 242).

40. Chapiro, *La Montre française*, 28.

41. Bruton, *The History of Clocks and Watches*, 115.

42. Quoted in Cardinal, *La montre*, 78.

43. Catherine Cardinal explains the significance of Protestantism for horology in France:

French horology included numerous masters who were members of the Reformation. They played an important role in the development of this science from the middle of the sixteenth century to the middle of the seventeenth by participating in the creation of great horological centers like Blois and Lyon. Out of 90 Lyonnais clockmakers whose religion is identified by archival documents, 50 were Catholics, while 40 were Protestants. The Huguenot masters brought horology to cities favorable to the Reformation, like Rouen, Sedan, and La Rochelle. In these places, a veritable correlation was created between the degree of development of horological arts and the proportion of Huguenots who worked there. (Cardinal, *La montre*, 38)

44. Ibid., 38.

45. Cippola, *Clocks and Culture*, 64.

46. Quoted in Cardinal, *La montre*, 30.

47. The listing offers these specificifications: "Une grande montre ronde sonnante à boîte d'or sous émail gravée dont le mouvement est de Macé horlogeur à Blois, prisée la somme de mille livres;" "Une autre grande montre sonnante ronde à boîte de laiton doré dont le mouvement est de Grégoire à Blois, prisée la somme de trois cents livres tournois;" "Une autre grande montre sonnante ronde dont le mouvement est de Pierre Le Roux à Blois à boîte d'or sous émail . . . cadran émaillé de vert, prisée la somme de mille livres tournois;" "Une autre grande montre sonnante ronde dont le mouvement est de Jean Roux à Blois à boîte d'or le cadran émaillé de vert, prisée pareille somme

mille livres;" "Item une autre montre sonnante ronde à boîte d'argent dont le mouvement du nommé . . . à Saumur, prisée la somme de cent cinquante livres" [A large
round watch with alarm in a gold case under engraved enamel, mechanism by Macé,
clockmaker in Blois, evaluated at the sum of 1,000 livres; Another large round watch
with alarm in a gilded brass case, mechanism by Grégoire of Blois, evaluated at the sum
of 300 Tournois livres; Another large round watch with alarm, mechanism by Pierre Le
Roux of Blois, gold casing with enamel . . . watch face in green enamel, evaluated at
the sum of 1,000 Tournois livres; Another large round watch with alarm, mechanism
by Jean Roux of Blois, gold casing with green enamel, priced equally at 1,000 livres;
Also, another round watch with alarm, silver casing, priced at the sum of 150 livres]
(BN, *Département des manuscrits, mélanges Colbert*, 75, 6v–7r).

48. Ibid., 9r–9v.
49. Pardailhé-Galabrun, *La Naissance de l'intime.*
50. Ibid., 86.
51. Ibid., 131.
52. Ibid., 141.
53. Ibid., 144.
54. Ibid., 145.
55. Ibid., 146.
56. Ibid., 147.
57. Ibid., 396.
58. Balthazar de Bonnecorse, *La Montre*. Subsequent quotations from this work are
cited parenthetically in the text.
59. Flotte, "Les poètes de Marseille. Balthazar de Bonnecorse," 121.
60. Aphra Behn, *La Montre: or the Lover's Watch.*
61. Boileau, *Œuvres complètes de Boileau*, 234.
62. Balthazar de Bonnecorse, *La montre, seconde partie*. Subsequent quotations from
this work are cited parenthetically in the text.
63. Aphra Behn, *The Works of Aphra Behn*, 284. Subsequent quotations from this
work, which I draw on for translations of selected passages from Bonnecorse (all other
translations are my own), are cited parenthetically in the text.
64. Half-hours were customarily marked on the faces of seventeenth-century
watches. Later in the century, some watches began to mark quarter-hours as well, in
anticipation of the eighteenth-century innovation of a consistent minute hand.
65. *Le Mercure galant*, March 1678, 172. Subsequent quotations from this periodical
are cited parenthetically in the text.
66. Sherman, *Telling Time*, 88.

## CHAPTER 2

Molière, *Œuvres complètes*, 1:831. Subsequent quotations from the Couton edition of
Molière are cited parenthetically in the text. This includes references to Molière (see
note 31 below), Félibien, and Benserade. This chapter will refer to the title—*Le Tartuffe
ou l'imposteur*—of the play's definitive version, first published in 1669. The guide to the
"Plaisirs de l'île enchantée" mentions "une comédie nommée *Tartuffe*" [a comedy named
*Tartuffe*] (1:828). The 1664 version also carried the title "L'Hypocrite," the name used
in the *Gazette*'s article of 17 May 1664 announcing the interdiction of the play by Louis

XIV, at the behest of the *Compagnie du Saint Sacrement*, a religious secret society with strong connections to the queen mother. While it had delighted some spectators during the "Plaisirs de l'île enchantée," the first *Tartuffe* shocked others by staging the character of a cynical manipulator and social parasite in the clothing of a priest (Molière, *Œuvres complètes*, 1:838). A revised version, in which Molière attempted to attenuate his satire of zealotry and to ward off further attacks from his harshest critics, would appear in 1667. This second version, called *L'Imposteur*, centered around a character named Panulphe, who appeared onstage wearing a sword, a wide collar (the opposite of the modest "petit collet" worn by the clergy), long hair, and lace. The idea was that men of religion would not see themselves in the flashy, wordly person of this impostor. A man of the world and not of the cloth, Panulphe was to deflect Molière's critiques away from the devout personages whom the playwright had so irked. However, Molière's trenchant attacks on religious hypocrisy continued to resound beneath the play's superficial alterations of 1667, and the work was banned until 1669, when the definitive version would take up once again the name of *Le Tartuffe* (Tartuffe himself wore somber, neutral clothing in 1669).

1. The version of *Le Tartuffe* that Molière presented on 12 May 1664 consisted of three acts, not the five of the 1669 version. The question of which three acts figured in the *Tartuffe* of 1664 remains open. La Grange, an actor in Molière's troupe who would become in 1682 the first editor of Molière's complete works, claimed that the three acts of the *Tartuffe* of 1664 were the first three. See Schérer, *Structures de* Tartuffe, 45. See also Cairncross, *Molière bourgeois et libertin*, 118–64. Cairncross has argued that La Grange committed an error of memory in recording events long after their completion. According to this argument, the first three acts could never make up an entire play, because the central character, Tartuffe himself, only appears in the third act, the ending of which could not serve as a dramatic dénouement according to seventeenth-century theatrical conventions. Cairncross claims that the first version consisted of acts 1, 3, and 4. The present chapter subscribes to neither view and analyzes time structures in the *Tartuffe* as a whole, accepting the calculated risk that some textual elements in the play's definitive version may not have factored explicitly in the "Plaisirs de l'île enchantée."

2. Levron, *La Vie quotidienne à la cour de Versailles*, 26. Le Vau built Vaux-le-Vicomte, which was a kind of model for Versailles. Fouquet's château was ornamented by Charles Le Brun (1619–90), who would be put in charge of decorating Versailles, and landscaped by André Le Nôtre (1613–1700), who contributed significantly to designing the gardens and fountains of Versailles.

3. *Versailles in the Age of Louis XIV*, 55.

4. Mitford, *The Sun King*, 22.

5. Molière, *Œuvres complètes*, 1:743.

6. 1st *intermède* [a kind of overture to the first act], scene 2.

7. Paris *Gazette*, 483. Subsequent quotations from this periodical will be cited parenthetically in the text.

8. The connection between virtually instantaneous acts of organization and royal authority, more specifically in the context of military prowess, would become more explicit in Félibien's account of the "Grand Divertissement Royal de Versailles" [Great Royal Divertissement] that celebrated the conquest of the Franche-Comté and the peace treaty of Aix-la-Chapelle in 1668:

> Mais comme il n'y a que le roi qui puisse en si peu de temps mettre de grandes armées sur pied et faire des conquêtes avec cette rapidité que l'on a vue . . . aussi n'appartient-il qu'à ce grand

prince de mettre ensemble avec la même promptitude autant de musiciens, de danseurs et de joueurs d'instruments et tant de différentes beautés. (Félibien, *Relation de la fête de Versailles*, 59)

[But since only the king can assemble great armies in so little time and conquer with the rapidity that we have seen . . . also it is only this great prince who can with similar quickness put together so many musicians, dancers and instrumentalists, and diversely beautiful things]

9. For a study of the codification of bodily attitudes in early modern times, see Vigarello, *Le Corps redressé*.

10. A mechanistic explanation for the functioning of the human organism figures in Thomas Hobbes, *Leviathan*, 61–62. For Descartes's mechanistic conceptions of man and nature and his theories of the separation of body and mind, see *Le Traité de l'homme*, *Le Traité de la mécanique*, and *Le Discours de la méthode* in René Descartes, *Œuvres philosophiques*. Especially revealing is Descartes's discussion of the circulation of blood, a topic that leads him to the concept of clockwork man:

[C]e mouvement, que je viens d'expliquer, suit aussi nécessairement de la seule disposition des organes qu'on peut voir à l'œil dans le cœur, et de la chaleur qu'on y peut sentir avec les doigts, et de la nature du sang qu'on peut connaître par expérience, que fait celui d'une horloge, de la force, de la situation et de la figure de ses contrepoids et de ses roues. (Descartes, *Œuvres philosophiques*, 1:623)

[This movement that I have just explained depends of necessity on the simple arrangement of organs that one can observe in the heart and on the warmth that one can feel with one's fingers, and on the nature of the blood that one can know from experience, just as necessarily as the movement of a clock depends on the force, the disposition, and the shape of its cogs and wheels.]

For studies of the impact of Cartesian rationalism on seventeenth-century culture, see Stone, *The Classical Model*, and Reiss, *Knowledge, Discovery and Imagination in Early Modern Europe*. A radically mechanistic explanation of human life would be developed in the eighteenth century by Julien Offray de la Mettrie — see *Machine Man and Other Writings*.

For a satirical representation of the mechanics of court life, see La Bruyère, *Les Caractères*. In "De la cour," La Bruyère compares the behaviors and attitudes of the courtier to the regular movements of a watch: "Les roues, les ressorts, les mouvements sont cachés; rien ne paraît d'une montre que son aiguille, qui insensiblement s'avance et achève son tour: image du courtisan, d'autant plus parfaite qu'après avoir fait assez de chemin, il revient souvent au même point d'où il est parti" [The wheels, the springs, the movements are all hidden; only the hands of a watch are visible, as they advance imperceptibly, going full-circle: this is the very image of the courtier, all the more perfect because, after he has covered enough ground, he often returns to the same point of departure] (*Les Caractères*, 205).

11. For a discussion of the etymologies of "machine" and "engin," in the context of Vauban's (1633–1707) military engineering under Louis XIV, see DeJean, *Literary Fortifications*, 22–23.

12. Du Crest, *Des fêtes à Versailles*, 95.

13. Quoted in Du Crest, *Des fêtes à Versailles*, 82.

14. Apostolidès, *Le Roi-machine*, 5.

15. Quoted in Elias, *The Court Society*, 131.

16. Verlet and Mesnage, *La Mesure du temps*, 86.

17. Levron, *La Vie quotidienne à la cour de Versailles*, 41.
18. Elias, *The Court Society*, 84.
19. Levron, *La Vie quotidienne à la cour de Versailles*, 41.
20. Quoted in Elias, *The Court Society*, 89.
21. Levron, *La Vie quotidienne à la cour de Versailles*, 48.
22. Ibid., 46.
23. Ibid., 49.
24. Mettam, *Power and Faction in Louis XIV's France*, 53.
25. Elias, *The Court Society*, 94.
26. Ibid., 111.
27. Moore, "Le Goût de la cour," 181.
28. Schérer, *Structures de Tartuffe*, 36.
29. Vernet, *Molière côté jardin, côté cour*, 36.
30. Artaud, *Le Théâtre et son double*, 134–35.
31. Poulet, *Etudes sur le temps humain*, 83.
32. All quotations from Molière are from the Couton edition and will be indicated parenthetically in the text in the following format: act.scene.line(s). For this first quotation, the citation would be referenced: (1.1.1). Translations of *Le Tartuffe* are all taken from Molière, *The Misanthrope and Other Plays*, trans. John Wood.
33. Richelet defines the idiomatic expression "la cour du roi Pétaut" as any place characterized by disorder and confusion. "Roi Pétaut" refers also to the king of vagabonds (Molière, *Œuvres complètes*, 1:1335–36 n. 1).
34. Chambers, "Gossip and the Novel," 213.
35. Both the notion of a host and of an attachment to the host can be understood in the biological terms of parasitism. See Serres, *Le Parasite*, 271–79.
36. Le Goff, "Au Moyen Age: Temps de l'Eglise et temps du marchand," 417.

## CHAPTER 3

1. For a survey of published correspondences from the early modern period, see Altman, "The Letter Book as a Literary Institution." See also Jean-Louis Guez de Balzac, *Œuvres de Monsieur de Balzac*; Rathery and Boutron, *Mademoiselle de Scudéry: Sa vie et sa correspondance*; Vincent Voiture, *Œuvres de Voiture*.
2. Marie de Rabutin-Chantal, marquise de Sévigné, *Correspondance*. The history of Sévigné's letters as literary works began when the marquise's cousin Bussy-Rabutin gave a small number of them to Louis XIV in 1680. These were letters the marquise had written during the years 1673–75 and represented, according to Bussy, some of his cousin's best writing. While Sévigné worried that she might be misinterpreted, she assured her cousin that he had "rien fait que de bien, et c'en est un fort grand de pouvoir divertir un tel homme, et d'être en commerce avec lui" [undoubtedly done a good thing, and it is a considerable good to be able to entertain such a man and to be in communication with him] (1.17.81, 3:60–61—Subsequent Sévigné references are to the Duchêne edition and will be indicated parenthetically within the text, in the format used above, with date, volume, and page numbers, respectively). Around the time of the marquise's death, selections from her letters appeared in 1696 and 1697, as part of Bussy-Rabutin's memoirs and correspondence, respectively. An anonymous collection of 28 letters appeared in Troyes in 1725. In the same year, an edition containing 134 letters was pub-

lished in Rouen. This latter book included a preface by Bussy, but did not have the approval of Sévigné's granddaughter, Pauline de Simiane, who was very protective of her family's letters. The marquise's granddaughter destroyed almost all of her own mother Mme de Grignan's letters and, though Mme de Simiane did work with publishers of Sévigné's writing, starting with Denis-Marius de Perrin in 1734, she eventually destroyed all but 40 or 4.65% of her grandmother's letters as well. See *Madame de Sévigné*. Almost a decade after a third unofficial edition of 177 letters appeared in the Hague in 1726, the first official edition of Sévigné's letters was published in 1734. Perrin's work of editing and presenting the letters to the public resulted from an often difficult collaboration with Mme de Simiane. He succeeded nevertheless in publishing, in his own revised form, over 700 of Sévigné's letters from 1734 to 1754. In the nineteenth century, the first critical edition of the marquise's correspondence appeared, in 10 volumes containing 1305 letters. This was Monmerqué's first edition of Sévigné. This careful editor would then present the Sévigné letters in 14 volumes, containing more than 1,500 letters, in 1862, as part of the "Grands Ecrivains de la France" series. Monmerqué drew on new manuscript sources and provided a critical apparatus of notes, biographical information, and sources. In 1873, Charles Capmas, a professor of law in Dijon, discovered a set of copies of Sévigné's letters. He published these new findings in the *Lettres inédites* of 1876. With the Gérard-Gailly edition of 1953–57 and the masterful Duchêne edition of 1972–78, scholars have access today to hundreds of what appear, through a complex history of anonymous and "official" editions and lost manuscript copies, to be Sévigné's letters (1:755–832). The difficulty of tracing Sévigné's letters back to their sources leaves questions of authenticity suspended, while the enigma of their historically and esthetically evocative power continues to intrigue scholars.

3. For analyses of the relation between the Sévigné correspondence and postal history, see Charbon et al., "La Correspondance de Mme de Sévigné"; Duchêne, "Mme de Sévigné et la poste."

4. Duchêne, "Art et hasard," 139–40.

5. These bi-weekly mail deliveries between Paris and other cities and towns date from 1630, when a royal edict required messengers to travel twice a week with mail cargo, under the supervision of the postal system, on all French mail routes passing through the capital. See Laurent, *Poste et postiers*, 10. In the early seventeenth century and during the Renaissance, mail was a service reserved for the use of the king or within the university system. A postal institution accessible to all citizens for a fee was a creation of Richelieu: "While . . . Louis XI had created a postal system devoted exclusively to the service of the state; while Henri III, with his edict of November 1576 had definitively created the service of messengers; and while Henri IV had organized the postal system with horses, Richelieu definitively placed the mails at the disposal of the public and truly created the modern postal system" (Laurent, *Poste et postiers*, 9). The standardization of cost for transport of mail dates from 1627, and the existence of a fixed date of dispatch for all courriers of the system dates back to 1622. When Henri IV created postal relays for messengers traveling by horse, in an effort to improve agricultural commerce, the faster relays served only the king and his ministers.

There was no centralized postal system serving both the government and population during the sixteenth century. For an account of difficulties and delays encountered by merchants in fourteenth-century Italy, who wrote an increasing number of letters at a time when no centralized postal system was yet in existence, see Jardine, *Worldly Goods*,

111. Daily life, which in the case of letter-writers was inflected by the postal schedule, changed from the sixteenth century to the seventeenth, and so did the understanding of time, which became more regularized and precise in the seventeenth century, as centralized institutions began taking shape.

6. Rothschild, *Histoire de la poste aux lettres*, 67, 90.

7. Graziani, *La grande aventure de la poste*, 47.

8. Belloc, *Les Postes françaises*, 116.

9. Rolland, "La naissance de la poste moderne," 52.

10. LeNain, *La Poste de l'Ancienne France*, 12.

11. Vaillé, *Histoire générale des postes françaises*, vol. 4, 13.

12. Ibid., 15.

13. Ibid., 20.

14. Ibid., 83.

15. Beik, *Absolutism and Society in Seventeenth-century France*, 280–81.

16. Quoted in Belloc, *Les Postes françaises*, 116.

17. Vaillé, *Histoire générale des postes françaises*, vol. 4, 82.

18. Louis XIV, *Mémoires*, 48.

19. Charbon, *Quelle belle invention que la poste!*, 40.

20. *Liste alphabétique des villes et lieux tant de ce Royaume que des païs Etrangers, où les Couriers des Postes de France portent les Lettres & Paquets, & les jours & heures de leur départ, pour l'année 1675*, 1–6.

21. Louvois correspondence, Archives nationales, t. 640, 14 avril 1680 (quoted in Vaillé, *Histoire générale des postes françaises*, 111).

22. Musée de la Poste, Carton 330, 23 mai 1666.

23. Belloc, *Les Postes françaises*, 133.

24. Musée de la Poste, Carton 330 D/289.

25. Quoted in Vaillé, *Histoire générale des postes françaises*, vol. 4, 94.

26. Ibid.

27. Belloc, *Les Postes françaises*, 114.

28. Vaillé, *Histoire générale des postes françaises*, vol. 4, 130.

29. Ibid., 106.

30. Quoted in Vaillé, *Histoire générale des postes françaises*, vol. 4, 107.

31. Vaillé, *Histoire générale des postes françaises*, vol. 4, 107.

32. Ibid., 110.

33. Ibid., 107.

34. Ibid., 108.

35. Ibid., 111. Louvois had authorized the *maîtres de poste* to search any packages weighing more than 60 *livres* "and to confiscate for their profit anything they may find." The messengers did not approve of their cargo being systematically inspected: "Naturally, even if the couriers could not protest Louvois's decision, they took advantage of this intervention of the postmasters, who searched all of them, in order to add a day to the trip from Paris to Lyon; but the Superintendent was not the kind of man who would give in to this." Delays were punished strictly and promptly in the continuing effort to minimize time lags.

36. B. N. Thoisy 433, f° 387–88.

37. B. N. Thoisy 433, f° 419.

38. Bercé, *La vie quotidienne*, 53.

39. Jacques Derrida points out what he sees as the inevitable link between postal

and penal institutions: "With the progress of the postal system, the state police has always gained ground" (Derrida, *La Carte postale*, 43).

40. Certeau, *L'Invention du quotidien. 1. Arts de faire*. To use Gaston Bachelard's terminology, individual temporal patterns of activity could be termed "chronotropismes." See Bachelard, *L'Intuition de l'instant*, 72.

41. Certeau, *L'Invention du quotidien. 1. Arts de faire*, 295.

42. Ibid., 134, 295.

43. Richet, *La France moderne: l'esprit des institutions*, 67.

44. I use the term "rhetorical," here and elsewhere in the chapter, to designate language strategies that Sévigné invented according to her own objectives for expression, in order to impart particular sentiments to specific readers. Sévigné's was a highly personal rhetoric that was in no way determined by the language codes established in seventeenth-century epistolary manuals, the use of which produced, in the marquise's estimation, a laughable "style à cinq sols" [five-and-dime style] (3.18.71, 1:187; 5.18.71, 1:258).

45. Duchêne explains the importance of Fridays for Sévigné in terms of the mechanics of mail delivery between Grignan and Paris, and between Paris and les Rochers:

> The marquise would receive both letters from Provence together because the first one, the one that got to the capital between Saturday and Monday, usually arrived too late to be taken to the postal bureau for Brittany Saturday, so it could be taken to Les Rochers two days later, on Monday. In Paris, it awaited the following *ordinaire*, on Wednesday, and was joined by the letter from Provence that would be arriving that day or the day before. Then both of them would make it to Vitry at the same time, on Friday, which spurred the marquise to write, in a parody of Saint-Pavin, who had previously asked the gods that he might see her more often at Livry: "Multiply the Fridays, I won't hold you accountable for anything else." Indeed, much more than the two dispatches of mail for Provence, it is the single receipt of the two letters from the countess that creates the rhythm of life at Les Rochers and gives Mme de Sévigné's letters their specific tone. (*Réalité vécue*, 295)

46. Bray, "Quelques Aspects du système épistolaire de Madame de Sévigné," 498.

47. Voiture, *Œuvres de Voiture*, 64–65.

48. Sévigné, *Correspondance*, 1:1100 n. 6.

49. Ibid., 2:1132 n. 2.

50. For a history of the time pressures that provincial consuls, councilors, and intendants faced in seventeenth-century France, see Beik, *Absolutism and Society in Seventeenth-century France*, 69–72, 80–85, 100–103.

51. See Longino, *Performing Motherhood*, for a detailed discussion of the complexities of the mother-daughter relationship in the Sévigné correspondence.

52. The peasants of Brittany violently protested increases in taxation in 1675. The government's response was brutal and included torture and hanging of numerous protesters. Sévigné's cool, ironic references to these events have become notorious: "on commence demain les punitions. Cette province est un bel exemple pour les autres, et surtout de respecter les gouverneurs et les gouvernantes, de ne leur point dire d'injures, et de ne point jeter des pierres dans leur jardin" [The punishments begin tomorrow. This province will serve as a nice example to others, especially on the necessity of respecting one's governors and governesses and of not throwing rocks into their gardens] (10.30.75, 2:147). In taking the side of state power, Sévigné was above all concerned for the well-being of her friend the duc de Chaulnes, governor of Brittany, and for the comte de Grignan, her son-in-law, who governed Provence at the time.

53. Derrida, *La Carte postale*, 34.

54. Altman, "The 'Triple Register,'" 310.

55. Bourdieu, *La Distinction*.

56. I have drawn the model of subjective experiences of temporal expansion and contraction from Paul Ricœur's analysis of St. Augustine (*Temps et récit*, 41). For a study of personal experiences of time in Sévigné, see also Mensher, "Problems of Time and Existence in the Letters of Mme de Sévigné."

57. Altman, "The Letter Book," 51.

58. See Hawcroft, "Historical Evidence and Literature," 62. Hawcroft carefully assesses the value of Sévigné's letters as documents: "As evidence about the trial, her letters may be wanting; but as evidence about the interpersonal relations of the aristocracy, they are highly suggestive."

59. Sévigné's letters contain numerous temporal indications that give an account of the trial's scheduling: "[Foucquet] n'est entré qu'à onze heures" [Fouquet only came in at eleven o'clock] (11.27.64, 1:63); "Sur cela, on a dit de faire entrer l'accusé; il était onze heures. Vous remarquerez qu'il n'est pas plus d'une heure sur la sellette" [At that point, the accused was asked to be shown in; it was eleven o'clock. You will notice that he is not on the stand for more than an hour] (11.28.64, 1:64–65); "M. Foucquet a parlé aujourd'hui deux heures entières" [M. Foucquet spoke today for two full hours] (12.2.64, 1:67); "Notre cher et malheureux ami a parlé deux heures ce matin" [Our dear and unfortunate friend spoke for two hours this morning] (12.3.64, 1:68); "Enfin cette interrogation a duré deux heures" [In short, this interrogation lasted for two hours] (12.4.64, 1:69); "Ce matin, Pussort a parlé quatre heures" [This morning, Pussort spoke for four hours] (12.17.64, 1:75); "Roquesante finit la matinée, et après avoir parlé une heure admirablement bien. . . . [Poncet] n'a pas voulu parler, quoiqu'il ne fût qu'onze heures" [Roquesante finished the morning, and after having spoken admirably well for an hour. . . . Poncet did not wish to speak, even though it was only eleven o'clock] (12.19.64, 1:77); "Ce matin à dix heures on a mené M. Foucquet à la chapelle de la Bastille" [This morning at ten Fouquet was taken to the chapel of the Bastille] (12.22.64, 1:79).

60. Duchêne explains the reasons for the messenger's slow rate of travel: "Livry was approximately halfway between Paris and Fresnes; the late hour of the decision and the shortness of the days of the end of December explain why the messenger wanted to stay over" (Sévigné, *Correspondance*, 1:917 n. 4).

61. The marquise reflected also, further in this passage, on how Fouquet himself came to know the nature of his sentence: "Le pauvre homme apprit cette bonne nouvelle par l'air, peu de moments après, et je ne doute point qu'il ne l'ait sentie dans toute son étendue" [The poor man learned this good news a few moments afterwards, and I have no doubt that he felt it through and through] (12.21.64, 1:78). These "peu de moments" specifically situated Fouquet's apprisal in time. Earlier in the trial, Sévigné commented on the temporal exactitude with which Fouquet had wished to be informed of his final sentencing: "[Fouquet] a demandé une chose qui me fait frissonner. Il conjure une de ses amies de lui faire savoir son arrêt par une certaine voie enchantée, . . . afin qu'il ait le temps de se préparer à recevoir la nouvelle . . . ajoutant que pourvu qu'il ait une demi-heure à se préparer, il est capable de recevoir sans émotion tout le pis qu'on lui puisse apprendre" [Fouquet asked something that made me shudder. He urged one of his friends to let him know his sentence by a certain enchanted means, . . . so that he may have the time to prepare himself to receive the news . . . adding that

provided he has half an hour to prepare himself, he is capable of receiving without emotion all the worst that one may pass on to him] (11.18.64, 1:58). The accused had made arrangements to be given a special signal, which would allow him time to compose himself before having to appear in public.

62. Longino, "Writing Letters," 237.

63. The poem "L'Horloge" depicts a second hand that announces the inexorable and destructive passage of time: "Horloge! dieu sinistre, effrayant, impassible, / Dont le doigt nous menace et nous dit: *Souviens-toi! / . . . /* Trois mille six cents fois par heure, la Seconde / Chuchote: *Souviens-toi!* — Rapide, avec sa voix / D'insecte, Maintenant dit: *Je suis Autrefois, / Et j'ai pompé ta vie avec ma trompe immonde!"* [Clock! sinister god, frightening, impassible, whose finger threatens us and tells us: *Remember!* Three thousand six hundred times an hour, the Second whispers: *Remember!* Rapid, with its insect's voice, now says: *I am Before, and I sucked out your life with my filthy snout!*] (*Les Fleurs du mal,* 87).

64. A night of insomnia led Sévigné to a diligent appreciation of temporal increments: "Je n'ai pas fermé les yeux; j'ai compté toutes les heures de ma montre et enfin, à la petite pointe du jour, je me suis levée" [I never closed my eyes; I counted all the hours on my watch and finally, at the break of day, I got up] (11.2.73, 1:609). In a typical moment of lament over delayed mail from Madame de Grignan, the marquise described her subjective relationship to the hands of a clock: "Je regardais ma pendule, et prenais plaisir à penser: voilà comme on est quand on souhaite que cette aiguille marche. Et cependant elle tourne sans qu'on la voie, et tout arrive" [I was watching my clock and taking pleasure in thinking: this is how we are when we want this minute hand to move. And meanwhile it turns without our seeing it, and everything keeps happening] (7.14.80, 2:1008). Sévigné thus at times sought mechanical help in charting the hours, minutes, seconds, and moments of her life. Along with increasing numbers of nobles and wealthy bourgeois who could own portable timepieces, Sévigné used the watch and the clock as a tool for self-tracking.

# Chapter 4

1. For studies of the constitution of a public for reading in seventeenth-century France, especially as concerns *La Princesse de Clèves,* see Merlin, *Public et littérature en France au XVIIe siècle,* 307–49; DeJean, *Tender Geographies,* 94–126.

2. Laugaa, *Lectures de Madame de Lafayette,* 25.

3. "Extraordinaires" were introduced beginning in January 1678. The "Extraordinaires" of April, July, and October 1678 contained letters that were contributed to the periodical publication by its subscribers.

4. Vincent, *Donneau de Visé et "Le Mercure galant,"* 363.

5. Mouligneau, *Madame de Lafayette, romancière?,* 161.

6. Laugaa, *Lectures de Madame de Lafayette,* 42.

7. [J.-A., Abbé de Charnes], *Conversations sur la critique de "La Princesse de Clèves,"* 6. Subsequent references to this work are given parenthetically in the text.

8. [J. B. de Valincour], *Lettres à Madame la marquise \*\*\* sur le sujet de "La Princesse de Clèves,"* 2–3. Subsequent references to this work are given parenthetically in the text.

9. Laugaa, *Lectures de Madame de Lafayette,* 30.

10. Ibid., 26.

11. Vincent, *Donneau de Visé et "Le Mercure galant,"* 221.

12. Ibid., 221.

13. Laugaa, *Lectures de Madame de Lafayette,* 29.

14. Chartier, ed., *A History of Private Life. III,* 111.

15. Ibid., 125.

16. In a discussion regarding the proper use of history for fiction, Valincour invokes Homer and Tacitus, along with Virgil, as models for contemporary writers to follow (90).

17. Genette, *Figures II,* 97.

18. Valincour is highly sensitive to the rhythms of subjective experience in *La Princesse de Clèves,* as evidenced by one of his more lyrical passages of critical prose: "Ces retours de Madame de Clèves sur elle-même, ces agitations, ces pensées différentes qui se détruisenet l'une l'autre, cette différence qui se trouve de ce qu'elle est aujourd'hui avec ce qu'elle était hier, sont des choses qui se passent tous les jours au-dedans de nous-mêmes, que tout le monde sent, mais qu'il y a très peu de personnes qui puissent dépeindre de la manière dont le voyons ici" [These returns of Madame de Clèves to herself, this agitation, these different thoughts that destroy each other, this difference between what she is today and what she was yesterday are things that take place every day in ourselves, and that everyone feels, but there are few people who can describe them in the way we see here] (186–87).

19. The passage in question is the following: "Vous avez de l'inclination pour M. de Nemours; je ne vous demande point de me l'avouer: je ne suis plus en état de me servir de votre sincérité pour vous conduire. Il y a déjà longtemps que je me suis aperçue de cette inclination; mais je ne vous en ai pas voulu parler d'abord, de peur de vous en faire apercevoir vous-même" [You have an affection for Monsieur de Nemours; I do not ask you to confess it, as I am no longer able to make use of your sincerity in order to guide you. It is long since I perceived this affection, but I have been averse to speaking to you about it, lest you should become aware of it yourself] (67; 28). See note 22 below for format of page references to *La Princesse de Clèves.*

20. Valincour does qualify his criticisms of digressions in *La Princesse de Clèves*: he admits that these passages are not extremely long and that they do afford a readerly "plaisir" (22).

21. There is a cynicism involved as well, in the recounting of events in which personal ambitions empty characters of any feeling of loyalty to friends.

22. Mme de Lafayette, *La Princesse de Clèves,* ed. Antoine Adam, 40. All subsequent quotations from *La Princesse de Clèves* are from this edition and are indicated parenthetically within the text. Except in offset quotations, where they are given separately, translations appear as a second page reference, after a semicolon in the same parentheses as the reference to the French text. This first reference, for example, appears as: (40; 7). Unless otherwise indicated, all translations are from *The Princess of Clèves,* ed. John D. Lyons.

23. Certeau, *L'Invention du quotidien. 1. Arts de faire,* 130.

24. Sarlet, "Le Temps dans *La Princesse de Clèves,*" 58.

25. For a study of the subjective significance of private space for the princess in Coulommiers, see Racevskis, "Solitary Pleasures."

26. Paige situates the role of interiority in Lafayette within the context of new forms of subjectivity exemplified by seventeenth-century spiritual autobiography (*Being Interior,* 30, 218–19).

27. See DeJean, "Lafayette's Ellipses."

28. See Francillon, *L'Œuvre romanesque de Madame de Lafayette*; Malandain, *Madame de Lafayette*: La Princesse de Clèves; Moore, "Temporal Structure and Reader Response in *La Princesse de Clèves*."

29. The task of interpretation again requires a calculated risk. For the equally valid study of *La Princesse de Clèves* in the context of sixteenth-century history, see Chamard and Rudler, "Les Sources historiques de *La Princesse de Clèves*."

30. Levillain, *Henriette Levillain présente* La Princesse de Clèves *de Madame de La Fayette*, 90.

# EPILOGUE

1. For further reading on the nature of modern and postmodern temporality and the temporal challenges faced by contemporary society, see Adams, *Timewatch*; Heise, *Chronoschisms*.

# Bibliography

Adams, Barbara. *Timewatch: The Social Analysis of Time*. Cambridge: Polity Press, 1995.

Alkon, Paul Kent. *Defoe and Fictional Time*. Athens: University of Georgia Press, 1979.

Altman, Janet Gurkin. "The 'Triple Register': Introduction to Temporal Complexity in the Letter Novel." *L'Esprit créateur* 1, no. 4 (winter 1977): 302–10.

———. *Epistolarity: Approaches to a Form*. Columbus: Ohio State University Press, 1982.

———. "The Letter Book as a Literary Institution 1539–1789: Toward a Cultural History of Published Correspondences in France." *Yale French Studies* 71 (1986): 17–62.

Ames, Glenn J. *Colbert, Mercantilism, and the French Quest for Asian Trade*. DeKalb: Northern Illinois University Press, 1996.

Apostolidès, Jean-Marie. *Le Roi-machine: Spectacle et politique au temps de Louis XIV*. Paris: Minuit, 1981.

*Archives de l'Armée de terre*. no. 231 (January–February 1669).

Artaud, Antonin. *Le Théâtre et son double*. Paris: Gallimard, [1938] 1964.

Augustine, Saint, Bishop of Hippo. *The Works of Saint Augustine*. Edited by John E. Rotelle, O.S.A., translated by Maria Boulding, O.S.B. New York: New City Press, 1997.

Bachelard, Gaston. *L'Intuition de l'instant*. Paris: Stock, [1931] 1992.

Bakhtin, M. M. *The Dialogic Imagination*. Edited by Michael Holquist, translated by Caryl Emerson and Michael Holquist. Austin: University of Texas Press, 1981.

Baudelaire, Charles. *Les Fleurs du mal*. Edited by Antoine Adam. Paris: Bordas, [1857] 1990.

Bedini, Silvio A. *The Pulse of Time: Galileo Galilei, the Determination of Longitude, and the Pendulum Clock*. Florence: Olschki, 1991.

Behn, Aphra. *La Montre: or the Lover's Watch*. London: W. Canning, 1686.

———. *The Works of Aphra Behn*. Edited by Janet Todd. 4 vols. London: William Pickering, 1993.

Beik, William. *Absolutism and Society in Seventeenth-century France: State Power and Provincial Aristocracy in Languedoc*. Cambridge: Cambridge University Press, 1985.

Belloc, Alexis. *Les Postes françaises, recherches historiques sur leur origine, leur développement, leur législation*. Paris: Firmin-Didot, 1886.

Belmont, Henry-Louis. *La Montre: Méthodes et outillages de fabrication du XVIe au XIXe siècle, de la naissance de la montre à la période proto-industrielle*. Besançon: Cêtre, 1991.

Bercé, Yves-Marie. *La vie quotidienne dans l'Aquitaine du XVIIe siècle*. Paris: Hachette, 1978.

Bergson, Henri. *Durée et simultanéité*. Paris: PUF, 1992.

Beugnot, Bernard. "Débats autour du genre épistolaire: Réalité et écriture." *Revue d'histoire littéraire de la France* 74, no. 2 (1974): 195–202.

Blaise, Clark. *Time Lord: Sir Sandford Fleming and the Creation of Standard Time.* New York: Pantheon, 2000.

Boileau. *Œuvres complètes de Boileau.* Edited by A. Ch. Gidel. Vol. 2. Paris: Garnier, 1870.

Bonnecorse, Balthazar de. *La Montre.* Paris: Louis Billiane, 1666.

— — —. *La Montre, seconde partie.* Paris: Barbin, 1671.

— — —. *L'Amant raisonnable.* Paris: Louis Billiane, 1671.

Bourdieu, Pierre. *La Distinction: critique sociale du jugement.* Paris: Minuit, 1979.

Bray, Bernard. "Quelques Aspects du système épistolaire de Madame de Sévigné." *Revue d'histoire littéraire de la France* 69 (1969): 491–505.

Brotton, Jerry. *Trading Territories: Mapping the Early Modern World.* Ithaca: Cornell University Press, 1998.

Brown, Lloyd A. *Jean Domenique Cassini and his World Map of 1696.* Ann Arbor: University of Michigan Press, 1941.

Bruton, Eric. *The History of Clocks and Watches.* London: Orbis Publishing Limited, 1979.

Cairncross, John. *Molière bourgeois et libertin.* Paris: Nizet, 1963.

Cardinal, Catherine. *Les Montres du Musée du Louvre.* Paris: Réunion des musées nationaux, 1984.

— — —. *La montre des origines au XIXe siècle.* Paris: Vilo, 1985.

Certeau, Michel de. *L'Invention du quotidien. 1. Arts de faire.* Paris: Gallimard, 1990.

Chamard, H., and G. Rudler. "Les Sources historiques de *La Princesse de Clèves*." *Revue du XVIe siècle* 2 (1914): 92–131, 289–321; 5 (1917–18): 1–20.

Chambers, Ross. "Gossip and the Novel: Knowing Narrative and Narrative Knowing in Balzac, Mme de Lafayette and Proust." *Australian Journal of French Studies* 23, no. 2 (1986): 212–33.

Chapiro, Adolphe. *La Montre française du XVIe siècle jusqu'à 1900.* Paris: Editions de l'amateur, 1991.

Charbon, Paul. *Quelle belle invention que la poste!* Paris: Gallimard, 1991.

— — —, et al. "La Correspondance de Mme de Sévigné: Trois lectures différentes de son œuvre." *Revue d'Histoire de la Poste* (December 1996): 11–39.

[Charnes, J.-A., Abbé de]. *Conversations sur la critique de "La Princesse de Clèves."* Edited by François Weil et al. Tours: Publications de l'Université François Rabelais, [1679] 1973.

Chartier, Roger, ed. *A History of Private Life. III. Passions of the Renaissance.* Cambridge, MA: Belknap Press, 1989.

Cippola, Carlo. *Clocks and Culture, 1300–1700.* New York: Norton, 1978.

*Collections du Musée international d'Horlogerie, La Chaux-de-Fonds, Suisse.* 1974.

Crest, Sabine du. *Des fêtes à Versailles: Les divertissements de Louis XIV.* Paris: Aux Amateurs de Livres, 1990.

Crosby, Alfred W. *The Measure of Reality: Quantification and Western Society, 1250–1600.* Cambridge: Cambridge University Press, 1997.

Defossez, Laurent. *Les Savants du XVIIe siècle et la mesure du temps*. Lausanne: Edition du Journal suisse d'horlogerie et de bijouterie, 1946.

DeJean, Joan. *"La Princesse de Clèves*: The Poetics of Suppression." *Papers on French Seventeenth-Century Literature* 10, no. 18 (1983): 79–97.

———. *Literary Fortifications: Rousseau, Laclos, Sade*. Princeton: Princeton University Press, 1984.

———. "Lafayette's Ellipses: The Privileges of Anonymity." *PMLA* (October 1984): 884–902.

———. *Tender Geographies: Women and the Origins of the Novel in France*. New York: Columbia University Press, 1991.

———. *Ancients against Moderns: Culture Wars and the Making of a Fin de Siècle*. Chicago: University of Chicago Press, 1997.

Derrida, Jacques. *La Carte postale de Socrate à Freud et au-delà*. Paris: Flammarion, 1980.

Descartes, René. *Œuvres philosophiques*. 3 vols. Edited by Ferdinand Alquié. Paris: Bordas, 1988.

Dessert, Daniel. *La Royale. Vaisseaux et marins du Roi-Soleil*. Paris: Fayard, 1996.

*Dictionnaire des horlogers français*. Edited by Paul Brateau et al. 2 vols. Paris: Tardy, 1971–72.

Dorling, Daniel and David Fairbairn. *Mapping: Ways of Representing the World*. Essex: Longman, 1997.

Duchêne, Roger. *Réalité vécue et art épistolaire: Madame de Sévigné et la lettre d'amour*. Paris: Bordas, 1970.

———. "Madame de Sévigné et le style négligé." *Œuvres et critiques* 1, no. 2 (Summer 1976): 113–27.

———. "Mme de Sévigné entre la communication et l'écriture." *L'Information littéraire* 35, no. 2 (March–April 1983): 54–59.

———. "Art et hasard: petit bilan de la correspondance de Mme de Sévigné." In *Ouverture et Dialogue: mélanges offerts à Wolfgang Leiner*, edited by Ulrich Döring, 133–45. Tübingen: Gunter Narr Verlag, 1988.

———. *Chère Madame de Sévigné . . .* Paris: Gallimard, 1995.

———. "Madame de Sévigné et la poste." *Revue d'Histoire de la Poste* (December 1997): 2–9.

Elias, Norbert. *The Court Society*. Translated by Edmund Jephcott. New York: Pantheon, 1983.

Félibien, André. *Relation de la fête de Versailles. Les Divertissements de Versailles*. Edited by Martin Meade. Maisonneuve et Larose: Editions Dédale, 1994.

———. *Relation de la fête de Versailles du dix-huit juillet mille six cent soixante-huit*. Edited by Allen S. Weiss. Paris: Mercure de France, 1999.

Flotte, Gaston de. "Les poètes de Marseille. Balthazar de Bonnecorse." *Revue de Marseille* 2, no. 3 (March 1856): 120–39.

Foucault, Michel. *Discipline and Punish*. Translated by Alan Sheridan. New York: Vintage, 1977.

Francillon, Roger. *L'Œuvre romanesque de Madame de Lafayette*. Paris: José Corti, 1973.

Genette, Gérard. *Figures II*. Paris: Seuil, 1969.

Gordon, Daniel. *Citizens Without Sovereignty: Equality and Sociability in French Thought, 1670–1789*. Princeton: Princeton University Press, 1994.

Graziani, Antoine. *La grande aventure de la poste*. Paris: André Bonne, 1965.

Hahn, Roger. *The Anatomy of a Scientific Institution: The Paris Academy of Sciences, 1666–1803*. Berkeley: University of California Press, 1971.

Harley, J. B. "Maps, Knowledge and Power." In *The Iconography of Landscape*, edited by Denis Cosgrove and Stephen Daniels, 277–312. Cambridge: Cambridge University Press, 1988.

Hawcroft, Michael. "Historical Evidence and Literature: Madame de Sévigné's Letters on the Trial of Fouquet." *The Seventeenth Century* 9, no. 1 (spring 1994): 57–75.

Heise, Ursula K. *Chronoschisms: Time, Narrative, and Postmodernism*. Cambridge: Cambridge University Press, 1997.

Hobbes, Thomas. *Leviathan*. Edited by John Plamenatz. Cleveland and New York: Meridian Books, 1963.

Jardine, Lisa. *Worldly Goods: A New History of the Renaissance*. New York: Doubleday, 1996.

Klein, Etienne. *Le Temps*. Paris: Flammarion, 1995.

La Bruyère, Jean de. *Les Caractères*. Edited by Pierre Ronzeaud. Paris: Librairie Générale Française, 1985.

Lafayette, Marie-Madeleine Pioche de la Vergne, comtesse de. *La Princesse de Clèves*. Edited by Antoine Adam. Paris: Flammarion, [1678] 1966.

Landes, David S. *Revolution in Time: Clocks and the Making of the Modern World*. Cambridge, MA: The Belknap Press of Harvard University Press, 1983.

La Rochefoucauld, François, duc de. *Maximes et Réflexions diverses*. Edited by Jacques Truchet. Paris: Garnier-Flammarion, 1977.

Laugaa, Maurice. *Lectures de Madame de Lafayette*. Paris: Colin, 1971.

Laurent, Benoît. *Poste et postiers*. Paris: Doin, 1922.

Le Goff, Jacques. "Au Moyen Age: Temps de l'Eglise et temps du marchand," *Annales* 15, no. 3 (May–June 1960): 417–33.

LeNain, Louis. *La Poste de l'Ancienne France, des origines à 1791*. Arles: l'auteur, 13 Chemin des Semestres, 1965.

Levillain, Henriette. *Henriette Levillain présente La Princesse de Clèves de Madame de La Fayette*. Paris: Gallimard, 1995.

Levron, Jacques. *La Vie quotidienne à la cour de Versailles aux XVIIe et XVIIIe siècles*. Paris: Hachette, 1965.

*Liste alphabétique des villes et lieux tant de ce Royaume que des pays Etrangers, où les Couriers des Postes de France portent les Lettres & Paquets, & les jours & heures de leur depart, pour l'année 1675*. Paris: François Muguet. B. N. Thoisy 433.

Longino-Farrell, Michèle. *Performing Motherhood: The Sévigné Correspondence*. Hanover: University Press of New England, 1991.

———. "Writing Letters, Telling Tales, Making History: Vatel's Death Told and Retold." *The French Review* 66, no. 2 (December 1992): 229–42.

Louis XIV. *Mémoires*. Edited by Jean Lognon. Paris: Tallandier, 1978.

Macey, Samuel L. *Clocks and the Cosmos: Time in Western Life and Thought.* Hamden, CT: Archon Books, 1980.

*Madame de Sévigné. Catalogue.* Paris: Paris-Musées/Flammarion, 1996.

Malandain, Pierre. *Madame de Lafayette*: La Princesse de Clèves. Paris: PUF, 1985.

Mensher, Gail Bussmeir. "Problems of Time and Existence in the Letters of Mme de Sévigné." *Dissertation Abstracts.* 38 4200A-01A (Iowa) 1978.

Merlin, Hélène. *Public et littérature en France au XVIIe siècle.* Paris: Les Belles lettres, 1994.

Mettam, Roger. *Power and Faction in Louis XIV's France.* New York: Blackwell, 1988.

Mitford, Nancy. *The Sun King: Louis XIV at Versailles.* New York: Harper and Row, 1966.

Molière. *Œuvres complètes.* Edited by Georges Couton. 2 vols. Paris: Gallimard, 1971.

— — —. *The Misanthrope and Other Plays.* Translated by John Wood. New York: Penguin Books, 1987.

Moore, Ann M. "Temporal Structure and Reader Response in *La Princesse de Clèves.*" *The French Review* 56, no. 4 (March 1983): 563–71.

Moore, W. G. "Le Goût de la cour." *Cahiers de l'Association Internationale des Etudes Françaises* 9 (June 1957): 172–82.

Mouligneau, Geneviève. *Madame de Lafayette, romancière?* Bruxelles: Editions de l'Université de Bruxelles, 1980.

Murat, Inès. *Colbert.* Paris: Fayard, 1980.

Musée postal. Carton 035 (038). Lois et Decrets, Messageries 1576–1746.

— — —. Carton 330. Chronologie, 1661–1700.

Paige, Nicholas D. *Being Interior: Autobiography and the Contradictions of Modernity in Seventeenth-Century France.* Philadelphia: University of Pennsylvania Press, 2001.

Pardailhé-Galabrun, Annik. *La Naissance de l'intime. 3000 foyers parisiens. XVIIe–XVIIIe siècles.* Paris: PUF, 1988.

Pernot, Michel. *La Fronde.* Paris: Fallois, 1994.

Perrault, Charles. *Parallèle des Anciens et des Modernes en ce qui regarde les arts et les sciences.* Vols. 1–4. Geneva: Slatkine Reprints, 1971.

Poulet, Georges. *Etudes sur le temps humain.* Paris: Plon, 1950.

Racevskis, Roland. "Solitary Pleasures: Creative Avoidance of Court and Convent in *La Princesse de Clèves.*" *The French Review* 70, no. 1 (October 1996): 24–34.

Rathery and Boutron. *Mademoiselle de Scudéry: Sa vie et sa correspondance.* Geneva: Slatkine Reprints, 1971.

Reiss, Timothy. *Knowledge, Discovery and Imagination in Early Modern Europe: The Rise of Aesthetic Rationalism.* Cambridge: Cambridge University Press, 1997.

Richardt, Aimé. *Louvois (1641–1691).* Paris: ERTI, 1990.

Richet, Denis. *La France moderne: l'esprit des institutions.* Paris: Gallimard, 1973.

Ricœur, Paul. *Temps et récit.* 3 vols. Paris: Seuil, 1983.

Rolland, R. "La naissance de la poste moderne." *Revue des P.T.T. de France* 35, no. 5 (1980): 46–58.

Rothschild, Arthur de. *Histoire de la poste aux lettres et du timbre-poste depuis leurs origines jusqu'à nos jours.* Genève: Slatkine Reprints, [1880] 1979.

Sarlet, Claudette. "Le Temps dans *La Princesse de Clèves.*" *Marche romane* 9, no. 2 (April–June 1959): 51–58.

Schérer, Jacques. *Structures de Tartuffe.* Paris: SEDES, 1974.

Serres, Michel. *Le Parasite.* Paris: Grasset, 1980.

Sévigné, Marie de Rabutin-Chantal, marquise de. *Lettres de Madame de Sévigné, de sa famille et de ses amis.* 14 vols. Edited by M. Monmerqué. Paris: Hachette, 1862–68.

———. *Lettres inédites de Madame de Sévigné à Madame de Grignan sa fille.* 2 vols. Edited by Charles Capmas. Paris: Hachette, 1876.

———. *Lettres.* 3 vols. Edited by Gérard-Gailly. Paris: Gallimard, 1953–57.

———. *Correspondance.* 3 vols. Edited by Roger Duchêne. Paris: Gallimard, [1646–95] 1972–78.

Sherman, Stuart. *Telling Time: Clocks, Diaries, and English Diurnal Form, 1660–1785.* Chicago: University of Chicago Press, 1996.

Shirley, Rodney. *The Mapping of the World: Early Printed World Maps, 1472–1700.* London: The Holland Press, 1983.

Sobel, Dava. *Longitude: The True Story of a Lone Genius Who Solved the Greatest Scientific Problem of his Time.* New York: Penguin, 1996.

———. *Galileo's Daughter.* New York: Penguin, 2000.

Stone, Harriet. *The Classical Model: Literature and Knowledge in Seventeenth-Century France.* Ithaca: Cornell University Press, 1996.

Sweetser, Marie-Odile. "Madame de Sévigné: Ecrivain sans le savoir?" *Cahiers de l'Association Internationale des Etudes Françaises* 39 (May 1987): 141–55.

Thompson, E. P. "Time, Work-Discipline, and Industrial Capitalism." *Past & Present* 38 (December 1967): 56–97.

Thrower, Norman. *Maps and Civilization: Cartography in Culture and Society.* Chicago: University of Chicago Press, 1999.

Vaillé, Eugène. *Histoire générale des postes françaises.* Vol. 4 *(Louvois, Surintendant général des postes, 1668–91).* Paris: PUF, 1951.

[Valincour, J. B. de]. *Lettres à Madame la marquise *** sur le sujet de "La Princesse de Clèves."* Edited by J. Chupeau et al. Tours: Publications de l'Université François Rabelais, [1678] 1972.

Verlet, Pierre and Pierre Mesnage. *La Mesure du temps.* Paris: Draeger, 1970.

Vernet, Max. *Molière côté jardin, côté cour.* Paris: Nizet, 1991.

*Versailles in the Age of Louis XIV.* Paris: Réunion des musées nationaux, 1993.

Vigarello, Georges. *Le corps redressé: histoire d'un pouvoir pédagogique.* Paris: J. P. Delarge, 1978.

Vincent, Monique. *Donneau de Visé et "Le Mercure galant."* 2 vols. Paris: Aux amateurs de livres, 1987.

Voiture, Vincent. *Œuvres de Voiture.* Geneva: Slatkine, 1967.

Williams, Charles G. S. *Madame de Sévigné.* Boston: Twayne, 1981.

Williams, Raymond. *Marxism and Literature.* Oxford: Oxford University Press, 1977.

Woolf, Virginia. *The Death of the Moth and Other Essays.* New York: HBJ, 1970.

Zumthor, Paul. *La Mesure du Monde.* Paris: Seuil, 1993.

# Index

Académie Royale des Sciences: founding of, 13, 31–33, 68; and Huygens, 39; new maps created at, 34, 37, 54
Africa, 32
Altman, Janet, 126, 131, 196 n. 1
ancien régime, 18
Ancients, 28
Apollo, 64–65, 87
Apostolidès, Jean-Marie, 67
Ariès, Phillipe, 17
Ariosto, Ludovico, 60, 64–65, 161
Artaud, Antonin, 73
astronomy: and accuracy in measurement, 26; construction of Observatoire, 31; use of Galileo's pendulum for, 27; uses for longitude, 33

Bachelard, Gaston, 199 n. 40
Baliani, Giovanni Batista, 26
Baltimore Aquarium, 188
Balzac, Jean-Louis Guez de, 90–91
Barbin, Claude, 45, 145
Baudelaire, Charles, 138, 201 n. 63
Bayonne, 97–98
Behaim, Martin, 35
Behn, Aphra, 44, 46
Beik, William, 95, 199 n. 50
Benserade, Isaac de, 65, 67
Bercé, Yves-Marie, 104
Bibliothèque Royale de Paris, 31
Blaeu, Joan, 36–37
Blaise, Clark, 191 n. 26
Blois, 25–26, 38, 192 n. 43
body, 20, 66
Boileau, Nicolas, 44–45
Bonnecorse, Balthazar de, 44–53
Bourdieu, Pierre, 128
bourgeoisie: and capitalism, 70–71; ownership of timepieces, 14, 43; as represented in *Le Tartuffe*, 86

Bray, Bernard, 110
Brittany, 108, 111, 199 nn. 45 and 52
Bussy-Rabutin, Roger, comte de, 121, 124, 131, 196 n. 2

Cairncross, John, 194 n. 1
Cape Verde Islands, 32
capitalism, 70–71
Capmas, Charles, 197 n. 2
Cardinal, Catherine, 37, 40, 192 nn. 38 and 43
*Carte du Tendre*, 53
cartography, 33, 35–37, 53, 191 nn. 28, 30, and 32
Cassini, Giovanni Domenico, 33–37, 191 n. 30
Catholics, 40, 192 n. 43
centralization, 17, 88; of postal system, 92–96, 105, 198 n. 5
Certeau, Michel de, 105, 170
Chambers, Ross, 76–77
Chantilly, 136–38
Charles II, 34, 37
Charnes, Abbé Jean-Antoine de, 147–49, 159–62
Chartier, Roger, 17–18, 105, 153
chronometry: critical chronometry of Valincour, 153; and epistemology, 53–54; history of, 13–14, 87, 187; Huygens and, 19; innovations in mechanics of, 26–27, 186; longitude and, 29, 37
Cipolla, Carlo M., 40
clergy: ownership of timepieces, 43
clocks: in contemporary life, 185; and education, 20; Galileo, Huygens, and pendulum, 13, 27, 186; influence on public and private life, 16; and longitude, 29–37; role in daily life, 21; in Sévigné, 139, 201 n. 64; support for science of

210